And Gently He Shall Lead Them

AND GENTLY HE SHALL LEAD THEM

ROBERT PARRIS MOSES AND CIVIL RIGHTS IN MISSISSIPPI

ERIC BURNER

New York University Press

NEW YORK AND LONDON

NEW YORK UNIVERSITY PRESS
New York and London

Library of Congress Cataloging-in-Publication Data
Burner, Eric.
And gently he shall lead them : Robert Parris Moses and civil
rights in Mississippi / Eric Burner.
p. cm.
Includes bibliographical references and index.
ISBN 0-8147-1209-6
1. Moses, Robert Parris.   2. Civil rights workers—Mississippi—
Biography.   3. Afro-Americans—Mississippi—Biography.   4. Afro-
Americans—Civil rights—Mississippi.   5. Civil rights movements—
Mississippi—History—20th century.   6. Mississippi—Race
relations.   I. Title.
E185.97.M89B87   1994
976.2′00496073′0092—dc20   94-5436
[B]   CIP

New York University Press books are printed on acid-free paper, and their
binding materials are chosen for strength and durability.

Manufactured in the United States of America

10   9   8   7   6   5   4   3   2   1

*To the men and women with the
courage to do what was right.*

CONTENTS

ILLUSTRATIONS

ACKNOWLEDGMENTS

Many people have given me encouragement and support, but I want especially to thank Professor Thomas R. West of Catholic University, who managed to teach me by example something of the difficulties and rewards of prose writing. Professor Hugh Hawkins of Amherst College, where this book originated as a senior honors essay, taught an excellent class on the 1960s and later extended warm encouragement. Professor Irwin Unger of New York University read an early draft of the book and steered me toward rethinking my thesis. In addition, Professor Doug McAdam of the University of Arizona generously sent a letter of inquiry on my behalf to dozens of former SNCC workers, enabling me to expand my understanding of Freedom Summer. Professor Anthony Rizzuto of SUNY Stony Brook helped me clarify my thinking about the influence of Camus on Moses.

A number of people involved in civil rights in Mississippi read drafts of the manuscript and gave me valuable insights, correction, or inspiration. They include especially Sally Belfrage, Howard Zinn, Miriam Cohen Glickman, John W. Blyth, Gordon Henderson, Roy Ginsberg, Robbie Ossman, Gar Alperovitz, Harris Wofford, Jane Adams, Kay Mischener, Richard W. Swanson, and Margrit Garner. I am also grateful to many archivists and librarians who freely gave me their time.

Moses' classmates at Hamilton College were most generous in their willingness to respond to my inquiries, and I want to thank in particular Emerson Brown, Jr., Richard P. Canuteson, Benjamin C. Carroll, W. Robert Connor, Preston Dawes, Peter Eckel, Thomas A. Fagan, Richard T. Field, William F. Fivaz, Frank J. Giruzzi, Jonathan G. Greenwald, Earl Herbert, Wayne Mahood, Harry Presberg, David Rothstein, James E. Schade, and Michael G. Sundell. Several others sent letters expressing interest and kind encouragement.

Three people offered a great deal of information and insight into Robert Moses' early years and later activities. I am especially indebted to his brother, Gregory Moses of Detroit, Michigan, for information about the family and early influences on the brothers. Moses' uncle, the late William Henry Moses, Jr., allowed a recorded transcript with him and his wife at their home in Newport News, Virginia.

Edwin King not only generously allowed me to peruse his unpublished memoirs, but also took the time to drive me to the Mississippi Delta and buy me a catfish dinner. For both my genuine thanks.

And finally, I would like to thank my parents, Sandra and David, for their years of support, encouragement, and help.

And Gently He Shall Lead Them

INTRODUCTION

L ate at night on August 17, 1962, Robert Parris Moses returned to a deserted Student Nonviolent Coordinating Committee (SNCC) office in Greenwood, Mississippi, that had just been ransacked by a white mob. Hours earlier three SNCC workers had just barely escaped the same mob by climbing to the next building over the roof and shimmying down a TV antenna. Moses stifled a yawn, made up a bed in the corner of the room, and went to sleep. The young black New Yorker had a job to do: go to Mississippi, register voters, and stay alive. And he was doing it. The offhandedness of that night's lodging was typical of him. "I just didn't understand what kind of guy this Bob Moses is, that could walk into a place where a lynch mob had just left and make up a bed and prepare to go to sleep, as if the situation was normal," observes Willie Peacock, a black Mississippian from the Delta who had made the one-

hour trip to the scene with Moses from Cleveland. "So I
guess I was learning."[1] The story added to the mythic
quality that Moses—the private, introspective leader
who doggedly shunned leadership—had already acquired among the black Mississippians and civil rights
workers living through these dangerous times.

Pensiveness, economy of speech, and action—rather
than the aggressive mastery of people and surround-
ings—defined Moses as a leader. He embodied ideas
and these, not leadership in itself, were his passion. As
Mary King remembers:

> In the same way that one listens more attentively to a
> whisper, people were drawn to Bob—he was so unob-
> trusive that in his quiet self-possessed stillness, he fixed
> additional attention on himself. He seemed entirely
> nourished from within. If Bob walked into a room or
> joined a group that I was in, I felt my chest muscles
> quicken and a sudden rush of exhilaration. He inspired
> me and touched me. I trusted Bob implicitly and felt
> deep affection for him.[2]

Cleveland Sellers, who would follow Stokely Carmichael as leader of SNCC in later years, has written of
Moses: "There was something about him, the manner
in which he carried himself, that seemed to draw all of
us to him. He had been where we were going. And more
important, he had emerged as the kind of person we
wanted to be."[3] A Mississippi black family had a picture of Moses cut out from the *Saturday Evening Post*
hung next to a picture of Jesus. According to the mother
in the family, "When he first came here I'd *cry* for him.
I thought sure they'd kill him. He'd jus' stand there and

talk to them.... Then they shot at him one day. I never thought they'd let him leave alive."[4]

Amzie Moore, a local National Association for the Advancement of Colored People (NAACP) leader in Cleveland whom Moses called "my father in the movement,"[5] gives a matter-of-fact description: "Well, I don't know whether I can explain Bob Moses, to be honest with you. Quiet, unassuming, a deep thinker, ordinary—you know, when I say 'ordinary,' just like a common shoe . . . and very seldom expressed himself unless asked."[6]

Robert Moses is one of the most important yet most elusive figures of the early period of the Second Reconstruction. During these critical years of the civil rights movement he was indispensable in Mississippi, its most dangerous ground. But like many other activists, he has had little of the national recognition accorded to Martin Luther King, Jr., Malcolm X, or Stokely Carmichael. Moses, perhaps more than anyone, shifted the emphasis of the movement from sit-ins, freedom rides, and other forms of direct action to voter registration. He orchestrated Freedom Summer, the ambitious and daring action that brought some 1,000 volunteers, most of them white college students, to the state in 1964 to register voters, teach black children, and provide food for impoverished Mississippians. And he led the Mississippi Freedom Democratic party (MFDP) challenge to the state's regular Democrats at that year's national Democratic party convention in Atlantic City. This was a pivotal event for Moses and for other participants, turning them away from working with liberal Democrats to a radicalism distrustful of all accommodation.

Moses was an early practitioner of what the New Left

would come to call participatory democracy, wherein active participation is as much end as means. Participatory democracy flourished in the later 1960s amidst the campus antiwar committees and the communes—more publicly and dramatically than at any time since the labor struggles of the depression era. In its more deliberate expressions, it was as sophisticated as philosophical anarchism, as primitive as the migrant camps imagined in *The Grapes of Wrath*. At its best, participatory democracy was simply primal democracy, the full realization of the citizen as individual and as an equal member of a community of individuals. It is only the customary modern reduction of the concept of democracy to the formal act of voting that requires the essentially redundant adjective "participatory" in reference to something larger. The black insurgents who walked and carpooled their way to justice in Montgomery, sat in at Woolworth's in Greensboro, or stepped through a hostile crowd to a Mississippi voting registrar were not using the term *participatory democracy*. But they made democracy happen; they enacted it. Participatory democracy in Mississippi found an instrument in Moses, a leader who encouraged but did not command.

The relations between Moses and the liberalism of the Democrats in the 1960s are also a study in the encounter between a demand for uncompromising purity and the political mentality that is prepared to coexist with evil for the sake of achieving partial good. It is an irresolvable encounter; neither Moses nor conventional liberalism could come to terms in the tangle of morality and practicality. Moses, in an effort to achieve the goal of civil rights for blacks, at times tried to force the hand of the federal government by using the techniques of politics. The Democratic administration and party—the embodiment of the liberalism of the 1960s—in turn rationalized that their practicality achieved some partial moral good. Together with the development of participatory democracy, that clash of moralities makes the voting registration campaign in Mississippi a microcosm of much that was to happen in the sixties.

Moses is known to have been a close reader of Albert Camus, and the analogies between the thought of the French writer and the example of Moses are sharp and pressing. He affirmed the relevance of Camus's writing to the situation in Mississippi in a February 1964 interview with Robert Penn Warren. Moses remarked that it was difficult to overcome the everpresent fear that surrounded him and those with whom he worked:

> When I was in jail this last time I read through *The Rebel* and *The Plague* again. The main essence of what he [Camus] says is what I feel . . . closest to. It's not a question that you just subjugate yourself to the conditions that are and don't try to change them. The problem is to go on from there, into something that is active, and yet the dichotomy is whether you can cease to be a victim any more and also not be what he calls an executioner. The ideal lies between these two extremes—victim and executioner.[7]

The explanation describes not the origins of Moses' conduct in Mississippi but what he represented there in the way of a morality beyond liberal accommodation, and a democracy beyond formal institutions.

During the 1950s the work of Albert Camus was enormously popular among U.S. intellectuals. In addition to the absurdity and darkness that surround human life, Camus expressed the strength of life to assert itself. It was "life without illusions," to use a phrase commonly associated with President Kennedy. Camus rejected revolution as a moral action, seeing it as a surrender of conscience and judgment to the pretended forces of history. He elected instead for what in *The Rebel* (1951) he called rebellion, a continuing personal assertion of conscience and freedom in the face of whatever, within the rebel or without, threatens freedom and life. Nonviolence, as practiced by the Montgomery, Alabama, bus desegregation demonstrators under King's leadership, had perfect resonances with the ethos of Camus. Nonviolence amounted to a defiance of authority and custom and at the same time a refusal to strike back against attack, whether by the police or by a white mob. This tactic exactly suited the decision commended by Camus to be neither victim nor executioner; yet Camus distinguishes between premeditated violence and capricious, spontaneous violence. For Moses, education and knowledge would allow the individual to decide, thus avoiding either pole. And a commitment to nonviolence in the presence of violence required precisely the self-knowledge and composure affirmed by *The Rebel*.

Camus addressed evil embodied in the worst experiences of the twentieth century: war and genocide. Germaine Bree calls that evil a force that envelops and surpasses the evil of specific men and women.[8] Segregation in Mississippi had something of that pervasive insidiousness. A purpose of Moses' civil rights work in Mississippi was akin to the purpose of Camus's outsiders: to heighten consciousness. Only by doing so could individuals decide for themselves what choices to make. This was necessary for participatory democracy.

Camus, though setting his rebel to resisting oppression, knew that violence in good causes has within it a capacity for oppression. He set for all use of power a test of scrupulosity that even the French resistance could not conceivably have passed. He recognized, more quickly than many on the left, that there was little difference between Hitler and Stalin. Moses' intense suspicion of all leadership, including his own, suggests Camus's insight that within the rebel there lurks the oppressor: that there is latent within life a power hunger that may war against beneficent instincts of goodness and purity. Moses, who in Mississippi consistently sought to apply the ethos of Camus to his own life and experience, would not attempt to change others; he would simply convince by his example.

The ethos of Camus, then, closely accorded with the conduct of Moses and the character of the voter registration campaign. Camus, who had put the responsibility for freedom squarely within the brains and conscience of the human being, captivated a young intellectual who wanted freedom for black Southerners and knew that it was already within them. And it is appropriate to what happened in Mississippi that Camus had urged a politics of small communities, where free individuals could discover their full selves and one another. He would have understood participatory democracy.

A book about a figure who spoke by silence and led by seeming only to respond cannot present itself as a biography in the full sense. Such is not my intention: I have no reason to invade the private Bob Moses. He was so naturally self-effacing, so consumed by his work, so determined to eliminate from it his own persona that his is essentially a public life. There are no personal reminiscences, just his moving words spoken at the time of his work in Mississippi. Even the delineations of Moses by coworkers in oral histories and books, or in personal interviews with them, are curiously unrevealing. Sometimes it is as though those who worked with him closely seem scarcely to have known him at all, and even the most painstaking searching has uncovered no detailed archival evidence. Various intellectual speculations, as well as a generous amount of his own words, come closest to getting at Moses' convoluted core.

Moses' most important achievement came in remote parts of Mississippi in the two- or three-year period when with the help of a handful of volunteers, most of them black, he was trying to awaken black Mississippians to their moral and legal rights. He did not then enjoy the protective encouragement and flattering publicity that national civil rights leaders were getting. His most important public moment was his role at the 1964 Democratic National Convention at Atlantic City, a turning point in the history of American liberalism that is extensively detailed here. My chief interest, though, is in the ways his presence and leadership style offer an entrance into the Mississippi registration project and into a decade that set radicals to pursuing purity and to practicing, at times, a democracy of incessant action.

ONE

"A LOT OF LEADERS"

Robert Parris Moses was born on January 23, 1935, and raised in Harlem, New York City. His grandfather, William Henry Moses, was a charismatic Baptist preacher who traveled throughout the South raising funds for the National Baptist Convention. William Moses was educated at Virginia Seminary in Lynchburg, where he met and married Julia Trent. He held pastorates in Knoxville, Tennessee; Newberry, South Carolina; Staunton, Virginia; Washington, D.C.; and Philadelphia.[1] He was also the author of several homiletic reviews for ministers and served a term as president of a four-year school to train black Baptist ministers in Guadalupe, Texas.[2]

Robert's father, Gregory, frustrated by the struggle to survive during the depression, inculcated in the young

Moses and his two brothers, Roger and Gregory, a drive
to succeed where he had failed. They lived in the four-
story Harlem River Projects, a small, contained complex with written exams to get in and a long waiting
list.[3] Moses' father—unlike his brother, a college professor—was a janitor at the 369th armory in Harlem,
an occupation Bob Moses has described as "a good job"
(for the Depression) that "didn't *go* anywhere.... That
ate away at him, and I think he himself never expressed
that in terms of frustration at society as a whole. It was
frustration that led to drinking that led to difficult
times in the family. There was a lot of that middle-class
frustration—a whole generation of people who were
intelligent, rooted in family, and industrious, for whom
there was just no opportunity. You'd always hear, 'It's
gonna be different when *you* grow up.' So you had a
slow buildup of frustration."[4]

But perhaps both his father's and his own frustration
impelled Moses to apply himself more rigorously to
make things different when he grew up. Moses entered
Stuyvesant High School, a school for gifted New York
City students who were admitted on the basis of com-
petitive citywide examinations. Stuyvesant was liberal
in politics and culture. Moses frequently attended hoot-
enannies, folk-singers' performances of a bohemian
cast, mild precursors of the experimental and insurgent
music of the 1960s. These, he has said, "helped orient
me."[5] In his senior year at high school he was elected
class president; he was also captain of the school base-
ball team. Moses graduated from Stuyvesant in June
1952, in the middle of his class academically.[6]

His parents pushed him in the direction of the good
small liberal arts colleges and away from the tradi-

tional black schools, which they believed too "social."[7] His father in particular thought that he would get a better education and be forced to prove his mettle at a white college.[8] Both parents were delighted when he won a scholarship to Hamilton College in upstate New York in the fall of 1952.[9]

At Hamilton, Moses was one of a few black students among upper-middle-class whites. It was not atypical for his classmates to respond that he was the first black person they had ever met when asked about Moses. One classmate speaks of the substantial difference between Moses and his peers "because so many of us had never really related to blacks in any significant way before. He lived . . . in some isolation. . . . Yet he was deeply, widely . . . universally respected."[10] A member of the honor court, co-captain of the basketball team where he exhibited "cool composure," the elected vice president of his senior class, and a Rhodes Scholarship candidate, he gained a reputation for being quiet and unaffected. As part of his scholarship arrangement, he worked as a waiter in the nonfraternity dining hall.[11] Moses also served for two years as head of the student advisors to freshmen. Perhaps the most influential student group to which Moses belonged was the Emerson Literary Society (ELS), a residential social organization that exhibited an uncommon social consciousness. As one classmate remarked, "By today's standards we were a largely racist, sexist, anti-semitic collection of white males. Fraternities completely dominated our social life and the Greeks didn't offer membership to minority or Jewish students. It was Korea, Eisenhower, and 25 cents a bottle Utica Club beer."[12] ELS was not the usual campus fraternal group: its members' average

grade, for example, exceeded that of any of the Hamilton Greek organizations. According to another ELS
member, Moses "was very hesitant to join ELS, and it
took considerable persuasion over two years before he
agreed."[13] One Greek fraternity did try to pledge Moses, Tau Kappa Epsilon, but he declined, not wishing to
be a token Negro in a Greek letter fraternity.[14] For a
time Moses served as the ELS rush chairman.

While only an occasional churchgoer during his
youth, at St. Mark's Church at 138th Street and St.
Nicholas Avenue in New York City, at Hamilton Moses
attended for a time a Christian study group, many of
whose members were fundamentalists. He debated
with his two freshmen Jewish roommates, fellow students from Stuyvesant High, about God's existence,
fairness, and justice, pitting Christian fundamentalism
against their very different religious backgrounds.[15]
Moses considered entering the ministry and, as part of
the college study group, even tried his hand at evangeli-
cal preaching on the streets of New York.[16] He wrote
to his father about entering the ministry; his father
responded that the ministry was "a calling, not just an
occupation."[17] His demeanor, as reserved as the Reverend Martin Luther King, Jr.'s was ardent, did not suit
the task. Yet it was later to be extraordinarily effective
for the work of civil rights organizing, in which impassioned oratory usually dominated. And doubtless Moses' experience as a novice preacher enabled him to
respond to the religion of Mississippi's rural blacks and
to that of many of his peers in the early days of the
movement. A fellow choir member at Hamilton stayed
with Moses' father when the group gave concerts in
New York during his freshman year: "His father read

the Bible during the evening, and I believe Robert was also very pious."[18]

Hamilton was politically conservative. A poll in the mid-1950s found President Eisenhower favored by students over the Democratic spokesman Adlai Stevenson by a margin of three to one. And forty-five percent of the faculty at this northeastern liberal arts campus shared that preference,[19] again reflecting the school's relative conservatism. One student recalls, "My campaigning for Stevenson was generally taken as odd."[20] Clarence Nixon, briefly head of the school's political science department, had been a distinguished member of the circle known as the Southern Agrarians, champions of the traditional landed culture of the South. Named "Southerner of the Year" by the Mississippi Council for Christian Action while Moses was at Hamilton, Nixon had pleaded for Northern understanding of Southern problems as well as a change in race relations in the South.[21]

The college was not the traditional place to achieve a black identity: "Hamilton's attitude was . . . it would admit black students who could handle the work academically, but that the college's business was liberal arts education (as Hamilton understood it) and students who didn't want what Hamilton had to offer should be elsewhere."[22] Elected to the sophomore honor society, Moses took no part in the minor hazing activities of the group toward freshmen—placing a new or recently painted toilet seat over the head of a transgressing freshman, for example—and "in his quiet style . . . tried not only to dissuade but to educate the rest of us," a classmate recalls. "He was simply practicing civil rights long before the rest of us came of age."[23]

Yet the students' focus and activities perhaps gave Moses some insight into what college students might be capable of doing when he would enlist their help some years later in Mississippi.

The atmosphere of the intellectually rigorous school can be described as genteel: "The tone was set by the boys from small towns and cities from upstate, many of them sons of teachers, ministers, and small businessmen."[24] In Moses' time Hamilton admitted about 175 students each year from an applicant pool of almost 1,000. In those days class attendance was mandatory, including Saturdays from 8:00 A.M to noon; skipping more than four during a semester without a wholly legitimate reason resulted inexorably in an F. Moses graduated with departmental honors in philosophy and a middle B average, which in those days placed him in the upper quarter of his class.

Moses encountered at Hamilton the Quaker pacifist beliefs that would illuminate his future career. Because he did well academically and showed an interest in things philosophical, his professors urged him to attend Quaker summer workshops abroad. After his junior year, Moses worked in Belgium with nine other volunteers to build a dormitory at a summer camp for underprivileged children in a mining district. In France, that same summer, he lived with pacifists whose commitment had been tested by Nazism, as racism was to test Moses. There in the Moselle region he helped to build houses for the homeless—hard manual labor, mixing cement, and pouring foundations. He met volunteers from Ceylon, West Africa, Egypt, and Jordan. He then traveled to a work camp near Bremen, Germany, operated by the American Friends' Service Committee, and

harvested potatoes for a missionary hospital.[25] The following summer he went to Japan, where he worked to
construct a stairway at a home for mentally disturbed
children and investigated Zen Buddhism. The American Friends' Service Committee evaluated Moses as a
"sociable, patient, and conscientious" young man who
displayed "natural leadership."[26]

Coupled with his concrete experiences was the intellectual tutelage of Francis Tafoya, Marcel Moraud, and
Frank Hamlin of Hamilton's French Department. Under
Tafoya, Moses read Albert Camus in what appears to
have been a continuing pursuit of a spiritual absolute.

Whatever benefits Moses gained from Hamilton, he
was to speak in a 1964 interview of being "deeply bitter
about some of the realities of the campus and of the
white attitude." Dominated by whites, the message of
higher education in the 1950s appeared to be saying:
"Well, we have to do our part—the society has the
overall problem, and our part as an educational institution is to try and open a door for two or three Negroes,
and let's see what happens."[27] And yet Hamilton was
racially progressive for its day. One fraternity during
that time elected to pledge students outside of the white
Christian pool and was promptly expelled from the national organization, its charter revoked.[28] The speaker
at Moses' commencement exercises on June 3, 1956,
was Chief Justice Earl Warren, the author of the landmark *Brown v. Board of Education* desegregation decision of 1954. Hamilton also eventually recognized Moses' achievements.[29]

After graduation from college, Moses entered Harvard's philosophy doctoral program and attended
Quaker meeting in Cambridge, where he also worked

part-time for nearly a year as a janitor in the meeting house.[30] At Harvard, Moses' focus was on analytic philosophy, which was well-suited to his penchant for mathematics, and he was awarded a Master of Arts in June 1957. His mother's death from cancer at forty-three, in February 1958, shortly after her first vacation with her husband,[31] interrupted Moses' doctoral studies, and he withdrew from Harvard the following month. Though the children suspected her condition, Louise Parris Moses had not permitted her husband to tell them about her illness. As he prepared to return to Harvard, Moses learned that his father, while retracing the steps he had taken to bury his wife, had hallucinated and been committed to Bellevue Hospital psychiatric ward, the victim of a breakdown brought on by despair.[32]

Moses did not return to Cambridge for two decades. He remained in New York to be near his father, who eventually recovered and returned to work. To pay for living expenses, Moses took a job from 1958 to 1961 teaching mathematics at Horace Mann, a prestigious private high school. During this period he took up folk dancing, and he traveled to Maine to attend a folk dance camp in the spring of 1960.[33] Later Moses would include such activities in group and staff gatherings—a much-needed antidote for the constant tension civil rights workers experienced. His uncle describes him during these years as being a "kindhearted, good-spirited" young man always "sympathetic to the needs of others."[34]

To supplement his income, Moses became a private tutor in 1958 to a fourteen-year-old black singer, Frankie Lyman. The job required travel by bus to the

black communities of various cities, and Moses soon
developed a sense of the emergent black ghettos and
the penalties of urban segregation.[35] Mississippi in the
late 1950s and early 1960s, and the rural South generally, was rife with rumors of the delights Chicago or
New York could offer an impoverished black. Racist
whites in Mississippi encouraged these rumors and
would occasionally offer to pay for the one-way bus fare
of blacks to Chicago. The reality, Moses soon came to
see, was far grimmer. He would come to believe that a
solution to racism was the enfranchising of the black
voting population in Mississippi.

In 1960, though, Moses was just beginning to see a
racial awakening. Watching on television and reading
in the newspapers about the events unfolding in North
Carolina, he was impressed by the determined faces of
the young black students who sat in at the Woolworth's
lunch counter in Greensboro, demanding they be served
along with whites. He has recalled:

> Before, the Negro in the South had always looked on
> the defensive, cringing. This time they were taking the
> initiative. They were kids my age, and I knew this had
> something to do with my own life. It made me realize
> that for a long time I had been troubled by the problem
> of being a Negro and at the same time being an Ameri-
> can. This was the answer.[36]

Greensboro was a forward current in what Moses
was to term the "ocean" of the civil rights movement.[37]
At Greensboro there were no waves of media figures;
the leaders were previously unknown college students.
Awakened by the 1955 Montgomery bus boycott, as
well as the activism that had stirred young black people

here and there in the South since the 1954 *Brown* decision, four students at the local black school, North Carolina Agricultural and Technical College, defied a
Greensboro ordinance and sat in at a white section of
Woolworth's lunch area. In the days that followed, their
numbers swelled and even included, if briefly, four
white students from the nearby North Carolina
Woman's College. The sit-ins were an early enactment
of what, in more conscious form, has come to be called
participatory democracy. As yet they were only spontaneous acts of rebellion, lacking the theoretical and con-
ceptual power that Moses, the disciple of Camus's morality of voluntary autonomous political action, would
give them. At this time, though, their style may have
helped Moses formulate his views on leadership.

A visit to his uncle, William Henry Moses, Jr., who
taught architecture at Hampton Institute (now Hampton University) in Hampton, Virginia, was Moses' first
encounter with Dixie.[38] This trip, during his 1960 spring
break, was memorable. He describes his feelings after
participating in a demonstration at Newport News:

> I had a feeling of release. From the first time a Negro
> gets involved in white society, he goes through the busi-
> ness of repressing, repressing, repressing. My whole re-
> action through life to such humiliation was to avoid it,
> keep it down, hold it in, play it cool. This is the kind of
> self-repression every Negro builds into himself. But
> when you do something personally to fight prejudice
> there is a feeling of great release.[39]

While in Newport News, Moses heard the Reverend
Wyatt Tee Walker deliver one of his sermons in support
of the sit-ins organized by the Southern Christian Lead-

ership Conference (SCLC) headed by Martin Luther
King. Walker referred to an upcoming rally for King at
Harlem's 369th Division Armory, where Moses' father
worked.[40] His eulogy of King provoked Moses to ask
Walker: "Why do you keep saying one leader? Don't
you think we need a lot of leaders?"[41] Walker's only
response was a puzzled look. Moses was drawing on his
own family experience. During World War II, through
the local Virginia Peninsula Teachers' Union, his uncle
had initiated a widely circulated petition, which was
sent to the president and the secretaries of war and the
navy and urged integration in the armed forces and
recognition of the right of blacks to become commis-
sioned officers.[42]

Seizing on an opportunity to express what he called
"a continual build-up and frustration . . . first that you
had to be treated as a Negro and you couldn't really be
accepted as an individual yet,"[43] Moses returned home
to volunteer his spare time to work with Bayard Rustin
on a rally planned for King in New York City.[44] Moses
had sought out Rustin earlier to discuss conscientious
objection to the military draft. At the committee office,
he requested that he be allowed to stuff envelopes. Rec-
ognizing Moses' potential, Rustin offered a more challenging job. Moses refused the leadership role, replying
that he would rather stay with his envelopes.[45] Rights
work in New York was not his calling. Upon Rustin's
urging and armed with his letter of recommendation to
Ella Baker, Moses headed south in June 1960 to work
for King's Southern Christian Leadership Conference
on a voter registration project. It was the beginning of
a five-year journey that would exhaust him and revolu-
tionize his core beliefs.

TWO

"TO 'UNCOVER WHAT IS COVERED' "

Twenty-five year-old Robert Moses arrived by bus in Georgia early in the summer of 1960 to find only three full-time workers in the Atlanta SCLC headquarters. The office was in transition, the publicity-seeking Wyatt Tee Walker replacing as executive director of SCLC the older but more radical Ella Baker. She had become a prime force behind the recently formed Student Nonviolent Coordinating Committee (SNCC) and was a leading early figure in the effort to make the left politics of the sixties radically democratic not only in objectives but in conduct.

Only weeks before, on Easter weekend, about three hundred Southern students joined by another hundred, mostly white Northern students had convened for the Southwide Youth Leadership Conference at Shaw University in Raleigh, North Carolina.[1] Brought on by the successes of the sit-ins and more tangibly by eight hundred dollars from SCLC, the conference was the work of Ella Baker. Meeting at her alma mater, where she had been valedictorian, the conferees listened to her encourage them to form their own organization and to work on broader issues. She has explained her convictions, "If I had any influence, it lodges in the direction of the leadership concept that I believe in . . . instead of having . . . a leader-centered group, you have a group-centered leadership."[2] Even in this birth of what first was named the "Temporary Student Nonviolent Coordinating Committee," there were two student contingents vying for leadership: one from Nashville, the other from Atlanta. As a compromise, Marion Barry, a young graduate student studying chemistry at Fisk University in Nashville (and future mayor of Washington, D.C.) was selected as chair, but the new group's office was placed in Atlanta with SCLC.[3]

From the start the marriage between SNCC and SCLC was at best an uneasy one. King's biographers debate whether he envisioned SNCC as a youth arm of the older organization or as an independent entity. Julian Bond, one of the students from Morehouse College in Atlanta attending the conference, recalls that representatives from SCLC, the Congress of Racial Equality (CORE), and the NAACP "wanted us, the students, to become a part of them . . . [as] . . . youth chapters."[4] Ella Baker has said of SCLC's intentions: "They were interested in having the students become an arm of SCLC. They were most confident that this would be their baby, because I was their functionary and I had called the meeting."[5] Instead she zealously guarded SNCC's independence and set it on its leftward course.

From the beginning, SNCC was resistant to the leadership of King and SCLC, or more precisely to leadership itself. In the style that they were soon to adopt on a public scale, the young SNCC workers came to differ from the prominent, solemnly ministerial spokesmen of the older organization. Moses himself, spare and understated in address and often clad in overalls well before proletarian clothing became a fad, was a stark contrast to King, a natty dresser with a magnetic public persona and enormous eloquence. The differences between King and Moses came to epitomize the differences in style between the two organizations.

But SCLC and SNCC had noticeable similarities as well. SCLC's discipline of nonviolence, informed by a religious ethic, was directed inward. It was akin to the conscience that Moses cultivated in his introspective self. Even in the pre-SNCC civil rights movement, the act of rebellion was both a means to freedom and a personal enactment of freedom by each participant: leaders, footsore black domestics, politely defiant students. And that empowerment of individuals was what Robert Moses would come to envision for black Mississippi.

When Moses arrived that June at the tiny SCLC office King was away and no one knew quite what to do with the young New Yorker. Moses had expected to find a room full of people organizing and training, or at least stuffing envelopes and collating reports.[6] Instead, he settled into the reality of a small Southern organization, understaffed and underfunded. At first, he was put to work preparing fund-raising packets for SCLC.[7] But he soon found the newly formed Student Nonviolent Coordinating Committee to be more compatible with his maturing political philosophy.

In addition to a secretary who worked solely for King, the staff included Jane Stembridge, a white volunteer for SNCC from New York City's Union Theological Seminary. She occupied a corner in the SCLC office, from which she was soon exiled to even smaller quarters on nearby Auburn Avenue. Here and in the back room of B. B. Beamon's, a soul-food restaurant where SNCC had temporary meeting space, she and Moses talked philosophy: Camus, Kant, Buber, Gandhi, and Tillich. Theories of nonviolence, especially the ideas of Camus and Gandhi, voicing the idealistic hopes of the movement in these early days before it became disillusioned and discordant, were earnestly debated. Connie Curry, a young white Southerner working for the National Student Association (NSA) in Atlanta, often joined in the discussions and remembers the heated debates over nonviolence as a technique or a way of life. In those first months her funding, a grant from the Field Foundation, helped support SNCC activities as well.[8] Moses' work for SNCC and SCLC was unpaid, though he received free room and board. During July, Moses and Jane Stembridge sent out a mailing advertising a SNCC general conference on October 14 as an opportunity for young students around the South to discuss and plan the next phase of their heartening new revolution. At the time, however, SNCC remained a small and ad hoc group that had enjoyed little success organizing the movement.

Meanwhile Moses also joined in the activities of the

Atlanta students, which included picketing Atlanta su-
permarkets that refused to employ black clerks. Moses
took to picketing, not simply on a one-hour shift like
the other students, but often all day and sometimes
alone. As he would do for the rest of his time with the
movement, he expressed himself by example. He stood
out in his reserved manner, his intellectuality, and his
lack of interest in the bickering, factional politics of the
movement. But whereas this style would invoke awe
and respect in Mississippi, it aroused uneasiness and
some suspicion among his Atlanta co-workers. Moses
was an outsider in external ways as well. He was a
New Yorker a few years older than the other student
demonstrators; most of the SNCC activist volunteers
were from Southern segregated colleges. These differences sometimes led to suspicion. A student activist in
Atlanta is reported to have told anyone who would lis-
ten, "Bob is so quiet and intense that he must be a
Communist."[9] Julian Bond explains, "We thought he
was a Communist because he was from New York and
wore glasses and was smarter than we were."[10]

While picketing a local A & P grocery store, Moses
was arrested with a group of older radicals whose protest was sponsored by the Southern Conference Education Fund (SCEF), a group to which Ella Baker belonged and which the House Un-American Activities
Committee had investigated in 1954. Moses' identification with the protest in the Atlanta media created
somewhat of a stir, for SCLC was still employing him.[11]
Asked by some cautious students how he had heard of
the picket line, Moses responded that he had picked up
the information while attending a mathematics lecture
entitled "Ramifications of Goedel's Theorem." None of

this did anything to reassure the anxious young black bourgeoisie.[12] The arrest was the first in a long series of encounters with the South's white police.

The SCEF case raised a thorny issue, redbaiting, which Moses disdained as a distraction. In his opinion, expressed a few years later,

> we can't call up people in the field one day and say now the Communist issue will be imposed, and call up another day and say now the dress-up-and-clean-up issue will be imposed, or now the white girl issue will be imposed. These people are risking their own lives. They have to make their own decisions, and they tend to emphasize their involvement rather than disguise it. We really look upon all these things—the political arguments of the thirties and forties, the impressions of the whites—as impositions of the whites—as impositions from the outside.[13]

But with the cold war raging, middle-class Atlanta blacks still shared with most Americans an overriding hostility to communism. Early student leaders of sit-ins who became deeply involved in SNCC, such as Diane Nash and Charles Jones, were committed to the belief that the student movement was part of the anticommunist struggle.[14]

The Atlanta students illustrate the generational distance between the early and the late 1960s. They were "good Americans" who did not yet question the system; perhaps the heady optimism inspired by recent successes in Greensboro and elsewhere across the South kept them from doing so. Some students, including one of the initial four to sit in at Greensboro, would, in a few years, find themselves on the battlefields in Vietnam.[15] Black students later were to question not why they were being excluded from American society but whether they wanted to be integrated into a "sick" society. They came to distrust their religious and conservative elders in the movement for being willing to buy into a system of laws and institutions they perceived to be corrupt by their very nature. In essence, they came to distrust liberalism, which promised no solution within the system. But in 1960 the movement fought to gain access to prevailing institutions and not to destroy or to withdraw from them. That meant, among many other things, shunning radicalism as incompatible with the basic redeemable American institutions. And the conservatism extended to social institutions as well. Despite Bayard Rustin's status as King's advisor, SNCC would withdraw the leftist homosexual Rustin's invitation to its upcoming October conference after the Packinghouse Workers' Union threatened to withhold funds if he attended.[16] This liberal micromanagement went unchallenged by the cautious young SNCC members.

Acting on their concerns, the Atlanta students called Moses in for an interview which proved maddening when Moses failed to share their worries. Since Moses was still technically a volunteer for SCLC, his inquisitors requested that King investigate and he agreed to do so. This meeting in King's study at Ebenezer Baptist Church was not confrontational. Moses, though not much younger, was too respectful to challenge the famed King, and King was too uncomfortable with red-baiting itself to upbraid him. "Some people think it's Communist, and that's what matters," King told Moses of the Southern Conference Education Fund, but he did not press the issue.[17] In the end, Moses had the support of Ella Baker, who refused to let the question of leftist association disqualify him.[18]

After this inauspicious introduction to the Southern civil rights movement, Moses sought a way out of the office in Atlanta. When the opportunity arose to become a field representative for SNCC and to experience the countryside where Jim Crow reigned unchallenged, he quickly volunteered. With partial financial support from SCLC, on August 13 Moses embarked on a recruiting drive among the underrepresented states of the deep South for the upcoming SNCC October conference in Atlanta.

He had prepared himself for the Southern brand of institutionalized white supremacy, but his background in Harlem and other Northern cities could not ready him for the grinding, inescapable poverty of the region. Class differences hardened the racial animosity that they had, in part, bred. Whites saw black Southerners living listlessly in subhuman conditions, and took this to be their natural state. Blacks, kept in ignorance, could not imagine a different way of life. In "the Delta of the early 1960s the white planter's word was still the law. . . . Conditions and situations that seemed more appropriate to the first half of the nineteenth century" characterized this area of Mississippi.[19] One particular episode that took place in the Delta region greatly impressed Moses:

> Just this afternoon, I had finished a bowl of stew when a silent hand reached over from behind me and took a discarded neckbone from the plate under my bowl. A voice mumbled some words of apology. Five seconds

later, the hand was back again, groping for the potatoes
I had left in my bowl. I never saw the face; I didn't look.
It was a man's hand, dark, dry and wind-cracked from
picking and chopping cotton. Lafayette and I got up and
walked out. What can you do when a man has to pick
up left-over potato from a bowl of stew?[20]

At Ella Baker's suggestion Moses visited Amzie
Moore, a grizzled longtime veteran of the struggle. She
explained: "I had gone down there and stayed with
them and helped with meetings, so I knew the person. I
knew he knew the state, and so Bob Moses was able to
have an entrée. Here was a man who had never been to
Mississippi, and he had somewhere to sleep, to eat, and
he had somebody who could be useful."[21]
    Moses' impression of Moore was of a man who "lives
like a brick wall in a brick house, dug into this country
like a tree beside the water."[22] Moore had worked
throughout the 1950s for voter registration projects.[23]
In addition to running a gas station and working part
time at the local post office, Moore was head of the
local NAACP chapter in the town of Cleveland, but was
evidently frustrated with that organization's plodding
legalistic approach. Moses remarks that Moore was
"the only person in the leadership of the NAACP that I
met at that time that was willing to welcome SNCC."[24]
Moore says opaquely of Moses, "He came down and
spent a while.... I don't know yet why Bob came to me,
but he found me and spent most of the time that summer at my house."[25]
    There were numbers of Amzie Moores in the South,
some of them black local activists, a few others representatives of a phenomenon remarkable at the time,
Southern white liberalism. Citizens' Councils—a more

upscale and genteel version of the Klan that formed the de facto government in many areas—effectively checked both their numbers and activities.[26] Anchored to their independence like the brick wall that is Moses' metaphor for Moore himself, these activists would have made the ideal citizens of a democracy of unresting civic participation, but they were too old for the 1960s. They were too worn down by life's oppression with few exceptions, like the fieldhand-turned-activist Fannie Lou Hamer. The young were the ones susceptible to the ideas and approach of SNCC.

Moore influenced Moses enormously and in a direction that nourished the roots of Freedom Summer. He talked with Moses about voter registration as a means to "uncover what is covered."[27] Through Moses he was soon able to shift the movement away from picketing, integrating public places, and other direct action strategies prevalent in other states toward a more focused attention to core problems of Southern blacks. These, he believed, could be handled only through the ballot box. Moore also believed that direct action was simply too dangerous in the deep South, especially the Mississippi Delta. Moore's ultimately more radical approach had the contradictory virtue of being for the moment safer, at least in the Mississippi heartland. A later comment by Moses on direct action explains, "Sure we could go to the desegregated restaurants. But could the Jackson Negro who might get fired for it go there? And how about the Negro who makes fifteen dollars a week?"[28]

Moore's local contacts would later prove to be indispensable to young SNCC workers. "We met at his house, we stayed at his house," a volunteer remembers.

"He had a hell of a network of individuals throughout the state.... Whenever anyone was threatened, Amzie Moore was sort of an individual protection agency."[29] Moses was deeply impressed by Moore. As he explained in an enthusiastic letter to Jane Stembridge in Atlanta:

> Amzie is the best I've met yet.... I would trust him explicitly and implicitly, and contact him frequently. Amzie thinks, and I concur, the adults here will back the young folks but will never initiate a program strong enough to do what needs to be done. Amzie thinks he can lay his hands on a bus if we can gas it up. The idea is to tackle the 2nd and 3rd Congressional districts, about 25 counties in all . . . . The main thrust is to take place next summer.... Nobody [is] starry eyed, these are nasty jobs but we're going to find some nasty people to do them, so put me down 'cause I'm not only getting mean I'm getting downright nasty.[30]

Moore, according to Moses, "wasn't very interested in the sit-ins and integration of lunch counters and so forth. So we mapped out the areas where a voter registration drive could take place and an idea for a program which I sent back to Atlanta."[31]

Moses soon formulated a plan for Mississippi voter registration and returned briefly to Atlanta with a list of local blacks interested in SNCC. He would later insist on the need for indigenous leadership, but at the time he met Moore he believed it essential to import SNCC workers into Mississippi to register new black voters. People would have to be brought in as a spark—to educate—and then the fire would begin. His aim compounded means and objective: to "awaken black people to stand up, respect themselves, dignity."[32] Moses told

Jane Stembridge that two thousand copies of the state's constitution would be needed to prepare would-be voters for rigorous examination by county registrars. She could not contain her enthusiasm: "This VOTER REGISTRATION project is IT!"[33] Moses was soon to learn that "in Mississippi voter registration was itself an act of confrontation."[34]

Moses' rendezvous in Mississippi was a journey into the heart of darkness, a racial past still alive in that land of black sharecroppers and white overlords. Later, some SNCC student members were to romanticize the black population of the deep South for having a culture more authentic than their own, and to seek, as one author has suggested, to be reborn themselves in the rebirth of these people.[35] Bob Moses too could perceive a distinctive virtue in black Southerners. He spoke of "people who come off the land . . . and simply voice . . . the simple truths you can't ignore because they speak from their own lives." Such were the people he wished to awaken to their collective existence and power. Moses wanted power for the black community in the South, an empowerment they would win in the action of willing it. But at least in his Mississippi field work he himself never displayed a need to search for an authentic black culture. Having his own palpable authenticity, he had no reason to take on another. Moses was seeking not to be reborn but simply to do right.

THREE

"THIS IS MISSISSIPPI, THE MIDDLE OF THE ICEBERG"

After Labor Day 1960 Moses returned to New York to his father's apartment and his teaching contract at the Horace Mann School in Riverdale. Late in the spring of 1961, he left for the South, honoring a commitment to work for SNCC in Mississippi "with no timetable or agenda other than the radical notion that blacks in the state should be able to vote."[1] He remained there for almost four years.

That spring the national press began to cover the Freedom Rides organized by the Congress of Racial Equality (CORE). The idea of testing national integration laws was not new: late in the 1940s CORE had taken a similar action in some of the border states to test integration aboard buses in interstate travel. Now the plan was for integrated groups to travel throughout the South, including the deep South, testing the Supreme Court ruling of December 1960 in *Boynton v. Virginia*, which required the desegregation of facilities used in interstate travel. The act was likely to provoke a visceral response in a region already edgy over the sit-ins.

The first freedom riders, led by James Farmer of CORE, left the nation's capital on May 4. As the two buses, filled with CORE members, student sit-in activists, and reporters, moved farther south, the riders encountered increasing violence, culminating in the well-publicized burning of a Greyhound bus near Anniston, Alabama, on May 14. The picture of the burning bus hit the front pages across the world, embarrassing President Kennedy, electrifying the black community, and shocking white America. After Klansmen beat CORE riders in Birmingham, Attorney General Robert Kennedy urged the group to have a cooling off period— affording the administration a breather before SNCC and student activists from CORE and SCLC announced continuation of the rides. This first round ended on May 23 in Jackson, Mississippi, with all the students jailed.[2]

The Freedom Rides won SNCC national attention for the first time and in turn the project, initiated by CORE, attracted students to SNCC. The result was a continuing stream of volunteers for the Freedom Rides and a burgeoning jail population in Jackson. But the Freedom Rides also highlighted the growing conflict in SNCC between advocates of direct action and supporters of voter registration projects.[3] Factionalism, which tore apart SNCC in the later 1960s, had already begun.

The Kennedy administration, working hard but silently to prevent the kind of negative worldwide publicity that had resulted from the Freedom Rides, threw its power behind the voter registration projects in which Moses believed. Timothy Jenkins, the National Student Association's vice president and an undergraduate at Howard University, describes a fall 1961 meeting with Assistant Attorney General Burke Marshall and the president's advisor on civil rights, Harris Wofford, in which representatives from the Taconic and other private liberal foundations promised funds to civil rights groups that would work on voter registration. Wofford offered protection and announced that the administration was committed to protecting voters' rights—to the extent of filling every jail in the South with obstructors.[4] But, for the moment, Washington was simply hoping to divert the energies of the rights workers into relatively safe political activity; helping blacks to register to vote would be less dangerous to the more enthusiastic student rights workers as well as to the government's reputation. That wish accorded with the pragmatic character of the Kennedy presidency, the inherent preference on the part of government for social peace, and the political realities of the times.

John and Robert Kennedy were northeastern Democrats and at least ambivalently liberal. Liberalism, along with an upper-class commitment to sportsmanship and fair play, predisposed them toward racial justice. But each had his own individual priorities: John was chiefly interested in foreign policy: Robert preferred to chase labor racketeers. Both were politicians, inclined to recognize that for the moment holding the white South and white Northern blue-collar workers was more promising to Democratic fortunes than any potential modest gains in black voter registration. And both were practical in the way that impatiently hard-headed people habitually are when they take the immediate visible contours of their world as given and enduring.

The practical eye, in the case of Mississippi, saw a landscape biracial yet white-supremacist in its leading features, with no visible trace of integration in it and no tolerance for race mixing. Between 1882 and 1962 the state had achieved the national record for lynchings of blacks, with approximately 538.[5] This history would move a pragmatist to choose voter registration over sit-ins and civil disobedience. Voter registration would have to be slow and plodding, which for the moment meant that it might be less volatile than direct integrationist action—particularly in Mississippi, where only five percent of voting-age blacks had been allowed to register. Yet for the long run it promised deeper changes than racial integration of a handful of sleepy early-morning customers at a roadside diner. But the same pragmatist would shrink back whenever registering voters threatened to become dangerous. Even at the cost of injustice, the most democratic governments seek to avoid disorder. It was therefore natural for the Justice Department to favor reining in Moses and his SNCC co-workers, rather than protecting them as they marched into white mobs sanctioned if not encouraged by the Mississippi police.

In the 1980s, Moses contrasted voter registration work in the South with activity in the Northern cities:

The tool for organizing in the Northern cities is political activity. Running people for office. But you couldn't get people [in Mississippi] to think like that. It was hard to get people to think about using the electoral process as an organizing tool. You couldn't export sit-ins or voter registration to the North. Community action [in the North] was a government funded program, which is different from the Mississippi Freedom Democratic Party, which was an independent political effort. The traditional route in the cities is through politics. That was not clearly articulated during the 1960s.[6]

Many in SNCC were wary of voter registration, thinking that the Kennedy administration was promoting it solely for the benefit of votes for the Democratic party.[7] As described by SNCC field worker Lonnie King, a boycott of AT&T in Southern states by blacks was in place to force the hiring and integration of blacks in the company:

We would . . . ask people to cut off their telephones for thirty, sixty days. . . . And what we were gonna do was to negotiate . . . until they agreed. . . . And within a few months, we're all summoned to Washington. . . . From their point of view [the Kennedys], our moving into voting rights would be more beneficial for them in terms of image than it would be to us. . . . I thought we could do both of them.[8]

Meanwhile, in July 1961, Moses began to initiate plans made the previous summer with Amzie Moore at his home in Cleveland, Mississippi. Moore, however, was alarmed and distracted by the Freedom Rides, which he believed to have worsened race relations. As the days passed in inactivity, Moses looked for a way out of an increasingly tense situation with a man whom he respected enormously.[9] In a later interview Moses has said that it was merely a lack of equipment and a meeting place that postponed his work.[10] For either, or more likely a combination, of these reasons, he accepted Moore's suggestion that he respond to a request for help with voter registration from the head of the Pike County chapter of the NAACP. Moore suggested to Moses that a team of students embark on the project. McComb, Mississippi, a town of twelve thousand people, lay in the southwestern corner of the state, about twenty miles north of the Louisiana border. All of Pike County boasted a total of two hundred registered black voters; the bordering counties of Amite and Walthall totaled one.[11] McComb had been the first stop in Mississippi for freedom riders on a Greyhound bus coming from New Orleans. Claude Sitton, a *New York Times* reporter for several Southern states, was in McComb in the cafe having a cup of coffee with *Time* magazine reporter Sim Fentress when the freedom riders entered and a riot erupted.[12] Sitton comments that FBI agents sat in a car down the street during the melee and later asked the reporters to fill them in on what had happened. The local newspaper mistook the two reporters for FBI agents.

Moses wanted to stay out of the conflict between the SNCC advocates of direct action and the members urging voter registration programs. An article on the freedom movement written a few years later underscored the propensity of Moses to avoid such debates: "While the others were talking, he was quietly working in Mississippi: contacting people, finding places for civil rights workers to live, looking for meeting places."[13] Moses was not at the SNCC meeting in mid-July when his request that SNCC consider his voter registration project, developed with Amzie Moore, was debated. The group also discussed "Mr. Bob Moses request for Official Status, Voluntary Field Sec'y." Because he was still on the staff of SCLC, there was some concern about the relationship; the decision was to form a committee to work with Wyatt Tee Walker of SCLC.[14] Charles McDew, elected SNCC chairman at this meeting, hoped to gain stature for the voter registration faction similar to that achieved by Moses' courageous lone travels through the deep South the previous summer.

SNCC put off acting on Moses' request, noting he was still technically associated with SCLC; the larger contest was over what course the young organization should take. Charles Sherrod, SNCC's first field secretary, had visited Amzie Moore in Cleveland to discuss voter registration; he reported to the group that Moore believed students would be best used to recruit blacks to attempt voter registration and they would be more likely to succeed at it. At the same time another report was given regarding a meeting with the prominent black singer Harry Belafonte in which it was agreed "that voter registration was the most important issue." Although the Belafonte meeting was basically a fundraising venture, it was suggested even at this early stage that the student movement be expanded to include from one hundred thousand to two hundred thousand students.[15]

By the first week in August Moses had cut his SCLC affiliation and volunteered himself as a field secretary for SNCC in Mississippi. He wrote Wyatt Tee Walker, the executive director of SCLC in Atlanta, to assure him that SCLC would be given some credit and publicity for the McComb project. Moses said that henceforth he would be unable to work for SCLC and was devoting his energies solely to SNCC. "The job needs to be done," he noted, "so I have made my choice." Moses' choice illustrates the early determination of SNCC to be independent of SCLC, despite the wishes of King and others. It also suggests Ella Baker's influence on the young organization. Moses did ask Walker whether SCLC could contribute money to the McComb project, beyond what it had received from the black community.[16]

Charles McDew gave Moses some measure of protection by handing him the private telephone number of John Doar of the Civil Rights Division of the Department of Justice. In a letter to Doar, Moses described his upcoming plans for voter registration in southern Pike County. In his July 17, 1961, response, sent to Moses in care of Amzie Moore, Doar directed Moses to call him at his office in Washington and report "any economic or other reprisals against citizens of Mississippi who attempt to register to vote," citing the penalties for interfering with the right to vote in a federal election. Moses' problem, however, was simply getting people registered so that they then could vote in any election. Doar missed the point: federal law appeared to protect not registration to vote, but only the vote itself. Nonetheless, Doar promised he would "vigorously investigate all alleged violations."[17] He instructed Moses to contact the local FBI office.

Instead of attending the SNCC meeting scheduled for August at the Highlander Folk School in Tennessee where the group was to determine its future direction,

Moses presented himself to C. C. Bryant in McComb as the voter registration "team." Bryant represented a small class of blacks relatively free of the economic pressures of whites. Numbers of black Protestant ministers had gained that freedom by working directly for the black communities. Other blacks achieved it by working for Northern companies. Bryant drew his paycheck from a railroad based in Chicago. As the president of the county NAACP chapter and an official in the Freemasons, he was able to secure a room at the black Masonic Temple for Moses to hold his voter registration school.[18]

Voter education schools prepared their participants for the details of the registration process and for the test questions about the law or other matters that applicants needed to answer in order to qualify. Black applicants could expect questions designed to stump them. A typical question would read, "Write and copy in the space below Section _____ of the Constitution of Mississippi." The registrar designated the section— any one of 285. Then the applicant would be asked to write a "reasonable interpretation" of that particular section.[19] As Lawrence Guyot, a student at Tougaloo in Jackson, put it: The registration test "was clearly devised . . . to make sure illiterate whites would be registered but no Negro, regardless how literate, would be registered."[20] In addition, a poll tax had to be paid two years in succession prior to voting; sheriffs collected the poll tax.[21] As one college volunteer noted: "A poll tax is still required for state and local elections, and there is widespread ignorance of the fact that it is not required for national elections, and the $2.00 tax seems like a considerable amount to people who are making

$3.00 a day for ten hours of chopping cotton, if they are lucky enough to have a job at all."[22] Beyond the immediate practical goals of the schools, however, lay their larger contribution to the empowerment of black Southerners.

To have knowledge about the political system or about anything else, to seek that knowledge within a state that did not wish its black population to obtain it, to gather together in what were at once learning and strategy sessions—these actions inevitably instilled a sense of awareness and self-assertion. They meant at the very least a rejection of the white-supremacist definition of black people as powerless and passive. They were, in themselves, acts of power. The notion of informal schooling for the sake of empowerment had been a concept both practiced and expounded in the Highlander Folk School in Tennessee, a continuing workshop for exchange of ideas among radicals and poor people who wanted to organize their communities. Highlander had opened in 1932 as a training school for union organizers in the Congress of Industrial Organizations (CIO). Originally located in the mountains outside Chattanooga, it had been one of the few places where integrated meetings could be held.[23] Highlander, the voter registration schools, and the freedom schools anticipated the movement for alternative education among privileged radical white students later in the decade.

Once he had a place to train blacks in the intricacies of Southern voter registration requirements, Moses somehow had to convince them that it was worth the effort to confront the hostility of whites, realizing that at best they would be denied registration and at worst they would face violence and even death. Under the influence of Amzie Moore, Moses had familiarized himself with the strategies of the local whites. But it was not merely a matter of countering strategies. For the average Mississippi black, appearing before the white county voting registrar was an excruciating and humiliating experience. Beyond the many obstacles the registrar's office could set up lay the psychological barriers built up by Jim Crow. Mississippi had conditioned generations of blacks to defer to whites. Most blacks who had even seen the inside of the county courthouse had been there not to register, but to stand trial at the whim of what was called justice. SNCC worker Lawrence Guyot talks about getting people to register: "With a program and with a concentrated effort you can get people to go to a courthouse. In '62 there was a hell of a job to even consider voting 'cause that meant going to the courthouse, that meant the possibility of being beaten—the probability of being beaten—the probability of not having a job and of being cut off of welfare. [The white authorities] had ... complete rigid control."[24] Moses considered it a victory even to get a black to think of entering the registrar's office:

> We went around house-to-house, door-to-door in the hot sun everyday because the most important thing to do was to convince the local townspeople that we meant business, that is, that we were serious, that we were not only young, but that we were people who were responsible. What do you tell somebody when you go to their door? Well, first you tell them who you are, what you're trying to do, that you're working on voter registration. You have a form that you try to get them to fill out. Now the technique that we found best usable, I think,

was to present the form to them and say, "Have you ever tried to fill out this form? Would you like to sit down now and try to fill it out?" And then, psychologically they have to complete the gap and imagine themselves at the registrar's office.[25]

According to Travis Britt, a freedom rider from New York who had been jailed in Jackson and came to join Moses, the youth of McComb were different from their parents: "They had no fear whatsoever. The ones who did not participate were kept away by their parents."[26] Two local high school students, Curtis Hayes and Hollis Watkins, volunteered to help and soon were not content with canvassing for possible registrants; they staged a sit-in at a Woolworth store and were charged with breach of the peace.[27] Still, there was sometimes an internal mechanism that limited even their horizons. As one young worker would later acknowledge: "While I was canvassing we discussed that the problems of some of the Negro race who are afraid, and do not understand their rights as being citizens simply because all their lives they have been taught that the Negro race isn't as good as any other race in the South."[28]

Out-of-state rights workers soon became interested in Moses' activities in McComb; he was joined by John Hardy of the Nashville movement and Reggie Robinson, who had worked in Baltimore. And other former freedom riders followed Britt to McComb. Funds for the activities came from the singer Harry Belafonte, who was instrumental in raising money for SNCC projects and later in helping to finance Freedom Summer.

The voter education classes produced some quick results. After the first meeting on August 7, 1961, four blacks pronounced themselves ready. Moses accompanied them to the registrar's office at the county seat in Magnolia. It must have seemed a mission behind enemy lines. "The courthouse," according to a rights worker, "represented the whole Mississippi society."[29] Yet three were registered.

After two days with similar success, local officials realized the surge of blacks registering was no accident and began summarily to reject applicants. Soon an article appeared in the local *Enterprise-Journal* reporting the sudden interest of blacks in registration. This served to alert local toughs and segregationists, and the undercurrent of threatened violence quickly frightened blacks in the nearby rural areas.[30] Nonetheless, a few of them beseeched Moses to begin similar projects in the surrounding counties of Amite and Walthall. These counties were more typical of Mississippi, and far more dangerous than McComb. While some 250 blacks had already been registered in McComb itself, not a single black, in local accounting, had voted in the countryside since the early days of Reconstruction. Moses lacked the people to expand his recruiting program. Yet after discussions with Bryant, it was decided that the only way to win the trust of local blacks was to face up to trouble spots:

> The position is simply this: that farmers came over and were very anxious to try and register and you couldn't very well turn them down; one, just from the human point of view, they had greater needs than those people in Pike County where we were working and, secondly, from the psychological point of view where the whole problem in Mississippi is pervaded with fear. The prob-

lem is that you can't be in a position of turning down the tough areas, because the people then, I think, would simply lose confidence in you; so, we accepted this.[31]

On August 11, Moses again wrote John Doar detailing the difficulties his registration pupils faced. This time Doar's response was a bit less hopeful. "We are not," he wrote, "able to provide observers at any particular registration office at any particular time. As for the specific questions which you ask, the registrar must treat Negroes as he treats whites. If he does not, and we have specific facts to establish that he does not, we will proceed promptly to court to seek an injunction prohibiting such practices."[32] This letter reflected, more accurately than Doar's first, the role of the Justice Department in the early civil rights era. Doar later remarked of Moses' decision to go into the most resistant areas: "He has to go where it's tough, to prove he has courage."[33]

Moses set up a voter registration school on a farm in Amite County. After securing a car and places to stay—no small task for a shy, introspective Northerner—he set out on August 15 to register three volunteers. In Liberty, the county seat of Amite, Moses had his first real encounter with Southern harassment:

We arrived at the courthouse about 10 o'clock. The registrar came out, I waited by the side for the man or one of the ladies to say something to the registrar. He asked them what did they want, what were they here for in a very rough tone of voice. They didn't say anything, they were literally paralyzed with fear. . . . Then our people started to register one at a time. In the meantime, a procession of people began moving in and out of the registration office. The sheriff, a couple of his deputies, people from the tax office, people who do the driver's license, looking in, staring, moving back out, muttering. The first person who filled out the form took a long time. . . . We finally finished the whole process at about 4:30, all of the three people had a chance to register, at least to fill out the form. This was a victory, because they had been down a few times before and had not had a chance to even fill out the forms.[34]

Once the whites had recovered from the shock of this breach of black deference, they were determined to punish Moses and his students. The local policeman followed them on their way back to McComb. Though they tried to shake him in every way possible, he finally succeeded in pulling their car over. The officer asked Moses whether he was the "nigger that came down from New York to stir up a lot of trouble?" He replied, "I'm the Negro who came down from New York to instruct people in voter registration."[35] He then jotted down the officer's name and was promptly told, "Get in the [police] car, nigger!"[36]

Moses, the educated Northerner, the "outside agitator," was the only one taken to the station in McComb, where the prosecuting attorney and the arresting officer looked through the law books for a charge. At first they booked Moses for interfering with an officer in the process of arresting someone; they soon looked for another reason because he was the only one arrested. Before being tried and found guilty on vague charges, Moses asked for his one phone call. He dialed the Justice Department collect and asked to speak with John Doar. Doar accepted and Moses described to him the viola-

tion of the Civil Rights Acts of 1957 and 1960 and suggested the possibility of a federal investigation.[37]

And so began a working relationship between these
two representatives of differing ethos: Moses, the
moral, philosophical activist; Doar, the legalistic representative of tempered liberalism. Doar describes the
Justice Department's activities in Greenwood: "We
brought suits against the county officials and the state
officials, and they were in court on these cases of [voter]
intimidation. At the same time, we were trying to get
more registrars to open up the rolls. We were battling.
We weren't making any significant progress, but we
had a lot of presence in Mississippi."[38] At first, the
two shared the hope that the federal government would
have an impact on Mississippi, but incompatibility in
method and thinking between SNCC and the Justice
Department would become increasingly apparent.

Facing enormous political obstacles, the federal government—despite Doar's protestations to the contrary—maintained only a minimal presence in Mississippi, due in part to constitutional limitations on its
power. "I can't keep a crime from being committed,"
John Doar explained. "We try the very best we can to
eliminate the lawlessness by seeking injunctions and
restraining various forms of economic retaliation. But
it is very difficult to win. We have to prepare and check
out those cases very carefully."[39] SNCC workers discovered that the promise made by Assistant Attorney General Burke Marshall to accept collect calls was stopped
when key congressmen objected: "Can you imagine
what that really is? Here's a guy down here surrounded
with all these cats about to eat him up with the billy

clubs and what have you and dogs, and he's in the police station calling his *one* call, and it's refused on technical grounds that the federal government can't receive a collect call."[40]

Doar's *apologia* was both right and wrong. Legally, it was very difficult to prepare cases against the local Southern county officials. It took much diligent research and interminable time under the anemic civil rights acts then in force. Yet as a federal suit that Moses filed in 1963 made clear, there were laws on the books that the Justice Department simply did not use. The Federal Bureau of Investigation was concerned far more with fighting a small and fading communist movement than with working on domestic civil rights issues. Some federal judges in the South, moreover, were staunch segregationists, including a few patronage appointees of the Kennedy administration. Robert E. Gilbert has noted, "One of the most controversial aspects of John Kennedy's civil rights record lies in his appointments to the federal courts, particularly those of the Fifth Judicial Circuit which includes much of the South. As many as a quarter to a third were estimated by scholars as segregationists."[41] One such judge, William Harold Cox, of the Southern district of Mississippi, hailed from Sunflower County, where his father had been sheriff and the population was seventy-four percent black. President Kennedy had appointed him in deference to Senator James O. Eastland, a staunch segregationist and a resident of Sunflower County. In 1961 Cox refused to permit the Justice Department to inspect public voting records for Clarke County, and in October 1967 it was Cox who heard the conspiracy case against the murderers of Goodman, Schwerner, and Chaney.[42]

Kennedy had chosen at the beginning of his administration to forego the legislative route to civil rights and took instead the slower but politically safer judicial way.[43] Taken as a whole, the combined forces of the federal government often hid behind the safety of excuses, never fully understanding the moral fervor propelling Moses and others in the civil rights movement.

But in 1961 Moses' telephone call from the McComb police station to John Doar in Washington, D.C., may have saved his life. Charles Jones, an early civil rights worker in McComb, remembers a rumor that the Ku Klux Klan had "told some Negroes that they were going to take Bob Moses out of jail. . . . We got the word they were going to take Bob out and kill him. . . . Bob [had] moved up to number one on the list of the Klan to be killed."[44] Perhaps Moses' connection with the federal government did scare away the Klan just as it was coming for him.

Moses refused the offer to pay a five-dollar fine to cover court costs and instead spent two days in Liberty's jail until an NAACP lawyer bailed him out on August 17. Surprised officials asked, "Boy, are you sure you know what you're about?"[45] Though on this occasion there was a measure of cooperation, differences in approach to civil rights strained the relationship between SNCC and the NAACP. The older organization, preferring to work through the courts, was annoyed to have to bail out SNCC workers who were doing things that the NAACP neither sponsored nor endorsed. An NAACP official in McComb advised Moses to discontinue his work and prudishly related to the FBI investigating the New Yorker's draft status that he was an "occasional drinker," was "evasive about things he did not want to discuss," and did not have a Bible in his lodgings.[46] One NAACP field secretary commented with pride, "In all my years of voter campaigning no one in my group has been arrested. When they bring in sit-ins and freedom rides and someone is arrested, my campaign is shot. That's it." On entering the most intransigent areas of white resistance, he said, "We should go in on a test case, and then pull out and go where we can get people on the books and registered."[47] That Moses debated to himself the morality of accepting bail, of accepting the benefits of an impure system, defines the distance between the ideologically motivated SNCC volunteers and the pragmatic NAACP.

After leaving the Liberty jail, Moses returned to McComb. He found the area flooded by SNCC volunteers from recent sit-ins at Jackson as well as SNCC leaders fresh from a meeting at the Highlander Folk School. Moses' dramatic arrest appealed to the proponents of direct action who had been stymied in Jackson. It made clear that voter registration was just as subversive of the existing racial order as sit-ins in a region where the authorities and the establishment were sufficiently determined not to yield anything to peaceful processes.

From McComb, Moses went to E. W. Steptoe's farm in Amite County, where he had been lodging. Steptoe had been the president of the county NAACP before the sheriff shut it down. He let Moses set up classes at his farm, but soon found a church in the woods for the sessions when the rights workers ran into trouble.[48] Moses had returned to Amite County to calm fears created by his arrest and the unsuccessful registration attempt in Liberty. Rumor had it that the Citizens' Council was discussing the registration project and that was worrisome. While Moses was at Steptoe's farm, there was fear among would-be registrants of additional trouble if any more people made the attempt. In his nightly meetings Moses softened his exhortations, yet it took nearly two weeks for two men to agree to come forward to register.

On August 29, Moses and his recruits set out for the courthouse in Liberty. On the way, three whites stopped them—including Billy Jack Caston, the cousin of the local police officer and the son-in-law of a local state representative. Questioned about where he was going, Moses simply replied, "to the courthouse." The response was several blows to the head with the handle of a knife.[49] After his beating Moses said to the others accompanying him, "We can't let something like this stop us. We've got to go to the Registrar. That's the whole point."[50] The three continued to the courthouse; there the unnerved registrar informed them that he was just closing the office. "I remember very sharply," reads an account by Moses, "that I didn't want to go immediately back into McComb because my shirt was very bloody and I figured that if we went back in we would probably be fighting everybody. So, instead we went back out to Steptoe's farm where we washed down before we came back into McComb."[51] There Moses got stitches for three head wounds—"I was beaten to the tune of eight stitches," he testified before a congressional hearing in 1963[52]—and during the treatment persuaded the doctor to lend the movement his car.

The beating inflamed both the local black community and the SNCC workers. But that was all to the good. Anger and indignation were essential emotions for action. "Only when metal has been brought to white heat, permitting it to be molded while it cools; this is the annealing process," Moses declared. "This is what we intend to do to the South and the country, bring them to white heat and then remold them."[53] In time white thugs, having discovered the unintended effect of their actions, would turn to beating civil rights workers away from the eyes and ears of the national media.

Stirred by the beating of Moses, SNCC called a mass meeting in McComb to hear both Moses and the rights activist James Bevel of SCLC. Bevel, who had been working in Jackson, was a moving orator and former student at the American Baptist Theological Seminary. The contrast between the two leaders was stark: detached, cerebral Northerner; passionate, engaged Southerner. Much as the Reverend Ralph Abernathy warmed up the crowds for the content of King's speeches, Bevel moved the crowd to fury, preparing it for Moses. The New Yorker proceeded to speak in a soft monotone. Yet his message was as powerful as if a charismatic orator had delivered it: "The law down here is law made by white people, enforced by white people, for the benefit of white people. It will be that way until the Negroes begin to vote."[54] Moses repeated what he had told the two men in Liberty: the important thing was to persevere. He announced he would return to Liberty the next day. A local white reporter who observed the meeting wrote that "the Negroes might be serious."[55]

The following day Moses swore out a complaint against Caston. Surprisingly, Caston was put on trial. But the character of the proceedings was not untypical of Southern racial justice: white farmers jamming the courthouse, ready for a show, shotguns resting on their knees. Right after Moses testified, the sheriff drove him to the edge of town, explaining the need to protect him from possible white violence. This apparently was the "first time any Negro had ever pressed charges against any white person in this county for anything. They still feared Moses for this," in the judgment of Travis Britt. "They couldn't understand how any Negro could have so much nerve."[56] Boldness, Moses could believe, gave him "some kind of immunity."[57] The trial ended in an acquittal that Moses read about the next day in the newspaper.

Meanwhile, direct action proponents in McComb, following an earlier attempt to integrate some downtown stores, organized a sit-in at the local Greyhound station lunch counter on August 30 in which sixteen-year-old Brenda Travis and four other high school students were arrested and jailed. The sit-in at the bus station aroused anger in both white and black communities: among whites toward SNCC for "corrupting" minors, among middle-class blacks toward the authorities who had jailed Travis. The local black high school expelled the girl, demonstrating in no uncertain terms how much control Southern whites wielded over the black community. (She later was given an indefinite sentence in reform school.)[58]

Brenda Travis's jailing scared off SNCC's whisper-thin support among older residents of McComb. As August ended, Moses had registered no blacks in Amite county and only a few in Pike County. But in failure he achieved success. Like a handful of American politicians, he was seen (in his case accurately) as above partisan struggle; he quickly became an almost mythic figure, working unobtrusively and with unostentatious courage among the wretched. Local people had begun to call him "Moses in the Bible,"[59] and SNCC workers were circulating the story that during beatings Moses would look up and say, "Forgive them."[60] Moses' simplicity and directness, cutting through oratory and grandiose ideology, was the essence of his ability to command respect and a following. Betty Garman, a SNCC worker in the Atlanta office, commented on Moses' style:

> In a meeting situation, he would never get involved in the kind of petty details of the problem at hand that was being discussed, but he would hold back all of his comments until an appropriate time when he felt he could summarize and direct the entire course of discussion.... He would come in with a brilliant statement, which just clearly cut through all of the mess and all of the tangle and all of the debate, said exactly what probably three-quarters of the people wanted to have said, and allowed the discussion to move on.[61]

This simplicity was reflected in the basic and utilitarian bib overalls he wore—later to be styled the SNCC uniform.[62]

By now Moses, like it or not, was a leader. His style was to be marked by "example and directional discussion."[63] He and others involved in the movement in these early years believed that real progress would come only if the leaders became less important than the ideas they advocated.[64] It was a style that invited contradictions. For example, Moses' policy of removing himself from discussion was an attempt to preserve the spontaneity of other participants, and to that extent was consonant with his affirmation of a democracy deriving its energy from autonomous individuals. But in a sense his practice of silent distance from discussion and debate was in conflict with those beliefs. If speaking is an act of the free mind and conscience, then he had some obligation to speak, if only because his speaking would affirm the right of everyone else to do so. And in sparing others the force of his persuasiveness, he was in effect protecting them against having fully to think for themselves, to argue against a strong and convincing intellect. Yet argument is part of the process of education, leading people to make informed decisions.

Soon after the arrests of the high school students, community tensions notched upward. On September 5 Moses and Travis Britt brought four blacks to the Liberty courthouse to register. In the turmoil, the registrants and SNCC workers attracted the attention of a small white mob. Someone screamed: "Why are you niggers from New York stirring up trouble down here?"[65] Not only was SNCC disturbing the way things had been for a century, but Moses and Britt were outsiders, Northerners in a land where the Civil War was sometimes referred to as the War of Northern Aggression. Britt was badly beaten by the mob despite Moses' nonviolent attempts to keep him from harm. The rest of the group escaped. The registrants, of course, were rejected. This beating, on the heels of others, drove people away from the registration schools SNCC had set up in Pike and Walthall counties. Amite was particularly hard hit. John Doar has remarked that all three counties "retained the character of the 17th century."[66]

Two days later John Hardy, another SNCC member, attempted for the fourth time to register blacks at the courthouse in Tylertown in Walthall County, on the other side of McComb from Amite. When the registrar claimed that he "wasn't registering voters that day," Hardy leaned forward to ask why his two applicants had been refused. The registrar returned to his desk and pulled out a gun, smashing it against the side of Hardy's head in response. Following Moses' example, Hardy set off for the local police station to report the incident. He was met in the street by the sheriff, who refused to arrest the registrar and instead arrested Hardy for disturbing the peace.[67] Fearing lynching, the sheriff removed the prisoner to the Pike County jail in the town of Magnolia.

In a significant historic step the federal government acted to block Hardy's trial. Perhaps, as Taylor Branch suggests, it was simply the Southern mockery of federal authority that in time shamed the Justice Department into acting rather than simply gathering information.[68] The case went before Harold Cox, who dismissed the government's petition for a restraining order. In a subsequent appeal before the Fifth Circuit Court of Appeals in Atlanta, two judges appointed by Eisenhower agreed with the Justice Department. The rest of September, in Moses' words, was "a tough time."[69]

John Doar, again more willing than most other federal officials to act, flew to Mississippi to investigate the charges of violence and landed in a situation charged with fear. He met with Moses on September 24, 1961,[70] just five weeks after the collect call from McComb.

Having read the dry technical reports Moses submitted to the department, Doar was unprepared for the graphic evidence of intimidation in the South. Moses and the FBI had understated rather than exaggerated Moses' considerable head scars and stitches, and this and other evidence convinced Doar of the likelihood of further trouble in Amite County. Doar met with E. W. Steptoe, who told him he feared for his own life and that of Herbert Lee, another black farmer actively aiding SNCC. Moses has said about Doar's visit:

> Whatever the shortcomings of the Justice Department, they certainly made a visible impact on the black population of Mississippi. People like E. W. Steptoe, down in Amite County. His face lit up when John Doar and the Justice Department came out . . . so different from when a local resident FBI agent came.[71]

Doar felt similarly: "These people see you and get to know you. They begin to have some confidence that you mean what you say."[72]

Two days later, on September 26, Doar returned to his office in Washington. He learned that Lee, a middle-age farmer supporting a large family, had been shot to death the day before in front of witnesses near a cotton gin. The body lay on the ground for several hours, because no one in town dared to touch it. Moses left the message for Doar after a tearful Mrs. Lee screamed at him, "You killed my husband! You killed my husband!"[73] Lee's death deeply disturbed Moses. In a wider sense Moses knew that white Southern bigotry, not the civil rights movement, had killed Lee. Yet Lee had died specifically for helping SNCC and an abstract knowledge of the inherent depravity of man hardly assuaged Moses' conscience. The murder was to have continuing ugly consequences.

Lee's killer was state Representative E. H. Hurst, who claimed Lee had attacked him with a tire iron. Witnesses, one white and one black, testified that Hurst had shot Lee in self-defense. Yet Hurst was over six feet tall and weighed about two hundred pounds; Lee was less than five-and-a-half-feet tall and fifty pounds lighter. A doctor who had examined the corpse said it showed no trace of powder burns, indicating that Lee had been shot at some distance.[74]

The FBI, without a nearby office in Mississippi, relied on the local police and failed to act until after Lee's burial. The investigation was perfunctory, without even the thought of an exhumation.[75] Moses and others sought out those said to have been witnesses—three black men—and on three separate nights heard the same story. Two admitted they had been pressured to describe the shooting as self-defense.[76] A SNCC fund-raising handbill said of the murderer: "This representative of the people was never arrested, never spent one hour in jail, and was acquitted by a coroner's jury."[77] The Justice Department filed a suit against the registrar but no intimidation suit against Hurst. Lee, Moses told a congressional committee in 1963, "happened to be a farmer who was very active in our voter registration campaign. Now there has been no real further voter registration activity since 1961, primarily because of . . . fear." In response to questioning, Moses reported that since Lee's death only one black had been registered to vote, in the winter of 1963.[78]

There was to be a worse sequel to the case. A black witness, Louis Allen, later informed Moses that he wanted to tell the truth about the incident—there had been no tire iron in Lee's hand—and asked whether

Moses could obtain federal protection for him: "If you give me protection, I'll let the hide fall with the hair."[79] Moses approached the Justice Department, which informed him that protection was impossible and evidently passed to the FBI news of Allen's change of mind. This intelligence leaked to the local police, and Allen was repeatedly harassed over the next several years. A SNCC news release issued in early August 1962 by Moses from the Lynch Street headquarters in Jackson related the incidents of harassment endured by Allen since Lee's killing, including intimidation for assisting others in jail and incarceration on trumped-up charges of aggravated assault.[80] After the divulgence, SNCC's already minimal trust in the FBI vanished. Moses described the organization's view of the bureau:

> [Allen's] jaw was broken by the deputy sheriff who knew that he had told the FBI that he had been forced to tell a lie to the grand jury and to the coroner's jury, because the deputy sheriff told him exactly what he had told the FBI. It's for reasons like these that we believe the local FBI is sometimes in collusion with the local sheriffs and chiefs of police and the Negro witnesses aren't safe in telling inside information to local agents of the FBI.[81]

On January 31, 1964, just before he was to leave Mississippi, Allen was shot to death.[82]

Moses, returning to McComb in early October 1961 after Lee's death, learned that the principal of the local black high school had refused to readmit two other students involved in the Greyhound bus station sit-in. The expulsion ignited other black high school students: some one hundred students walked out in solidarity.

The students called for a march on October 4. Moses opposed it on the grounds that the march would further stall the registration drive and accelerate white violence. After a discussion and argument very much in the participatory democracy mode, he acquiesced. The demonstration resulted in the arrest of all the local SNCC members—most while praying—along with a dozen high school students.[83] Despite the efforts of Moses and SNCC chairman Charles McDew to avoid violence, Bob Zellner, a white SNCC field representative from Alabama, was held by a policeman while a white mob beat him:

> My hands were on the railing and they got two, three guys on each leg. . . . They'd pull and they couldn't get me loose. And then they got even more excited and they started trying to hit my hands with the objects that they had: pipes and so forth. . . . Then one of the guys . . . started putting his fingers into my eye sockets and he actually would work my eyeball out of my eye socket. . . . He was trying to get my eyeball between his thumb and his index finger so he could get a grip on it and really pull it out.[84]

The attack on Zellner, however grisly, was undoubtedly less violent than the beatings given to numbers of blacks who did not live to relate their horror.

Curtis C. Bryant, the local NAACP leader who had originally requested the student voter registration teams, became enraged over the jailing of the teenagers. Blaming SNCC's confrontational ways, he accused Moses of encouraging the youngsters and threatened to withdraw all support, including the meeting place in the local Masonic Lodge he had secured for them. The students were released on bail after a month in prison and offered readmission by school officials on the condition that they accept a ten percent reduction in their grades and agree never to walk out of school or participate in protest marches again. The students refused the deal.[85]

SNCC saw here an opportunity to pursue Amzie Moore's strategy of organizing the young and quickly enrolled the students in the newly formed Nonviolent High School. Moses and others, all released on bond through the generosity of Harry Belafonte, served as their teachers during the next few weeks, instructing them in an eclectic range of subjects. The school was really one large room with fifty to seventy-five students at any one time and lasted less than a month.[86] One student—revealing the scope of the job that needed doing—had asked whether they would cover the War for Southern Independence.[87] The staff intended not only to teach general high school topics, but also to erase whatever submissiveness to white supremacy might remain in these defiant students; like others of its kind, it both taught and embodied empowerment.[88]

Moses and the other members of SNCC returned briefly to Atlanta during these few weeks for a meeting to discuss the tactics that had produced so few tangible results at so great a cost in legal expenses, in white violence, and in human life. At this tactical planning meeting held hurriedly in October, Moses was his usual reticent self. When he spoke, he stated only his desire to return to Mississippi.[89] According to his interview with Taylor Branch some years later, Moses "thought the students [at the meeting] were grandstanding, trying to surpass one another in eloquence, but he would not say so, any more than he would pressure Mississippi farmers to register, because he recoiled from seeking to dominate others with his presence."[90] The newest member to join the group, James Forman, who had worked as a teacher in Chicago, was elected executive secretary of SNCC. His recollection of the session is more elaborate: the group came to compromise by dividing its work between voter registration and direct action. Forman, who had served in the Air Force, felt hampered by the group's lack of discipline and organization, yet he was attracted to the values and energy of the young SNCC workers, most of them born a decade later than he.[91]

In mid-October Moses again returned to McComb and Nonviolent High. The school lasted through the month, until some of the students returned to the regular high school, pledging to refrain from civil rights activities, and the remainder were accepted in the high school section of Campbell College in Jackson, a private black church school. Nonviolent High ended not because the students had lost interest, but because the faculty were scheduled to go on trial at the end of the month.

The trial itself threatened further to immobilize the SNCC activists. The judge warned them: "Some of you are local residents, "some of you are outsiders. Those of you who are local residents are like sheep being led to the slaughter. If you continue to follow the advice of outside agitators, you will be like sheep and slaughtered."[92] Addressing Moses directly, the judge then asked, "Robert, haven't some of the people from your school been able to go down and register without violence here in Pike county?"[93] Moses, Zellner, and McDew, along with local residents active in SNCC, were quickly sentenced to four to six months in jail for disturbing the peace and contributing to the delinquency of a minor. The police sought to use the troublemakers as examples, bringing contingents of whites to stare at the three SNCC workers they believed must be communists. One young girl asked McDew to say something in communist; he obliged by saying a few words in Yiddish. Moses recounts the ordeal: "The police brought the people down, the white people, the so-called good citizens of the town, to come down and take a look at this Moses guy, and they would come down and stand at the front of the jail and say, 'Where's Moses?' And then the kids would point me out and I was again, very, very quiet."[94]

John Doar, alerted by SNCC, again flew to Mississippi. He entered a SNCC safe house under the cover of darkness, an incident that nicely suggests the impotence of the federal government in the face of the Klan and the Citizens' Council. But Doar had not been so inactive as it must have appeared. He had been preparing a "b-suit" based on the strongest provision of the Civil Rights Act of 1957,[95] authorizing the government to punish anyone interfering with the act of registration or voting, and he planned to use Louis Allen as a witness. The aim was to get Hurst arrested and tried, to thrust him into the public spotlight. The plan was never implemented. Doar's superior, Burke Marshall, rejected the case, fearing chaos in Mississippi. Although Attorney General Robert Kennedy believed the Justice Department's strongest authority to act rested in the 1957 and 1960 Civil Rights Acts that addressed voter registration, he also preferred legal court actions pursued within the narrow technical limits of the law that insured calm, controllable activity. And in the killing of Lee the defense might draw on *Screws v. United States of America* (1944), in which the Supreme Court had overturned a conviction on the grounds that an intention to interfere with the civil rights of the victim had not been proven. The problem here was similar. Even if it could be established that Hurst had murdered Lee, it also had to be proven that he had specifically intended to interfere with Lee's right to vote, not simply to harm or kill him.[96]

Such torturous legalities plagued Doar's effort throughout the period and increasingly stretched his credibility with the SNCC workers. The most important tool that the 1960 Civil Rights Act provided was the authority not only to inspect but also to photograph voter registration records. Local county officials and registrars were, of course, uncooperative. The task of photographing records was given to the FBI. And John Doar later remarked, "A singular characteristic of thirty-four FBI reports was that we got exactly the information we asked for—no more, no less."[97] Assistant Attorney General Burke Marshall testified before a congressional subcommittee in January 1964 that as its part in the analysis of voting registration records "the FBI only snaps the shutter on the camera."[98] In the same month, the FBI, with six thousand special agents and eight thousand clerks and technical assistants, said it was unable to spare the personnel to analyze voter registration records in three Southern counties. Thus the civil rights division, with its fifty-three lawyers and fifty-five clerical employees, was obliged to conduct these analyses of masses of records on its own.[99] The FBI similarly worked within its own internal and external constraints: the position that the bureau was an investigative, not a protective agency; the need to cooperate with local authorities in pursuing investigations; and an almost pathetic helplessness or unwillingness to proceed when Southern sheriffs and police were not forthcoming.[100]

With or without the support of the federal government, Moses and his companions in the Pike County jail in Magnolia soon discovered that support for their cause and immediate situation was being generated within the larger civil rights movement. C. C. Bryant, impressed by the support parents were giving their imprisoned children, abandoned his earlier conservatism: "Where the students lead, we will follow," he declared.[101] Martin Luther King sent Attorney General Robert Kennedy a telegram calling the events in Mississippi an "apparent reign of terror."[102] The registration campaigners needed support, for the enemy was gaining in strategy and sophistication. Over the summer of 1961, the white community had learned how to respond to the threat of SNCC. Besides using violence and economic intimidation, it blamed "outsiders," a term with great resonance in a region of tight-knit towns and neighborhoods. Even SNCC workers from a different place in Mississippi were deemed outsiders. Moses spoke of Mississippi as though it were its own world, a separate state of mind.[103] And indeed it was to most Americans, black or white.

During his time in jail, Moses was able to sneak out a letter to SNCC's Atlanta headquarters:

We are smuggling this note from the drunk tank of the county jail in Magnolia, Mississippi. Twelve of us are here, sprawled out along the concrete bunker: Curtis Hayes, Hollis Watkins, Ike Lewis and Robert Talbert, four veterans of the bunker, are sitting up talking— mostly about girls—Chuck McDew ("Tell the story") is curled into the concrete and the wall; Harold Robinson, Stephen Ashley, James Wells, Lee Chester Vick, Leotus Eubanks, and Ivory Diggs lie cramped on the cold bunker; I'm sitting with smuggled pen and paper, thinking a little, writing a little; Myrtis Bennett and Janie Campbell are across the way wedded to a different icy cubicle.

Later on, Hollis will lead out with a clear tenor into a freedom song. Talbert and Lewis will supply jokes, and McDew will discourse on the history of the black man and the Jew. McDew—a black by birth, a Jew by choice, a revolutionary by necessity—has taken on the deep hates and deep loves which America and the world reserve for those who dare to stand in a strong sun and cast a sharp shadow. . . .

This is Mississippi, the middle of the iceberg. Hollis is leading off with his tenor, "Michael row the boat ashore, Alleluia; Christian brothers, don't be slow, Alleluia: Mississippi's next to go, Alleluia." This is a tremor from the middle of the iceberg—from a stone that the builders rejected.[104]

On December 6, the defendants were released from Pike County jail on a bond appeal of one thousand dollars each.[105] After the trial, the movement in the McComb area lost momentum. Fear of violent repercussions kept people away from the registration classes. Carrying out an earlier threat and probably under pressure, C. C. Bryant allowed the Masons to close their temple to SNCC. Most local blacks wanted the SNCC workers to leave. Bowing to these pressures, the SNCC members retreated to Amzie Moore's house in the northern Delta country almost three hundred miles away and decided to scale down operations for the winter and retain only the most reliable workers.

Toward the end of the year Moses ventured to Jackson, where at a Freedom House he met with Medgar Evers, Jackson NAACP field representative, and Bill Higgs, a white Mississippi lawyer who had run a liberal protest campaign in 1960 against Congressman John Bell Williams. Higgs broached the idea of running a black candidate for Congress. Evers was the first choice, but he backed away from the idea, instead suggesting Bob Smith. Smith also rejected the offer but proposed his father, the Reverend Robert L. T. Smith, a NAACP member, who agreed.[106] Moses volunteered to serve as his campaign manager. He and SNCC staffers also helped Reverends Theodore Trammell and his replacement W. W. Lindsey, who ran for Congress after Trammell died of a heart attack midway through the campaign.

The campaigning was essentially a matter not of winning an electoral contest but of consciousness raising, of introducing black Mississippians to an indigenous, assertive black politics. Using the federal government's provision of equal time to get Smith on television fitted that objective. After one appearance on WJTV, a local television station, Smith's two additional appearances were canceled. WLBT, the other station in Jackson, was not interested. Prominent liberals, including Eleanor Roosevelt, wrote protest letters to the Federal Communications Commission (FCC) chair, and Smith himself reported his rejection to President Kennedy and the FCC.[107] Eventually both stations cooperated, but only after the manager of one tried desperately to talk Smith out of appearing. He discussed the extent to which the station would undoubtedly have to go to protect itself from physical destruction and concluded that he believed once Smith was seen on television, "our two bodies will be found floating in the Pearl River," a stream across the road from the station. The river remained unburdened.[108]

Moses also used his travels with Smith to recruit young people for SNCC and voter registration. The New Yorker spent most of the winter and early spring of 1961–62 in this endeavor, which included an attempt to integrate the all-white spectator section of the state legislature. In the end the black candidates lost handily.

The young SNCC workers stayed around Jackson in the late fall and early winter of 1961, getting ready for the next spring and summer campaigns. They took some trips to the McComb area as well as to southwestern Mississippi, but these were in preparation for the next year. Moses recalls:

> We had, to put it mildly, got our feet wet. We now knew something of what it took to run a voter registration campaign in Mississippi; . . . First there were very few agencies . . . that could act as a vehicle. . . . The Negro churches could not. . . . The Negro business leaders could also not. . . . In general, anybody who had a specific economic tie-in with the white community could not be counted on when the pressure got hot. . . . The only way . . . was to begin to build a group of young people who would not be responsible economically to any sector of the white community and who would be able to act as free agents. . . . [They needed] a conjunction between the young people and some indigenous farmers, independent people, or some courageous businessman able to stick his neck out, which was the combination which worked in the voter registration drive.[109]

Moses would later trace to this period the idea of launching a separate political party in Mississippi.[110] Emily Stoper credits him with being the "mastermind" of a plan to set up a four- to five-year program to win local, state, and Democratic party delegates and congressional representation for blacks.[111] But Moses had a much more skeptical view of the length of time it would take blacks to achieve such goals. And he was too wedded to reaching decisions through group consensus to mastermind anything. "The movement from the rural to the urban is irresistible," he nonetheless remarked, "and the line from Amite to McComb to Jackson straight as the worm furrows. Accordingly, I have left the dusty roads to run the dusty streets."[112]

However authentic and admirably modest his behavior, Moses contributed to the early image of SNCC as being an isolated organization. He rarely left the state, keeping in touch largely with the rural poor and working almost incommunicado behind the geographical boundaries of segregation. Unique in its challenge to racism, his was in fact a style and method repeatedly found in radical or insurgent movements: the early Christian community, gathered with little care for comfort, safety, or acclaim; or the union local that forms among downtrodden workers when an organizer comes to town. The civil rights movement through SNCC was repeating an age-old response of oppressed groups. Moses wished to evoke a local, indigenous black insurgency, an excellent strategy against the racists who fattened on suspicion of outsiders. It also placed energy where it was needed: in the local Mississippi community, and its individual black members.

Whatever may have been Moses' understanding of

what he was doing, his work in the South during these early years suggests a self-contained young philosopher hoping that each of the people he reached could be similarly centered. It implies again the disciple of Camus, whose writing on political morality projects a social order consisting of human beings each refusing to submit to injustice or to tolerate the subjugation of anyone else, and refusing the temptation to turn resistance into a quest for rule and subjection. The voter registration campaign in Mississippi that he increasingly led by refusing leadership was democratic not merely in objective, the winning of the vote, but in the daily action of organizing and sustaining itself. Motivating young people to encourage their elders to attempt to register widened the movement and doubtless introduced an element of practical stability; yet a thirst for moral purity continued to dominate it. And in Moses' refusal to perpetuate his role of leader there was something of Camus's sense that the rebel threatens to become the oppressor. Leadership he could shun; but his image was commanding.

FOUR

"FOOD FOR THOSE
WHO WANT TO
BE FREE"

Mississippi was the hardest state for the civil rights movement to crack. It therefore offered the cause its greatest prize. In the early spring of 1962, SNCC workers resumed the drive to register the poor to vote, this time targeting the heavy black population in six counties of the Mississippi Delta, mostly farmland tilled by poor and uneducated blacks for absentee own-ers.[1] While other rights workers were busy during the summer months with fruitless negotiation in Albany, Georgia, Moses had returned to Mississippi's LeFlore County, operating out of headquarters in the Delta city of Greenwood.[2] A description in 1964 by Moses of the effort in Mississippi will do as well for 1962: "This movement is pointed in a different direction—not toward the downtown white but toward the rural Negro, not toward acceptance by the white community but toward the organization of political and other kinds of expression in the Negro community, or really toward the organization of a Negro society."[3] And for Moses the rural areas proved to be the most difficult yet the most rewarding to organize.

In June 1962, Moses and his workers attended the Highlander Folk School training session on voter education techniques in Knoxville, Tennessee. There the SNCC team listened to Highlander founder Myles Horton and passed on lessons learned the previous summer in McComb about the techniques of nonviolent action and the methods to be used in working with illiterate and poor rural blacks in remote farm areas. After the workshop, Moses persuaded Bernice Robinson, who had taught the first adult literacy classes for Highlander in South Carolina, to conduct sessions in Mississippi during the summer and again in the spring and summer of 1963.[4] And in July Moses submitted a report to the governing board of the Mississippi Adult Education Program summarizing the first workshops on adult voter registration education and leadership training. Held at the Mt. Beulah Christian Center located midway between Jackson and Vicksburg, the workshops were conducted by Harvard law students and a political science major from Brandeis under the direction of Moses and Bernice Robinson. Amzie Moore led evening program discussions, and Moses noted: "We mapped plans for voting drives in Greenwood, Ruleville, and the mid-Delta rural counties ... and are planning a workshop for 60 to 75 students the week of July 22nd–

27th."⁵ Moses worked throughout the summer with these black youths, most of them Mississippians, who had been recruited in the spring while he was engaged in the congressional campaign of the Reverend R. L. T. Smith.⁶

So Moses was again trying to persuade black Mississippians, who had no reason to be confident about the political system, that they must persevere. He sought to make tangible to his audiences the need for collective assertion. He noted, for example, the probable effects of automation on agriculture. His argument about the disempowering role of technology to a group of black farmers was simple, concrete, and powerful:

> This spring, you're going to see a plane over-head and something is going to come out of the back, and that will be weed-killer, and it will kill all the weeds in the cotton field. That means that nobody will be chopping cotton this spring. Then, this fall, you're going to see a machine go up and down the rows of cotton, and that will be an automatic cotton-picker. And that means there will be nobody picking cotton this fall. That airplane and that cotton-picker together are automation. . . . "Automation" means that a lot of people won't be eating this winter. But don't go to Chicago, because you won't be eating there, either. So we'll set up a food program to hold you for a while . . . and see what we can do.⁷

Without the right to vote, blacks would be powerless in the face of such developments, having no access to any federal programs for retraining or the like. Moses was placing black rural workers between a rock and a hard place. Ultimately advancing technology threatened their economic livelihood; immediately not only their incomes but also their personal safety was endangered should they act on his urging. Nonetheless, Julian Bond wrote that summer: "SNCC is working in the South in areas no other civil rights group has ever been to, with farmers, domestics, laborers, and people who really want to be free."[8]

Counties in the Mississippi Delta with the most registration potential were Washington and Coahoma, for there a confident and powerful white elite had protected its field hands from lower-class white physical intimidation. But even in these two counties the work was hard: "The kind of operation there was day-to-day drudgery, going around in the hot sun, talking to people, trying to get them to overcome their fear, trying to convince them that nothing would happen to them if they went down, that their houses wouldn't be bombed, that they would not be shot at, that they wouldn't lose their jobs."[9] The *Mississippi Free Press*, a weekly issued from Jackson and established largely to serve as a diary of the civil rights movement, recounted the kind of retaliation experienced by blacks attempting to register.

In Sunflower County alone a black city employee in Ruleville was told he would be laid off because his wife had registered to vote, two black cleaning establishments were closed for violating vague city ordinances, and a church allowing voter registration training classes lost its tax exempt status and no longer received free water.[10] A press release issued by Moses listed a daily log of events taking place in Ruleville throughout August and early September. After a mass meeting of whites on Sunday, September 2, 1962, Moses notes: "All the Negro businesses were closed by the mayor." During this period lawyers from the Justice Department were in the town, gathering statements from blacks victimized by the systematic intimidation.[11]

And in LeFlore County, Moses observed, "We couldn't convince people [that they would not come to physical or economic harm if they attempted to register to vote] because for one, it wasn't true."[12] Lawrence Guyot, a black college student from Tougaloo and a native Mississippian, has left a description of trouble in Greenwood, the major city of LeFlore County:

> It took us three months to get a meeting place and every time we would move into a place and attempt to rent some place to stay, the Klan would come that night. They would not bother us—but simply park outside all around the place and shine their lights from their cars. And when we attempted to use the telephone, the telephone operator would call back and say, "Look, you got some trouble-makers in there, you better get them out." This went on for four months.[13]

In late July a young fourteen-year-old black boy had been arrested and brutally beaten as a peeping Tom in a case involving a white woman.[14] This atrocity attracted some national attention. Moses and Sam Block, a vocational college student from Amzie Moore's town of Cleveland who had been assigned as field worker to the Greenwood office, seized the opportunity to bring twenty-five registrants to the courthouse on Saturday, August 10, 1962, followed by a national television network crew and scores of reporters. The media's response to events in Mississippi ebbed and flowed with the level of confrontation.[15] One week later, on August 17, came the predictable Mississippi reaction. The few blacks who had shown up for registration classes picked careful positions, out of possible sniper range. The caution was justified. In the early hours of the morning, several carloads of whites surrounded the office. Sam Block, Lawrence Guyot, and Luvaghn Brown escaped by climbing across the roof and shimmying down a TV antenna.[16]

Forty miles away in Cleveland Moses learned of the trouble when Block hurriedly telephoned him. Moses also informed John Doar and Burke Marshall, Doar's Justice Department superior, at their homes. He then quickly returned to find the office pilfered and in disarray after an invasion of whites armed with chains and shotguns. Then Moses took the celebrated nap that added to his already legendary presence within SNCC. As though this intimidation were not enough, SNCC members were forced out of the office after local authorities charged their landlord with bigamy, possibly the first time this law had been applied to a black.[17] A SNCC field worker reported an interrogation of a black by the police in Greenville, the Delta city on the Mississippi River some forty miles west of Greenwood. "God damned black bastards think they're going to be taking over around here. Well, you and the other god damned Moses' niggers around here ain't gonna get nothin but a bullet in the head."[18]

Yet the rights workers had gained a presence, at least in Greenwood. Lawrence Guyot's comment on the effort there suggests the strategy and strength of the whole SNCC project:

> I guess the reason we got away with what we did in Greenwood was for a couple of reasons. One, we were soundly based in the churches. Two, our objectives were

very clear. It was not to desegregate the two or three good local white restaurants. It was simply to register people to vote.[19]

In the midst of all this, the various groups working in Mississippi needed to discuss the use of registration funds, provided mostly from the newly reactivated Voter Education Project (VEP). Founded in 1954 as a tax-exempt foundation that gathered contributions from various philanthropic groups, VEP attracted the favorable attention of the Kennedy administration as a moderate vehicle through which to channel the energies of the movement. Late in August in the basement of a church in Clarksdale, an hour's drive northwest of Greenwood, Moses and his few coworkers assembled with Wiley Branton, the head of VEP, Dave Dennis of CORE, James Bevel and Jack O'Dell of SCLC, James Forman of SNCC, and Aaron Henry and Amzie Moore of the NAACP. The disparate groups agreed that to alleviate the bureaucratic wrangling and turf wars among the various organizations they would revive the Council of Federated Organizations (COFO).

COFO had been formed in 1961 as a united front of rights groups opposed to segregationist Governor Ross Barnett. Its revival was designed especially to accommodate the conservative Roy Wilkins of the NAACP, who regarded SNCC as irresponsible. To placate the NAACP, which considered itself the presiding civil rights group in the state but felt slighted by the other more militant groups, the organizers chose Aaron Henry of the Clarksdale NAACP to head COFO. An NAACP leader is reported to have said some years later, "They [SNCC] say they speak for the people, but they

have three Mississippi or eight Mississippi natives
working with SNCC, whereas we have 15,000 people
who are members of NAACP. We speak for Mississippi."[20] Yet the national NAACP viewed Mississippi as
a state to stay away from; most of the local organizations were helpless against the state's legal and political power structure. Lawrence Guyot's remarks suggest
how hated this cautious and socially conservative organization once was among Southern whites: "In Yazoo
City [forty miles north of Jackson] . . . it was unthinkable to hold a membership card in the NAACP, absolutely unthinkable. And register to vote—good God,
man, you're talkin' death."[21] The NAACP feared that
Mississippi would be a waste of the VEP funds. At any
rate, activists realized that a successful registration
project depended on Moses and his fellow workers in
SNCC. Moses was appointed program director of COFO,
in charge of voter registration.[22] He has observed that
the COFO political activities formed the basis on which
the Mississippi Freedom Democratic party was built.[23]

Some participants were arrested as they left the
meeting. The next day, August 30, Moses was taken into
custody in Indianola, in Sunflower County, for distributing literature without a permit.[24] James Bevel, who
had come to the Delta area to help Moses, bailed him
out. White extremists meanwhile were discovering evidence of the sinister forces behind the assault on their
traditions. Redbaiting came easily to them, and now
Southern papers were linking Moses to a reputed Communist, Carl Braden, who was active in the Southern
Conference Education Fund (SCEF), an organization
suspected to be a communist front.

Moses and Carl Braden had traveled "about 925

miles up and down and across the state in a period of six days—from July 13 to 19" conducting workshops on "civil liberties, nonviolence, and the First Amendment" from Jackson to Hattiesburg, Tougaloo, Greenwood, Clarksdale, and other places. In his report to the director of SCEF, Braden estimated they had "reached about 300 of the key leadership in Mississippi, including a few whites." He added that fewer people were being "beaten to death in the jails and on the streets.... Nowadays it seems that police content themselves with beating prisoners . . . Beatings at Greenwood are regularly administered with a leather whip about four feet long." Braden's report speaks of a planned seminar for the fall on news media and of the need for funds: "One field secretary at Greenwood told me he eats once a day—about 2 o'clock in the morning before going to bed for a few hours. I guess he doesn't like to go to bed hungry."[25]

News of this trip instigated charges of communist influence in SNCC, spread by the Southern press. Moses had joined Braden on the picket line organized by SCEF in Atlanta back in the summer of 1960; now his picture was published in the *Jackson Daily News* under the headline "Commies Active Over State."[26]

Moses realized it would be wise to avoid Sunflower County, where he had been arrested. But his ambition to nourish local black activism held him to his promise to help eighteen blacks from the rural town of Ruleville register the next day at Indianola, the county seat.[27] All eighteen were rejected. While returning with the group in a rented SNCC yellow bus Moses was again arrested. The charge was driving a vehicle that too closely resembled a school bus. Moses was soon released on bail.

One of the attempted registrants was Fannie Lou Hamer, who was to become an important figure in the Mississippi Freedom Democratic Party. By her account, the driver of the bus at first was fined one hundred dollars, a sum later reduced to thirty dollars; among themselves the riders managed to raise the money.[28] Her description of what followed demonstrates how persuasive Moses and his co-workers had to be:

> The thirty-first of August in '62, the day I went to the courthouse to register, well, after I'd gotten back home, this man that I had worked for as a timekeeper and sharecropper for eighteen years, he said that I would just have to leave.... So I told him I wasn't trying to register for him. I was trying to register for myself.... I didn't have no other choice because for one time I wanted things to be different.[29]

Eight days later, on September 8, Moses and Amzie Moore were accosted by a white man in a pickup truck as they were walking down the street in Ruleville. The man asked whether they were the "folks getting the people to register." When they answered affirmatively, he responded, "O.K., I have a plantation and don't try and register anybody on that plantation. I got a shotgun waiting for you, double barrel."[30]

Meanwhile, those who had agreed to house the SNCC volunteers suffered constant harassment in Ruleville. Night riders came by and fired shots into their homes, on one occasion wounding two SNCC volunteers. In one simple frame home twenty-four bullet holes were found. And on September 10, two girls on their way to college were shot, one critically.[31] The mayor of Ruleville came to the scene, where he said in a conversation

with the police chief, "Bob Moses is the cause of all of
it. I knowed something like this was going to happen."[32] The drive from Jackson to Cleveland in the
early morning hours en route to the shooting scene in
Ruleville had been harrowing on its own. The car, by
Moses' account,

> was in bad condition and we couldn't slow down under
> 30 miles an hour because the car would stop. . . . This
> meant that we had to change drivers while we were
> driving, and added to the general fatigue and ner-
> vousness. Finally, all of us fell asleep in the car, includ-
> ing the driver. . . . We plunged straight off the road . . .
> through a road sign, and settled down into somebody's
> cottonfield.[33]

When Moses appeared the following day to gather facts
for a report to the Justice Department, the sheriff
threatened to arrest him for interfering with a police
investigation. The mayor, who also served as justice of
the peace and sole judge in town, ordered the water to
be cut off and tax exemption status revoked for Williams Chapel, which housed SNCC meetings; the building's insurer also dropped its coverage. The newspaper
published the names of all blacks who attempted to register.[34]
    Moses reported these incidents to the Justice Depart-
ment although he knew it would do little good. In a
letter to the Atlanta headquarters of SNCC, he observed
that the federal government "must [file a] broad suit to
stop economic reprisals and physical violence to pro-
spective registrants and those who work to get others
registered," but complained that "there would probably have to occur more evictions and widespread pub-

licity before they will file a suit to stop economic reprisals in Sunflower County."[35] On August 28 the Civil Rights Division of the Department of Justice filed a statewide suit, *United States v. Mississippi*, charging racial discrimination; it "itemized hundreds upon hundreds of specific incidents of racial discrimination in voting occurring in Mississippi after March 24, 1954."[36]

SNCC workers attempted to hold classes in tents, seeking the trust and participation of local blacks by running errands and chopping wood for them. "It's very important," Moses wrote, "that the Negroes in the community feel that you're . . . going to ride through whenever trouble arrives. And in general, the deeper the fear, the deeper the problems in the community, the longer you have to stay to convince them."[37] SNCC needed to have "an image in the Negro community of providing direct aid, not just 'agitation.' "[38] As always, Moses tried to publicize the plight of impoverished blacks, who were dependent on whites for economic control, especially on the plantations where many worked as sharecroppers. The *Mississippi Free Press* noted that the routine reactions to the attempt to register to vote by blacks was a notice of eviction on the part of white landowners. The National Sharecroppers Fund reported numerous incidents of eviction, refusal of credit, and other forms of economic intimidation in Indianola during 1962.[39] Terrorist acts had their effect. Local blacks soon stopped attending meetings.

By late 1962, Moses had come to realize that without some sort of new outside intervention to protect the rights and safety of Mississippi blacks, progress would continue at a crawl.[40] The rights workers could not protect blacks, local authorities would not, and the actions of the federal government were tardy and feeble. Conditions did not allow the kind of action that the Kennedy administration took to permit the enrollment of the first black, James Meredith, at the University of Mississippi. After Governor Ross Barnett defied a court order in the fall of 1962, the president sent 550 federal marshals to Ole Miss to protect Meredith, federalized the National Guard, and delivered a televised speech promising to uphold the laws of the land and the orders of the court. He ultimately had to order 23,000 federal troops to the state.[41] But this was a focused, central event. Moses' work, if more expansive and far-reaching, was much less amenable to sensational national publicity and could not be protected with one massive assault. This problem of affording minimal protection would especially trouble Moses and COFO in the fall 1963 Freedom Vote when Moses decided not to open polling places in certain counties where there were no COFO workers to be with the people in the aftermath. But without some way of showing local blacks that the terror could be overcome, the movement was stymied. The recognition that the system was inadequate to meet their needs contributed to the radicalization of SNCC workers.

Moses sought ingenious ways of prying open the black community. At a news conference he was asked about the best way to organize: " 'By bouncing a ball,' he answered quietly. 'What?' 'You bounce a ball. You stand on a street and bounce a ball. Soon all the children come around. You keep on bouncing the ball. Before long, it runs under someone's porch and then you meet the adults.' "[42] SNCC often found that its entrance was through the young. Deference to whites was not second nature to them, mainly because they were not directly dependent on whites for jobs like their parents.

News of the Ruleville incidents made its way into President Kennedy's news conference. Calling the shootings of the two young women "cowardly as well as outrageous," he declared: "I commend those who are making the effort to register every citizen. They deserve the protection of the United States Government, the protection of the states. . . . And if it requires extra legislation, and extra force, we shall do that."[43] The words were an appropriate and sincere verbal gesture, Kennedy's strongest statement on civil rights to date, but SNCC resented the continued lack of federal action in Mississippi. Moses wrote to the Voter Education Project that "we are powerless to register people in significant numbers anywhere in the state." Change, he said, would require the removal of the Citizens Council from control of Mississippi politics; action by the Justice Department to secure safe registration for blacks; and a mass uprising of the unlettered, fearful blacks, demanding the immediate right to vote. "Very likely all three will be necessary before a breakthrough can be obtained."[44]

While SNCC was acting to prod the Justice Department into action, the local Mississippi authorities were widening their own strategy of potentially violent persuasion. If they could not completely intimidate blacks from cooperating with SNCC, they could make the consequences of participation painful and possibly deadly. State legislators enacted into law a policy started by the Ruleville local paper: all new registrants' names had to be published two weeks in advance of acceptance. Current registered voters would be allowed to object to the moral character of potential registrants. The white government also sought to use broad economic coercion. The federal government had long been supplying agricultural surpluses to the states for distribution to those in need. In October 1962 the LeFlore County Board of Supervisors voted to cease its participation in the federal surplus program, affecting twenty-two thousand people in the predominantly black county, about fifty percent of the county's population. The contribution of the county to the program had amounted to $4,150 per month.[45] As the white power establishment abandoned the black poor who had been structurally dependent on it, COFO attempted to take up the task of provisioning and thereby liberating the impoverished. It was, as Moses, said, "food for those who want to be free."[46] Indicative of the attempts to prevent aid from reaching needy families was the arrest in Clarksdale in late December 1962 of Ivanhoe Donaldson and Benjamin Taylor, both students at Michigan State who had driven into town in the early hours to deliver supplies, including medicine, to Aaron Henry's Fourth Street Drug Store. They were arrested on drug charges, and with bail set at $15,000, Donaldson managed to alert COFO leaders to his plight by slipping a note to one of the black inmates whose job was to collect the money in parking meters during the day and who could deliver a message to Henry at his drug store.[47]

The resupply effort soon began to falter for lack of resources. It revived, however, as the winter ground on and reports in various newspapers around the country noted the number of the needy. Harry Belafonte and another prominent black entertainer, Dick Gregory, donated money and time to help the cause; Gregory even flew supplies to Mississippi himself.[48] In a letter of late February 1963, Moses observed that food and clothing had been given to only one thousand out of the twenty-two thousand needy, and cited yet another violent means local whites used to subvert the effort:

> Nine thousand pounds of food arrived Feb. 19, by truck from Chicago. That night four buildings, including a community center and a store, were burned down. At least one worker received an anonymous phone call gloating that no food would be distributed the following day. But they missed the storage place and food was distributed to six hundred people.[49]

In the aftermath of the arson, Sam Block, a SNCC field worker heading the program in Greenwood, was arrested and jailed because he had stated that the burning was a reprisal against the food drive. The charge was "public utterances designed to incite breach of the peace."[50]

The tons of food and hundreds of blankets received were not nearly enough. Most of those affected by the cutoff were unlikely to take or pass the registration test. Yet the effort was better than nothing. The registration campaign had apparently failed, but SNCC's courage strengthened its influence among black Mississippians. Unita Blackwell, one of the LeFlore County blacks who participated in the food project, has described the impression Moses had on her: "Bob Moses was a little bitty fella. And he stood up to this sheriff and Bob said,

'I'm from SNCC.' I had never saw that happen before.
From that day on, I said, 'Well, I can stand myself.' "[51]

As the story of Mississippi unfolded, the appropriate
federal agencies became increasingly embarrassed.
They had good reason. In five years the federal Civil
Rights Commission had never held hearings on Mississippi, undoubtedly the worst state violator in the nation. The creation of Eisenhower's Attorney General
Herbert Brownell, the commission had been established as an independent fact-gathering committee to
investigate voting rights violations and charges of economic retaliation against blacks attempting to exercise
the vote. Under the Democratic administration, moreover, the Justice Department had been working to keep
the commission out of Mississippi; realizing this, the
chairman, John Hannah, finally approached the president. Kennedy rebuffed Hannah, telling him that hearings under the Civil Rights Commission would under-
mine a strategy of litigation, county by county,
currently planned by the Department of Justice.

At the time that it created the commission, the Eisenhower administration had set up the Civil Rights Division of the Justice Department to strengthen the attorney general's legal status in enforcing federal laws on
voting rights in the federal courts. John Doar was hired
in 1960 under the same Republican administration to
serve as first assistant within the civil rights division.
Doar himself admitted late in 1962, "We have moved
from no Negro registration to token registration."[52] No
cases brought by the Justice Department against Mississippi as of January 1963 had been won. Yet several
suits were pending in the slow, methodical, and difficult process of establishing a pattern of discrimination.

An example of progress at the time was the way the state's authorities condescended to consider black schoolteachers with doctorates as qualified to pass registration tests.

It was characteristic of the Kennedy administration to avoid public crises and exert quiet pressure. In response to the LeFlore County crisis, the Justice Department ultimately threatened to have the Department of Agriculture take over the distribution of surplus food. In April 1962 county officials reversed their decision.[53] A federal presence would have been an anathema to local whites. Kennedy, throughout his presidency, sought to keep the national spotlight off of the South. Hearings on Mississippi would do nothing for him politically, especially in this important region.

So by the beginning of 1963, a line had been drawn. It was as significant for what it defined in proper human conduct as was the line of blood between SNCC and the Mississippi white supremacists. On one side was the Democratic and at least mildly liberal administration: it was well intentioned and convinced of the efficacy of carefully applied legal processes, which it had not really gotten around to applying at all. On the other side were the young SNCC militants. To call them moral purists of the kind soon to burn flags and draft cards would not be correct. They asked only for the full force of the law. But that much they did demand. Their moral anger would increase in the face of the government's hesitancies. And in the absence of major federal intervention, they were learning for themselves and for black Mississippi the way of free, democratic organization and action. The Mississippi story would not go away.

FIVE

"ONE MAN—
ONE VOTE"

The plodding zigzag efforts of the Justice Department frustrated and discouraged SNCC workers. This contributed to a heightened radicalism within the growing group. On January 1, 1963—with the support of both Martin Luther King, Jr., and the Gandhi Society—Moses filed suit against the department and the FBI. The suit named Attorney General Robert Kennedy and J. Edgar Hoover in an attempt to force them to perform their legal duties.[1] Specifically, the plaintiffs wanted the court to enforce six sections of the federal code that forbade the harassment or intimidation of anyone attempting to vote.[2] The suit also stated that it was not indicting the Justice Department's Civil Rights Division, where John Doar worked. But that disclaimer did not mollify the Kennedy administration, which suc-

cessfully blocked the action. The government, Moses
has explained, "didn't want a case moving through the
courts that opened up the issue of the federal government protecting voter registration workers and black
people attempting to register."[3] As he came to appreci-
ate those Justice Department lawyers, such as Doar,
who sought to work within Kennedy administration
politics, he increasingly despaired of the policies of the
FBI, which maintained its distance and investigated
only after events. From his experiences during 1961 and
1962 Moses would move toward more assertive action
in an attempt to garner national publicity and participation. Accompanying the increasing disillusionment
with federal cooperation was swelling factionalism
within SNCC itself. Not all of SNCC's difficulties came
from its implacable foes and its dubious friends. At the
end of 1962 SNCC was suffering from a disorganization
rooted in its aversion to hierarchy. Shunning the need
to raise money as at best a hindrance to its work and at
worst a compromise with a corrupt society, it lacked
the resources to finance critical strategies. SNCC members usually lived very modestly. In a memorandum to
the COFO executive committee in 1963, Moses noted
that the monthly budget for the entire project was
about $5,000 and the expense for each staff member
"roughly $23 per week." Such specificity indicates that
Moses was well aware at this point of the daily operations and management of COFO—not an idealist removed from daily, tangible business.[4] The sparseness of
resources often showed up in the sparseness of results.
Organizers considered a turnout of twenty sharecroppers for voter education meetings a success. New black
voters registered in preceding months had numbered

only in the dozens. Yet by 1963 Moses and SNCC were incrementally succeeding in doing what Martin Luther King, Jr., had already achieved by calculated design.

Moses was seeking, like Camus, to find a balance between pragmatism and purity. And in doing so he was also coming to represent, not only in manner but in action and goal, a concept of the struggle quite different from that of the great ministerial orator. King was much too pragmatic and accommodating for Moses' taste. King concentrated on the national consciousness with showy efforts that could be abandoned if unsuccessful. Moses looked to local programs to awaken the docile spirits of Mississippi's blacks. He would have liked to register blacks in small-scale local projects across the state.

Seeking to draw out potential black voters, Moses planned for a literacy program. The idea belongs in the lineage of Highlander, the voter registration schools, and Nonviolent High. To learn and to come together for learning meant defiance, solidarity, self-awareness, and a capacity for further action.

To this end, Moses began in early 1963 an extensive correspondence with a former Hamilton College philosophy teacher, John Blyth, a pioneer in programmed learning who at this time was director of the Programmed Learning Department for The Diebold Group, management consultants. Their aim was to devise programmed learning for illiterate people and to secure foundation grants to support it. By mid-February Blyth reported to Moses that he had written to a variety of foundations and set up appointments with representatives; among the foundations he was seeking out were the Field, Taconic, and Carnegie. On February 24 Moses wrote Blyth: "I am looking for a place to rent here in Greenville [the major Delta city in Washington County] which may be used as a center, not only for the reading, but for other kinds of teaching as well. I think we could do a great deal of informal research and experimentation within the program as budgeted."[5]

Moses himself repeatedly, and sometimes successfully, applied for support to a variety of Northern liberal foundations.[6] In mid-July he wrote to Philip Stern of the Stern Foundation, proposing a work study program at Tougaloo and Miles Colleges with the aid of college students.[7] Mendy Samstein, a history professor at Morehouse College and later prominent in the Mississippi struggle, first became involved in SNCC when asked to participate in the seminars at Miles College provided for students in the work study program during the fall of 1963.[8]

In a memorandum to the COFO executive committee, Moses sketched out the venture, which was established as the Literacy Project, administered by Blyth and financed by an anonymous donation. Moses described the project as a pilot program staffed by SNCC members with the grant funded through Tougaloo College. Its purpose was to test the use of materials that related to economic and social problems as a means of facilitating the teaching of reading and writing to illiterates.[9] In late April, he went to his college alma mater and gave a talk to the Emerson Literary Society. He observed courses using programmed instruction and planned to obtain a contribution for SNCC through the community chest drive even though, he noted, "the college campus is conservative."[10] Programmed learning might also help blacks pass voter registration tests. For this as for other activities, reports in SNCC archives reveal that Moses, the radical activist, at odds with establishments, could also effectively act as liberal social scientist and liberal bureaucrat.[11]

Meanwhile, Wiley Branton, the director of the Voter Education Project, found that Moses had been using VEP grant money to purchase food during the winter of 1962–63, replacing supplies cut off when local authorities voted to withdraw from the federal food surplus program. Branton evidently discovered this after reading a field report from Jack Minnis, research director for VEP: "Apparently Moses is unable to resist the temptation now and then to use VEP funds in a small way to alleviate some of the distress which their voter registration activity is causing some of the local people."[12] Realizing that this would jeopardize the project's tax-exempt status, Branton confronted Moses, who replied, "I know, Wiley, but what can you do when you're faced with all those people standing in line?"[13] Branton, though generally the bureaucrat's bureaucrat, yielded to Moses' persuasive manner—as so many others had. The voluminous correspondence Branton generated in his effort to secure precise facts, figures, and vouchers on exact forms, papers, and dates is almost humorous. A typical memo to Moses from Branton is dated November 20, 1962: "I am in receipt of a comprehensive report of your financial disbursement . . . together with a note . . . that the October report would be sent this week. We assume that this report will be accompanied by the vouchers since they did not accompany the financial statement. . . . It should be pointed out . . . that there is [an] . . . error on page 2 of your financial statement. Subtotal 4, under XI.D." On No-

vember 29, Branton withheld half of the monthly two
thousand dollar payment because not all of the progress
reports and financial reports had been received "for the
period ending November 30, 1962." Moses and the
other rights workers were trying to survive; they filed
reports on a catch-can basis. Jack Minnis, in reminding
Moses of a coming monthly reporting deadline, seemed
to have some appreciation of this: "We are not trying to
hustle you unduly, nor are we implying that you might
neglect such mundane matters as reporting in favor of
the more interesting problem of staying alive in Mississippi."[14]

Branton himself was sufficiently sympathetic to send
a VEP representative into Mississippi to determine
whether a significantly larger sum of money should go
into the state for stepping up voter registration drives.
Branton was responding to the moral power of the Mississippi project, the fearless, self-denying youth who
squabbled rarely if at all about salaries and position.
Those who measured by columns of numbers saw the
Mississippi project as an operation small in scale and
results. Yet voters were being registered. Inspired by
Moses and the other civil rights workers, by 1963 Delta
blacks were more often courageously standing their
ground in the county courthouses, more frequently willing to go to jail or to risk their lives; they were becoming psychologically and morally empowered. At their
side were the determined SNCC workers. And against
them were mobs and hard-faced police. SNCC had
brought morality to Mississippi; white-supremacist violence would in time bring segregation itself to practical defeat.

Before the VEP representative arrived in late February, the aftermath of the midmonth arsons and the outcome of Sam Block's trial had resulted in an uproar in Greenwood, site and symbol of the white South's intransigence. Block, who had worked in the community for over nine months and had been arrested seven times and repeatedly beaten severely, apparently possessed Moses' ability to draw support by example of perseverance under harrowing conditions. Some one hundred of Greenwood's blacks had marched to his trial. Offered a suspended sentence if he would stop working on the registration project, Block replied, "Judge, I ain't gonna do none of that." He was sentenced to six months in prison.[15]

Block's arrest and his defiance of the white system apparently cracked the fear of the black community. At a registration meeting on the night of February 26, 1963, Moses uncharacteristically exhorted the participants to register and seize their freedom. The SNCC workers' example of long-standing presence and suffering, combined with the food effort, had to some degree finally subverted the years of Jim Crow conditioning. The next day hundreds lined up outside the registrar's office demanding to be counted.[16] Although technicalities and the registrar's whim prevented most from registering, this was a significant victory for SNCC in awakening pride and militancy among blacks. The next day, Moses wrote an open letter: "We were relieved at the absence of immediate violence at the courthouse, but who knows what's to come next?"[17] Moses soon after termed it "the first real breakthrough in Mississippi."[18] His three-pronged effort was on its way to achieving his legal, political, and philosophical goals: giving power and control to black people through the vote; arousing the nation to the situation of blacks in the South; awakening black Southerners to a consciousness of their power.

But for every action there is a reaction. Every SNCC advance generated a backlash in the white community. Randolph Blackwell, the VEP representative sent by Wiley Branton, arrived on February 28. He could not have appeared at a better time for Moses; the events that followed graphically demonstrated the need for continued VEP funding of the Mississippi civil rights movement.

During that evening's meeting a SNCC worker noticed a car without license plates staking out the SNCC office. The SNCC members' response was to separate into different cars and head in different directions. In one car were Jimmy Travis, a twenty-year-old volunteer and former Tougaloo College student, as well as Blackwell and Moses. They attempted all the usual tricks to lose the Buick that followed their car. At first they thought they had shaken it off and headed toward Sunflower County. But then another vehicle, a 1962 white Buick without a license plate, suddenly appeared. When they slowed down to let the car pass, it moved alongside them and someone fired a machine gun, hitting Travis and just missing Moses. Finding a doctor who would treat a black in their bullet-riddled car depended on good luck. LeFlore County Hospital referred them to University Hospital in Jackson. There a surgeon removed a forty-five-caliber bullet lodged an inch from Travis's spine that had just missed paralyzing him.[19]

On the same evening of the shooting, Moses spoke to the students of Tougaloo College just north of the Jackson city limits about the incident. The Reverend Edwin King, the campus minister, has written of the conservative views of some administrators at this middle-class black school:

> While Moses was speaking the college business manager, a black man . . . walked into the building.. . . He was very upset and asked if I knew who the speaker was. I told him it was a friend of Jimmy Travis. Before I could say more [he] told me that this was Bob Moses, the leader of the SNCC work in the state. He told me that Bob Moses was an extremely dangerous kind of person and that it was not good to let such people speak to the Tougaloo students. [He] further stated that we should try to keep people like Moses from stirring up the Tougaloo students. I played the role of a foolish white minister, . . . I soon realized that spring that [his] thinking about the Movement probably represented the majority opinion of the Black faculty. Many of the Black faculty members just wanted to be known as teachers at the best (for Negroes) private college in Mississippi. It must have been a matter of embarrassment rather than pride to have to have their college mentioned so frequently as a place of agitation. There was no status or security in that.[20]

The FBI investigated the shooting and determined it was a local matter. It therefore turned its findings over to the local police, who in turn dropped the case after arresting some white men who were promptly freed on bail.[21] Timothy Jenkins, a National Student Association (NSA) leader and SNCC worker, has remarked: "I am absolutely certain that the FBI knew many of those things that were going to happen before they happened. . . . The close affinity of the FBI agents for the [South-

ern] police people was something that the FBI and Justice never faced.... The FBI was helping the police keep
track of us."[22] Nearly two years later, the Greenwood
district attorney, George A. Everett, dropped all
charges against the two white men arrested after the
Travis shooting. Everett had resigned from the FBI to
run for the job of district attorney.[23]

SNCC workers vowed not to let this latest shooting
incident deter them, especially because they had just
started making progress. The attack worked to SNCC's
immediate advantage. Many civil rights leaders converged on Greenwood, setting up registration classes in
suddenly welcoming churches. Wiley Branton fired off
telegrams to Governor Ross Barnett of Mississippi and
to both President Kennedy and the attorney general
announcing in the aftermath of Travis's shooting an all-
out campaign to register qualified blacks to vote in
LeFlore County.[24]

At about this time the national news media also began showing greater interest in SNCC's program. In
early March 1963 the *New York Times* published parts
of Branton's telegram: "This can no longer be tolerated.
We are accordingly announcing a concentrated satura-
tion campaign to register every qualified Negro in
LeFlore County."[25] The attorney general's reaction was
to send lawyers to investigate the suspension of the
federal surplus foods program, perhaps believing that
this alone had been the cause of the troubles. The Kennedy administration still appeared to be trying to keep
the movement from getting into the news and further
shaking the wobbly Democratic coalition. It was not
until February 1963 that President Kennedy sent his
first civil rights message to Congress. His proposed leg-

islation set a presumed literacy level at the sixth grade, attempted to expedite litigation regarding voting rights, and abolished double standards for voter qualification.[26] But the federal government could not end the conflict between SNCC and a white Mississippi community determined to keep up the fight against "outside agitators." One white voter commented: "We killed two-month-old Indian babies to take this country, and now they want us to give it away to the niggers."[27]

There was more violence in the ensuing weeks in Greenwood. Sam Block and another SNCC worker were shot at while driving at night, and the SNCC office was set on fire. The blaze ruined the office equipment and exposed the arsonists' further malicious act of ripping the telephone from the wall. During this time, Bernice Robinson from the Highlander Center was conducting a series of training workshops and citizenship classes in the area. In a report to Highlander director Myles Horton, she notes: "The calls kept coming in to Amzie's [Moore] house from everywhere, telling us about the burning down of the office.... But it seems to have stepped up the movement more. They had a mass meeting tonight ... and the church was filled to an overflowing capacity. So we go on with the work as though nothing has happened."[28]

But it was the shotgun blast that erupted on March 26 in the home of Dewey Greene, Sr., father of children active in voter registration and of a son seeking to enter the University of Mississippi, that inflamed the black community.[29] The next day a crowd of between 100 and 150 blacks walked to city hall to protest the lack of police protection for black citizens attempting to vote. Turned back by the mayor, who threatened to use po-

lice dogs, the group attempted to march to the courthouse a few blocks away to submit applications to register. The marchers were met by twelve policemen and
a German shepherd before they arrived. In response to
Moses' demand to speak with the authorities, the police
let loose the dog, who ripped at Moses' leg, sending the
crowd into retreat.[30] It then tore into the flesh of another demonstrator. Moses asserted to a crowd of cheer-
ing blacks, "And the dog? The dog is going to have to
bite every Negro in LeFlore County before we quit."[31]
The use of ferocious police dogs in Greenwood (and
earlier in Jackson) was a prelude to their more sensational use in Birmingham. At the church where the
march had started, the police promptly arrested the
returning Moses, along with James Forman, SNCC's
first full-time executive director, Lawrence Guyot, a
SNCC field secretary, and several SNCC workers.

Pictures of the day's events sent out by wire services
drew the nation's newspaper reporters and the next day
over a hundred police from Greenwood and surrounding counties obligingly repeated the scene in front
of the media. This time a police dog bit the minister of
the church, drawing blood. In an effort to get the federal government to file suit against the local officials by
means of a temporary restraining order, the eight SNCC
workers refused bail.[32]

The Kennedy administration attempted to find a way
out of what it saw primarily as a public relations mess.
Kennedy's civil rights commission (including the Mississippi members) was almost in open revolt, threatening to release its own report on Mississippi, and the
Justice Department tried to compel Greenwood's officials to relent without resorting to the use of force it

had finally and sparingly employed in the Freedom
Rides. As the news gatherers and other civil rights figures converged on Greenwood, John Doar informed Moses and other SNCC workers that he and Assistant Attorney General Burke Marshall were about to ask for a
broad injunction that would vacate the convictions of
the eight SNCC leaders as illegal interferences with the
right to vote, prohibit harassing or intimidating black
citizens wishing to register, and require fair and adequate police protection at the courthouse registration
office.[33] But Moses would learn on April 4 that the federal officials had compromised, abandoning the suit in
exchange for obtaining the release of the eight SNCC
leaders.[34] The suit would not be filed, even though President Kennedy had spoken at a press conference of its
having been filed. As part of the settlement, SNCC was
to discover later, the federal government agreed to pick
up the cost of distributing the surplus food in LeFlore
County.[35] Once more, by sidestepping the basic issue of
interference with voter registration attempts, the administration was ducking the moral challenge SNCC
had hurled at it.

One explanation for the compromise is that King's
activities in Birmingham were competing for media
attention.[36] In April, civil rights groups began a campaign against segregated establishments there, using
the techniques of sit-ins, marches, and mass demonstrations and receiving the response of police dogs and fire
hoses. In a broad-ranging article, the *New York Times*
discussed events in Birmingham and in Greenwood.
The mayor-elect of Birmingham blamed the arrests of
thirty-five blacks in a direct-action campaign on "outside elements and agitators."[37] Observing that the situ-

ation in Birmingham, having received little local coverage, had now attracted much national notice, the *Times*
recounted more vividly the events in Greenwood. And
Greenwood was getting increasing attention: the black
comedian Dick Gregory was in town (having brought
several tons of food from Atlanta), defying white officials as blacks had not defied them in a century. The
Times article noted that the Justice Department's filing
of a request for a federal court order to cease intimidation of blacks "marked the first time in the civil rights
struggle that the [Justice] department had interceded
to preserve the right of peaceful protest."[38]

John Doar was left to explain to Moses the government's definition of "civil rights politics," a concept
that SNCC would have abhorred. Doar accepted—
though not so unreservedly as his superiors isolated in
Washington—the idea that the government could not
take an exclusively moral approach to civil rights. Doar
believed the role of the government was to push for civil
rights within the much larger context of Democratic
liberalism. Unlike much of the federal establishment,
Doar could make that claim with authenticity, for he
had acted on behalf of justice in Mississippi, calculating
to the best of his ability how much justice was attain-
able. His position implied that compromises had to
be made; government had to concern itself with many
competing interests.[39] Above all, violence must not be
allowed to spread. Moses believed the law was right
and its enforcement requisite. And by now Kennedy's
civil rights commission and others were beginning to
join SNCC in questioning the administration's political
rationale.[40]

The Kennedy administration, suggesting that it

would provide significant help in the slow legalistic process of registering blacks, had encouraged voter registration as an alternative to the nonviolent direct action techniques of sit-ins or freedom rides. Moses had played along, filing his tedious reports with the Justice Department and trusting in Doar's ultimate cooperation when the situation demanded it. But the government now came to realize what Moses had understood all along: in Mississippi voter registration was direct action, as defiantly direct as sitting in at a white lunch counter, often provoking the most violent reactions of the white community. So now Washington began to paddle backward, agreeing to sacrifice the ballot to induce local police to restrain their dogs and release their prisoners. Of the fifteen hundred blacks applying in LeFlore County during the next six months, only fifty would be registered.[41] Blacks faced the same barriers they had before. These would not come down without federal intervention. Moses had every reason to be angry. And, in a 1966 interview about this period Moses was asked, "Didn't you get mad?" His simple answer was "Yes."[42]

The movement in Mississippi temporarily collapsed with the compromise. Only violence would attract the needed attention of the media and the government.[43]

SIX

YOUNG AMERICAN REVOLUTIONARIES

On Easter weekend 1963, at SNCC's fourth annual conference, Moses gave a speech outlining his plans for continuing voter registration in Mississippi's Delta. The need was for "not five hundred but five thousand" blacks to register to vote, but SNCC must realize that it was confronting a white monolith: "I don't for one minute think that the country is in a position or is willing to push this down the throats of white people in the Delta, and it will have to be pushed down their throats because they are determined not to have it done."[1]

This speech shows a different Moses from the young philosopher who had who came to work for SCLC in 1960. He was now talking explicitly of the need to force a confrontation between the federal government and the state, using more openly the vocabulary of power and competition. Blacks would have to take control of the political structure: education, jobs, and medical care would follow.[2] Moses now believed the black leaders already in positions of leadership were too cautious to be on the side of a radical group like SNCC. The answer was to persuade the majority of Mississippi blacks to elect leaders whom whites could not control. During this period the shift from middle-class black concerns to the concerns of the poor, unemployed, or marginally employed rural blacks quickened under SNCC's influence. SNCC and CORE field secretaries were increasingly arguing that the needs of the blacks they worked with in the cotton fields centered not in desegregation but in the right to vote. Criticism of the "black bourgeoisie" and "white liberals" began to be made publicly.

By almost any standard, Moses had become radicalized, or rather, further radicalized, because anyone in the deep South who challenged its racial system was by definition a radical. By staying in Mississippi, in the center of danger—slowly, steadily, patiently exhorting, failing, and trying again—Moses had become a revolutionary guerrilla chieftain deep in an enemy land. Yet it was a contradictory radicalism. The talk was of conflict and seizure of control; but the method and object remained the seemingly innocuous, traditional institution of the ballot, which was a sort of mirror image of Moses himself.

In the end, the direct action wing of the civil rights movement and the voter registration wing differed less in kind than in emphasis and strategy. The decision on the part of a Mississippi black to attempt to register

was an immediate act of rebellion and self-empow-
erment. But the disciplines of nonviolence (to an extent
still part of the ethos of SNCC, as its title announced)
and civil disobedience that King's legions employed
were also of that character; they were practices of self-
possession and self-transformation. And they too aimed
not merely at personal triumph and moral witness
against segregation but, in such forms as economic boycott, at a transformation of economic and political institutions. SNCC and SCLC, even in their differences,
together embody the dual character of the movement:
immediate liberation in empowering personal action
and permanent liberation through the redistribution of
power. They were, as Moses had originally realized,
both practicing direct action.

By the spring of 1963 in all of Mississippi some 6,700
of the more than 60,000 blacks who made the attempt
had been registered to vote.[3] Violence against blacks
continued. On May 8 Moses raced to Mileston, about a
dozen miles northeast of Lexington in Holmes County.
Mileston was the scene of a firebombing at the house of
Hartman Turnbow, the first black to attempt to register
in the county. With his own automatic rifle, he had
driven off armed whites who tried to prevent his escape
from the fire.[4] Turnbow represented a small but growing segment of blacks in Mississippi, often farmers, who
did not simply meet violence with disciplined nonviolent action. King, according to Turnbow, was the only
one to have urged him to practice nonviolence.[5]

Moses took meticulous notes as usual, and an FBI
agent dispatched by John Doar at Moses' request also
investigated. The sheriff came by and accused Turnbow
of firebombing his own house to generate sympathy for

SNCC's voter registration campaign. Moses, Turnbow, and three others were themselves arrested for interfering with a fireman in his investigation. Moses was also found guilty of obstructing the sheriff's investigation by taking pictures. The Greenwood *Commonwealth* quoted deputy sheriff Andrew Smith, who asserted that a Molotov cocktail had been thrown into Turnbow's home "to work up sympathy and excitement" for the voter registration project because "interest in the drive just dropped to zero. They were all at the scene the next morning and no other Negroes were there. The story they told was just too fantastic."[6] Fay Bennett, the executive secretary of the National Sharecroppers Fund, sent a telegram to Attorney General Kennedy referring to a *New York Times* report of Moses' arrest and jailing in Lexington and urging that the Justice Department take action. The message concluded, "Charges against Moses incredible. Fear for his safety."[7] John Doar and the Justice Department filed suit on May 11 to void the convictions as "false and baseless charges."[8] All charges were dropped two days later except for that against Moses of interfering in an investigation. All were released five days after the incident.

Moses testified before the House Judiciary Committee later that month about conditions in Mississippi. He pointed out that a Justice Department proposal to automatically register blacks with a primary school education would not do because many whites with a lesser background had been enfranchised. Only a quarter as much was spent on education for each black as for each white child and fifty percent of blacks dropped out of school after the eighth grade. The federal govern-

ment would need to spend vast amounts to educate
Mississippi blacks to bring them to the advanced primary school level; thus Moses urged that both races
be granted the vote regardless of literacy. Implicitly
reminding the committee that many rural blacks were
armed, he called the situation in the Delta "very dangerous.... They are not going to stand by much longer
and have people shoot in their homes."[9]

Moses' words proved prophetic. Within a few weeks
the nation and the administration were shaken by the
highly visible June 12 murder of NAACP's Mississippi
state field secretary Medgar Evers in Greenwood, Mississippi. Evers had just heard President Kennedy pro-
nounce at a national press conference: "We are confronted primarily with a moral issue.... I shall ask
the Congress of the United States to act, to make a
commitment it has not fully made in this century to the
proposition that race has no place in American life and
law."[10] Evers's murder was provoked by his attempt to
mobilize Jackson blacks to achieve the same conces-
sions of the white community that King had managed
to secure for Birmingham.[11] The funeral brought a
near riot.

On June 19 President Kennedy sent his civil rights
bill to the House of Representatives, timed to respond
to the anger that Evers's murder had awakened among
black Americans. Moses was disappointed in the bill,
for it failed to address voting rights, what he thought to
be the important issue. The most controversial provision prohibited discrimination in public accommodations. The earlier civil rights acts of 1957 and 1960 had
included provisions on voting rights, giving the Justice
Department the power to seek injunctive action against

officials practicing discrimination in voting activities and granting the civil rights division authority to inspect and photograph voter registration records. And in March 1961 the civil rights division had been instructed to use the FBI in conducting investigations of voting cases.[12] Perhaps Moses feared that a piecemeal bill would ease the pressure building on the administration to intervene for voting rights. Certainly the new legislation appeared to veer away from the explosive issue of voter registration, again reflecting the skittishness of the Kennedy administration once confrontations, killings, and controversy threatened to force it to react in ways that would antagonize the white Southern bloc. Moses resolved that he and the movement would need to create the conditions to force federal intervention.

SNCC meanwhile attempted to raise the spirits of people in Greenwood in the aftermath of Evers's assassination. The Delta Folk Music Festival, on July 6, was to be its first integrated public gathering. Local police continued petty harassment, putting up "no parking" signs on each side of the road leading to the gathering. Held in a cotton field a few miles outside of Greenwood on land under black ownership, the festival featured Bob Dylan, Pete Seeger, and Theodore Bikel.[13] The event failed to draw more than the COFO staff and a small group of blacks who knew nothing of the entertainers' reputations. And the local newspaper publicized the event in typical fashion by asserting that Seeger was a communist sympathizer and that "Negro vote workers here consider Communists their friends."[14]

Meanwhile Moses attempted once more to force the federal government into action. He telegraphed the fed-

eral Civil Rights Commission, complaining that "a ring
of killers operates out of Greenwood with an official
wink from the police and other law enforcement agencies in Mississippi."[15] He pointed to killings of blacks
in the previous six weeks. "The fact that the murderer
of Medgar Evers comes from Greenwood," he said in
reference to the most publicized violent event of the
moment, "is not insignificant by any means. It strongly
supports the theory" that Greenwood was the center of
an organized and violent group dedicated to eradicat-
ing opponents of white supremacy.[16] For its part, the
Civil Rights Commission had compiled a report after
the shooting incident at the home of Dewey Greene in
late March only to have the Assistant Attorney General
Burke Marshall persuade the six commissioners not to
release it until the president had met with them.[17]

An interview contains Moses' appraisal of the Mississippi situation at this time:

> So, the picture in the summer of '63 then, . . . after
> Medgar was killed and the demonstration people went
> to jail, you have the huge bail money, hundreds of thou-
> sands of dollars to raise which has to be raised outside
> of Mississippi. The people in the demonstrations [were]
> not really ready to stay in jail. That whole jail no bail
> movement really never took off the ground. . . . So then
> what does the Movement do? It can't demonstrate . . .
> you had that stalemate in Jackson, a similar stalemate
> in Greenwood around voter registration.[18]

Moses observes that what sustained him and his fellow
activists during these early years was their own growth
and that of the local blacks who were able to overcome

their fear and begin working themselves on voter registration projects.[19]

However much attention the murder of Mississippi NAACP leader Medgar Evers may have taken from Moses' activities, in the end it furthered the voting rights impetus. The killing produced a series of demonstrations in the black community in Jackson and elsewhere that attracted the attention of Allard Lowenstein, a liberal coalition builder, among others.

Lowenstein, a white Northerner, had been active in politics and liberal causes from the time of his involvement with the National Student Association, an organization for which he subsequently served as president. After graduating from Yale Law School he traveled to Africa as a foreign policy aide to Hubert Humphrey and began (possibly through the auspices of the CIA) working for an end to apartheid there. He then sought to enter U.S. politics in New York, cultivating a connection with Eleanor Roosevelt.[20] By the time he ventured to Mississippi, he had done a stint as teacher and administrator at Stanford; written *Brutal Mandate,* a book about his experience in South-West Africa; and accepted a teaching position at North Carolina State in Raleigh. He participated in the demonstrations in Jackson after Evers's assassination and ostensibly offered his services to replace Bill Higgs, the only white civil rights lawyer willing to work with SNCC for civil rights in Mississippi, who in January had filed Moses' suit against the attorney general and FBI director Hoover.[21]

In early July 1963 Lowenstein caught up with Moses in McComb. When efforts to register black voters once again bogged down, he suggested that blacks be encour-

aged to cast protest ballots in the state's early August
Democratic primary.[22] Moses attributed the idea to

> some of the law school students who were down in Jack-
> son doing research. In fact they were the first white
> students down there.... They uncovered a law which
> allowed for casting protest ballots in the primary....
> We had people do this in Greenwood. We had hundreds
> of people who had tried to register, go down on the day
> of the primary around the Governor's election and so
> forth and cast a vote as a kind of freedom ballot.[23]

About one thousand blacks cast protest ballots,[24] but
the Mississippi authorities, now alert, simply threw out
their votes. Moses had written letters to civil rights
leaders, asking them to come to Greenwood to serve
as poll watchers in the black precincts there.[25] The
campaign, which at an earlier time would have resulted
in open violence, died of a technical maneuver by a
state that was coming fitfully and partially to recognize
it had to reckon with both publicity and the federal
government. When the Democratic primary runoff
came three weeks later, a mock election organized by
COFO workers that allowed unregistered blacks to vote
in their churches and at other community gatherings
achieved a massive response of more than twenty-seven
thousand ballots, most voting for the more moderate of
the two candidates.[26]

Moses judged this effort on balance a success. When
Lowenstein offered to recruit white college students to
work in Mississippi on a full-fledged "Freedom Vote,"
Moses departed from his normal position of neutrality.
Through Lowenstein's contacts at Yale and at Stanford,
where he had worked as assistant dean of men,[27] he

could provide the access Moses needed to recruit and subsequently to fix national attention on civil rights activities in Mississippi. At that time no whites were working in the Delta itself; local black Mississippi students made up most of the staff. Moses knew that many in SNCC would object to such a plan; it went against the grain of developing an indigenous black leadership. But after pondering the issue for a number of weeks, he decided the benefits that might come from using the white students should ultimately outweigh the discord their presence might bring. These benefits would consist both of their direct working contributions and of the national attention these young members of the country's white elite could bring to the struggle in Mississippi.

During this time massive preparations were under way for the August 28 March on Washington, but Moses took no part in this activity. Although SNCC was represented by its new chairman, John Lewis, an early rights leader from Nashville and former theology student, the organization as a whole had little to do with the extensive preparations, funded largely by the Taconic Foundation. At initial meetings, SNCC urged that the route of march include the Justice Department, particularly because the government had recently brought charges against SNCC leaders in Albany, Georgia, for "conspiracy to obstruct justice"; they had picketed a juror's store after an acquittal of a sheriff accused of shooting and beating a black. Many SNCC workers viewed the action against the rights workers simply as another example of the Kennedy administration's efforts to toady to white Southern voters.[28] But the suggestion to demonstrate against the Justice Department was discarded by the group newly organized to manage the march, the United Civil Rights Leadership Council, composed of leaders of all of the major rights groups.

And so while thousands crowded the Lincoln Memorial to hear Martin Luther King, Jr., deliver his landmark "I Have A Dream" speech, Moses and a small group picketed the Justice Department. In an all-night vigil, Moses carried a philosophical picket sign that read: "When There Is No Justice, What Is the State but a Robber Band Enlarged?"[29] Moses' refusal to see the larger significance of the undertaking could be interpreted as petulant. Yet it is in keeping with his dislike of public displays, speeches, grand gestures—the large-scale demonstrations that King orchestrated so well. And for many SNCC workers who had toiled in the dusty, hot, poverty-stricken villages and farms of Mississippi, Alabama, and Georgia, the march seemed yet another compromise on the part of the SCLC, the NAACP, and CORE. These organizations, cooperating with the National Council of Churches and other religious organizations, seemed to be staging a grandstand display in support of the administration's efforts to promote and pass a flawed civil rights bill. The March on Washington, in fact, was perhaps the single most important event in raising the consciousness of blacks throughout the country that their needs and rights were legitimate and overdue. And the march engaged the support of thousands of Northern white liberals, precisely the tactic Moses would come to use in his own work during the coming months and the following summer in Mississippi.[30]

In a memorandum to the SNCC executive committee in early September, Moses summarized the past two

1. Martha Prescod, Mike Miller, and Bob Moses attempt to convince a woman to register in Ruleville, Mississippi. (Danny Lyon, Magnum Photos)

4. Moses ponders the direction of the movement after Atlantic City; Waveland, Mississippi, November, 1964. (Danny Lyon, Magnum Photos)

Facing Page:
Top: 2. The second person arrested on Freedom Day in Hattiesburg, Mississippi, January 22, 1964. (Danny Lyon, Magnum Photos)
Bottom: 3. Moses with coworkers Sam Block *(middle)* and Willie Peacock *(right)* at Amzie Moore's house in Cleveland, Mississippi. (Danny Lyon, Magnum Photos)

5. Frank Smith, Moses, and Willie Peacock in the Greenwood SNCC office in March 1963. The office was firebombed the day after this picture was taken. (Danny Lyon, Magnum Photos)

Facing Page:
Top: 6. Moses in quiet conversation with Freedom Summer volunteers in June of 1964 at Western College for Women, Oxford, Ohio. (Steve Shapiro, Black Star)
Bottom: 7. Moses orienting Freedom Summer volunteers in June of 1964 at Western College for Women, Oxford, Ohio. (Steve Shapiro, Black Star)

8. Moses explains a point to a student volunteer in June of 1964 at Western College for Women, Oxford, Ohio. (Steve Shapiro, Black Star)

Facing Page:
Top: 9. Moses talks with a registered voter, April, 1963. Claude Sitton *(The New York Times)*
Bottom: 10. On the floor of the Democratic National Convention in 1964, Moses talks with a reporter. (Bob Fletcher, Schomburg Center for Research in Black Culture)

Above: 11. Robert Moses in 1993. (Chester Higgins, Jr., *The New York Times*)

12. Robert Parris Moses. (Danny Lyon, Magnum Photos)

years' work in Mississippi, noting among the accomplishments "establishment of 'beachheads' or bases for operation in a number of towns and counties." In listing what had been learned, he remarked, "It is not possible for us to register Negroes in Mississippi. (There is reason to believe that authorities in Mississippi will force a showdown over the right to vote in large numbers.)" Perhaps the safety of a separate Freedom Vote, although outwardly meaningless in securing real enfranchisement for blacks, would contribute to their empowerment psychologically and symbolically. In this position paper, Moses makes his strongest statements about political power and anticipates coming programs:

> The only attack worth making is an attack aimed at the overthrow of the existing political structures of the state. They must be torn down completely to make way for new ones. The focus of such an attack must be on the vote and the Delta of Mississippi, including Jackson and Vicksburg.... That S.N.C.C. [should] launch a one-man-one-vote campaign for Mississippi aimed at obtaining the vote in Mississippi by 1964. That S.N.C.C. [should] organize local political clubs to support a Negro for Congress.... That it [should] begin now to explore ways and means of electing militant Negroes to local offices in Mississippi in the 1967 elections.[31]

Moses and others worked along with nearly one hundred Northern liberal white college students recruited by Lowenstein, helping local blacks cast ballots for their own candidates at "freedom" polling sites to parallel the official Mississippi gubernatorial election of November 1963.[32] Lowenstein had observed that blacks in South Africa held a day of mourning on the white election day. Some SNCC workers have since claimed that the idea for the Freedom Vote came from efforts in Alabama, where the state permitted voter registration only two days a month.[33] Some fifteen years later, Moses would say that he did not know who thought of the idea, adding that it was not important.[34] The purpose was to raise consciousness among blacks and to show, in the face of white claims to the contrary, that tens of thousands of blacks wanted to vote. The vote would be an assault on Jim Crow as a system of controls imposed by the white race and as a state of mind on the part of the oppressed. Moses said of it, "The freedom vote is a major step in getting Negroes into the workings of democracy. The next process we have to go through is to prepare people for the day when Negroes run for office."[35] Moses' own work for the congressional campaign launched in the winter of 1961–62 for the Reverend R. L. T. Smith had given him substantial knowledge about the possibilities of a comparable statewide gubernatorial campaign.[36] The endorsement suggests a turning on Moses' part toward a more pragmatic use of political techniques. He was prodded by the frustrating slowness and the high emotional and physical cost of achieving the vote for blacks; the agonizing deliberations of the federal government were spurring him to look for new methods outside of the courts and local community leadership. Moses hoped that between 150,000 and 200,000 blacks would take part.[37] The campaign would also publicize the lack of voting privilege: "Mississippi's so-called two-party politics," Moses explained, "means *no* politics for thousands of Negroes across the state."[38]

COFO held a convention on October 6, 1963, to select candidates for the coming parallel gubernatorial election. Its elected delegates nominated for governor Aaron Henry, head of the Mississippi NAACP and of COFO, and for lieutenant governor Edwin King, the white chaplain at Tougaloo College. Henry was a black pharmacist who operated a drugstore in the Delta town of Clarksdale. King, twenty-seven years old and a native of Vicksburg, Mississippi, had long been active in the civil rights movement. That summer he had been involved in a forced head-on collision by white terrorists and was recovering from disfiguring facial injuries.[39] The candidacy of Ed King makes clear the nature of Moses' work. As King relates in his unpublished memoir:

> About a week after the campaign had officially begun I received a phone call from Bob Moses. Bob . . . wanted to talk . . . about some important matters concerning the election. . . . In his quiet way he made his request— he wanted me to join the ticket as the candidate for Lt. Governor. Bob said that he knew that I was interested in interracial reconciliation and understanding, just as he was. This campaign could be an important step in that direction. The most important thing, obviously, was to have a Black candidate for Governor. But if I would join Aaron Henry then we could have a ticket with two native Mississippians, one Black and one white, working together, speaking together at campaign rallies, talking about the problems of all people of the state. . . . And so I entered politics.[40]

Although the Freedom Vote, as a parallel election in black communities, was less provocative than previous campaigns because it did not involve standoffs with regular registrars, it made the public statement its sponsors intended. And white supremacists, though a few had begun to show some awareness of what national publicity was doing to their cause, once again helpfully acted out their customary role of violent villains in the morality play. By the time of the vote, the state had been keyed up to combat "communist, outside agitators" regardless of what they did. One example is revealed in Ivanhoe Donaldson's field report for the week of October 30 to November 5, 1963. A small group that was to meet with Moses went to the airport in Jackson to pick up rental cars to use in canvassing for the Freedom Vote. Donaldson and his companions were followed by police, who proceeded to harass and threaten the group with remarks like "Goddamned NAACP Communist trouble maker, ain't you, Boy?" and "Nigger if I had your god damned ass over in Branden I'd kill you. Before you goddamned black communist sonafa bitches started coming *down* here, everything was all right. Niggers down here don't need to vote— ain't supposed to vote." At one point Donaldson, isolated in a police car and informed that he was under arrest for having illegal plates—although he had a proper license and rental papers—seemed close to death when a hysterical policeman cocked the hammer of his gun, held it to Donaldson's face, and announced, "Black son of a bitch, I'm gonna kill you nigger. God damn it, I'm gonna kill you!!"[41]

On election day the police arrested blacks without the slightest provocation and attempted to confiscate ballots of the mock primary. Local whites also stepped up their harassment, especially of the economic variety. Yet this November vote, unauthorized by state procedure, produced an even larger turnout than the August 6 Democratic primary. At least seventy-five thousand blacks voted for the two candidates.[42] These voters, according to Neil McMillen, represented the shift within the black community from the titular leadership of middle-class NAACP members to the farmers, share-croppers, and poor uneducated blacks of the state.[43] Ivanhoe Donaldson, a Mississippi SNCC worker, comments that after the vote "there was less fear in the Negro community about taking part in civil rights activities."[44] The psychological reward of the Freedom Vote was a much-needed impetus at a time when the movement was at an ebb in achieving its limited goals. It demonstrated that local people could set up a political network in the state[45] and instilled what Ed King describes as "the new spirit of pride in the black people of Mississippi and, in the staff, a revived feeling of hope that something worthwhile could be done in the worst state in America."[46] And it represented a breakthrough for Moses and SNCC, a chance to get away from the slow, low-reward effort of individual voter registration in a system rigged against blacks. The idea of the Freedom Vote had perfectly expressed the moral nature of Bob Moses and of SNCC, the reliance on a dramatic presentation of the moral issue that would at once mobilize black people and compel the federal government to take action. The December 9, 1963, issue of the *Student Voice* quotes him as saying that there was little possibility that the white population would voluntarily make any real change in the status of black people and would not accept any substantial changes in the power structure without federal intervention. SNCC's job is to "bring about just such a confrontation . . . to change the power structure."[47] At a "Victory Rally" in Jackson when the Freedom Votes were counted on the eve of the Mississippi regular November election, Moses spoke of the need for federal intervention: "We expect our efforts to dissuade those who believe that anything less than federal troops will work."[48] Whatever had been Moses' reservations about importing Northern white students and about confrontation, he was convinced by this time that both would be major factors in transforming Mississippi.

A few weeks later, the November 22 assassination of President Kennedy riveted the nation in mourning. Moses, as always, fixed on the cause and the larger issue; he had lost faith in the administration. He asked, "Will the country be moved to face real issues, and that which is to be done, or will it shift the blame outside of America and do nothing about the condition which fostered this act of violence?"[49] A few days later he was harsh in his opinion of the nation's grief. Concerning the coming SNCC conference in Washington, D.C., he said:

> The conference may be the one place in the country where people can get together and talk . . . without having to pay homage which is trivial . . . banalities. It just doesn't seem that anywhere in the country we have a counterbalance to the idea that if a president dies, he was a hero therefore we must eulogize him. So if there are any real issues at the bottom of this, we must cover them up and avoid real confrontation because it divides. See, SNCC doesn't have to go through this.[50]

Although the Freedom Vote confirmed to Moses that the presence of white college students could generate enormous interest, bringing in almost one hundred of them touched a raw nerve among the black Southerners who had worked to earn the trust of local residents for many months.[51] Mendy Samstein recounted that there were four main topics discussed at a weekend COFO staff meeting on November 14–16, 1963.[52] This meeting came at the end of an eight-day conference conducted by SNCC, CORE, and SCLC staff with seventy-five participants and a number of additional local residents attending evening sessions. One of the topics on the schedule was the role of staff members. But the weekend conference—composed of the smaller COFO group and led by Moses and Dave Dennis, with Howard Zinn as the resource person—listed three main discussion items: "(a) role of whites; (b) summer project; (c) federal involvement."[53] The first item included more precisely the number of Northern students to be brought into Mississippi again the next summer. Samstein's analysis was that the controversy over white participation was not so much the presence of Northern white students but the shift to the central office in Jackson where most of the decisions concerning the Freedom Vote campaign were made. People in the field felt left out, and the concentration of whites was in that central office. Samstein essentially agreed with Moses' defense of the situation that "it was more the result of necessity . . . than of design."[54]

At that November 14 COFO meeting Moses formally presented a plan to COFO's executive committee to make wider use the next summer of white students like those who had helped during the Freedom Vote.[55] His primary idea was to organize the black communities of Mississippi and thereby "to build a base of political power to effect radical changes in the political and economic set-up of the state."[56] He projected a voter registration effort that would begin on December 15 and last through February 29, 1964. Part of the goal was to put forward black candidates for five congressional seats and the Senate seat of John Stennis. Freedom candidates, Moses argued, would not win but would demonstrate the potential power and display the will of black voters in the state. In addition, he proposed the concept of parallel registration elections and voting coordinated by COFO. Moses also suggested sending delegates to both Republican and Democratic nominating conventions to challenge the seating of all-white Mississippi delegations.[57]

This far-reaching proposal represents a departure from Moses' earlier statements and actions. During the summer of 1962 twenty black field secretaries had worked with Moses, sixteen from Mississippi. And in the spring of 1963 he observed: "At this point it is too dangerous for whites to participate in the project in Mississippi—too dangerous for them and too dangerous for the Negroes who would be working with them."[58]

The limited success of the Freedom Vote and Lowenstein's undoubted organizational and oratorical powers ensured future success in gaining volunteers. All the same, Lowenstein antagonized veteran civil rights workers with his often "frenetic style and contacts in high places." Lowenstein, Moses has explained, "had lots of ties to important people in the government and the Democratic party like Hubert Humphrey. He was always on the phone with them and Ella Baker had reservations about it. That wasn't the way we were working at the time."[59]

A reliance on white volunteers, perhaps, came partially from the need to find a substitute for VEP. Its director, Wiley Branton, had come to the conclusion that unless the Justice Department could prevent Southern white officials from interfering with black voter registration in Mississippi, VEP funds were better placed elsewhere.[60] And VEP disavowed any financial connection with activities that could be called "partisan politics." In notifying Aaron Henry, president of COFO, of the fourteen-thousand-dollar grant from VEP in September 1962, Branton inserted a paragraph stating: "No part of these funds may be used to support partisan politics in any manner whatsoever, nor to influence legislation of any kind, nor in behalf of or against any political candidate."[61] After it became clear that a parallel gubernatorial campaign supporting Henry and Ed King would be launched in the fall of 1963, Moses wrote Branton that voter registration efforts would be suspended from early October until the beginning of December "in order that full forces may be mobilized behind the 'one-man—one-vote,' Henry-for-Governor Protest Election Campaign."[62] When Branton asked how Moses planned to finance the endeavor, Moses said that he was trying to collect twenty thousand dollars from individual donations and that Al Lowenstein had gone to New York to help raise funds.[63]

Moses' projected 1964 summer project would involve not only registration work but also Freedom Schools, community centers, and other substitutes for federal and state government. The community centers would offer children and adults the kind of facilities limited by the Jim Crow system: libraries, arts and crafts, day care, rudimentary health care, and literacy classes. Freedom Schools were to offer a general academic curriculum, with an emphasis on remedial work in a state where schooling for blacks was tucked in before and after the cotton season. As Fannie Lou Hamer remarked, "I started working when I was about six years old. I didn't have a chance to go to school too much, because school would only last about four months at a time.... We didn't have clothes to wear to that [school]."[64] They would also instruct students in African-American history and current events. Even activities without an obvious political bent Moses saw as an opportunity to teach the "politics of Mississippi" and begin to build a core of educated leadership in the state.[65] Typically, he sought a balance between direct political, pragmatic activities and the moral empowerment of Mississippi blacks.

Freedom Summer was an ambitious and heartening project. The sticking point was the importation of an army of Northern white volunteers. Throughout 1963 racial tensions had been increasing within SNCC as more and more whites joined the organization and, having more savvy in manipulating the media, using influence, and making political contact, rapidly moved into organizing and leadership positions. Howard Zinn minimizes the racial frictions within the organization. His claim that calls for violence against whites had "not found approval among the SNCC staff" is believable, but does not speak to the larger and later question of distrust and hostility.[66] At any rate, Moses recognized the growing racial antagonisms, noting racial outbursts in meetings and observing that it was "very hard for some of the students who had been brought up in Mississippi and are victims of this kind of race hatred not to begin to let all of that out on the white staff."[67] He believed, however, that blacks in the movement could "find a broader identification with individuals that are going through the same kind of struggle, so that the struggle doesn't remain just a question of racial struggle."[68] Allard Lowenstein would recognize, at least in retrospect, the reality of racial tensions in SNCC and the growing opposition of blacks to white workers: "Here were kids who had been risking their lives in Mississippi for a long time, and nobody even noticed it. I mean the white people who came down got the publicity. It would have taken an angel not to have resented that."[69]

The argument for bringing in the Northern volunteers was clear enough. In sheer numbers, they would bolster the project. As the children of the favored social classes of the nation's favored race, they would attract an attention that the hardened Southern black SNCC workers had not received. In that capacity as well, they could bring safety to the project as a whole. Lawrence Guyot, a Mississippian and Tougaloo graduate who had been involved in SNCC rights activities since 1961, noticed during the fall of 1963 when students from Yale and Stanford came to volunteer with the effort to register black voters that, "wherever those white volunteers went, FBI agents followed."[70] Stokely Carmichael, not yet a thoroughgoing black separatist, made the same observation: "While these people [white volunteers] are here, national attention is here. The FBI isn't going to let anything happen to them. They let the murderers of

Negroes off, but already men have been arrested in Itta Bena just for *threatening* white lives."[71] Mendy Samstein added that "during the Freedom Rally in Jackson which concluded the [Freedom Vote] Campaign, TV men from N.B.C. spent most of their time shooting film of the Yalies and seemed hardly aware of the local people and full-time SNCC workers."[72] Not lost on the embattled SNCC staffers was the recognition that the Justice Department "had people on hand in the *eventuality* of trouble."[73]

And there was the larger ethos of the rights movement, which at the time was staunchly integrationist. Charles Cobb, a Howard University student from Massachusetts, had been working in the Delta on voter registration for several months before Freedom Summer. Though he resisted the use of Northern white volunteers, believing it an admission of failure and an inability to handle Mississippi violence, he recognized that the principle to which the project had committed itself was that of an integrated society, a transcendence of race.[74] But against these arguments stood potent misgivings.

Part of the problem was Al Lowenstein, who probably originated the scheme of bringing in Northern volunteers for the Freedom Vote and whose support would be essential for the project. Although he was a major asset to COFO, he was also a potential liability. The aggressive and optimistic Lowenstein often took action without the consensus discussion—slow, methodical, and often inconclusive—that had been SNCC's modus operandi. "The genius of SNCC in Mississippi," Ed King explains, "was that . . . most things were done on a very practical basis. There really was no absolute philosophy or political ideology that guided people. Bob Moses and his staff spent most of their time listening to the people; programs geared to those needs ... were slowly developed—or discovered."[75] Amzie Moore has remarked that Moses wanted "the people in this area to do their own thing rather than have SNCC do it.... He felt like it was the people's thing.... Other people felt ... that it would take years of supervision for it to be a people's thing."[76] Lowenstein, as King puts it, "did not know how to separate his advice from his leadership."[77] Moses understood the promise that Lowenstein's personality and position offered and would continue up through the 1964 Democratic National Convention to seek his advice.[78] Yet the two could not have been farther apart in their concept of leadership.

Lowenstein's style was a problem in itself. More significant was what it suggested to the SNCC staffers about the conduct of the Northern volunteers.

During the Freedom Vote project, the indigenous leadership had been shaken by the presence of educated white college students who, as the local activists saw them, were aggressive and confident to a fault—much like Lowenstein himself. And like Lowenstein, these students believed in decision making and leadership from the top down. At the November 14 meeting, several staffers, discussing the possible 1964 Freedom Summer, argued that during the Freedom Vote Northern whites had bulldozed their way into positions of power. More particularly, they believed that whites had pushed blacks out of the Jackson office. Moses viewed the influx of white volunteers somewhat pragmatically: "We had a lot of work to do in Jackson. It was as simple as that."[79] There was reference to a white student's insistence that he had gotten instructions from Lowenstein and would follow them regardless of what Moses said.[80]

It was not merely the actual or suspected or anticipated conduct of white volunteers that scraped the staffers' nerves. The most modest and best behaved of Northern college students and others of their class might still be a threat to all that the SNCC workers had labored for. Hollis Watkins, a native of Pike County who was active in SNCC from the time he was a teenager and at the outset of Moses' work in Mississippi, remembers the question of the volunteers as a "tough issue." Bringing in Northern white students could hurt the community-based organization that the activists were trying to build: "For the first time, we had local people who had begun to take the initiative themselves. . . . Local indigenous people knowing that most of the students would be more educated than themselves . . . would become complacent, they would feel inferior and fall back into the same rut."[81]

The night before the November 14 meeting the Mississippi COFO staff, gathering in Greenville without Moses, discussed the possible Freedom Summer project. Remembering abrasive encounters with Lowenstein, and some irritating characteristics of the whites from the good schools, they decided to limit rather than expand the role of whites. The next night, Moses listened to the minutes of the previous meeting:

1. There would not be a white director of a project.
2. Whites would not write any party platform.
3. There wouldn't be a white WATS line operator.
4. Whites would be carefully selected to see where they

could fit in to work on a field worker basis, at the request of project directors.

5. The main function of whites would be to work in the white community, on a new white project.

Moses interjected, "In other words, get rid of the whites." A COFO staff member responded, "No, not at all." Moses continued:

> Well, it seems to me that's the idea, if you're sending them to work in white communities. I am concerned that we do integrate, because otherwise we'll grow up and have a racist movement. And if the white people don't stand with the Negroes as they go out now, then there will be a danger that after the Negroes get something they'll say, "Okay, we got this by ourselves." And the only way you can break that down is to have white people working alongside of you— so then it changes the whole complexion of what you're doing, so it isn't any longer Negro fighting white, it's a question of rational people against irrational people.... I always thought that the one thing we can do for the country that no one else could do is to be above the race issue.[82]

Some written notes on the weekend meeting outlined the range of discussion: "whether to have students, what racial composition of summer group should be, administrative problems of large number of people, whether their presence would force federal action, how to deal with repercussions."[83] The notes on discussion of the "White Students' Role" read: "Much discussion. Decision to choose roles on basis of qualified people. Will begin project in white community.... Still feelings about need for leadership to be Negro but no specific decisions made about how whites should be limited."[84]

When the plan for Freedom Summer again came under discussion in late December 1963, debate continued, often heatedly. On the first day of meetings, the plan was rejected. When Moses did speak, it was with a forcefulness that broke with his practice of allowing, by his own silence, the free formation of a consensus. Lawrence Guyot describes it: "Moses came on the second day and said, 'Look, I'm not gonna be a part of anything all-black. We're gonna have the Summer Project. We need it. We need it for these reasons.' And suddenly, there was a reconsideration of the vote.... See, had Moses not wanted it to happen, it wouldn'ta [sic] happened."[85]

The SNCC staff arrived at something of a compromise. A hundred white students who would be allowed to come down for the Summer Project—only a fraction of the real number finally recruited.[86] The persistence and determination of the opponents of the use of whites boded ill for future integrated rights activities.[87]

On December 30 the SNCC executive committee finally discussed the project. Opposition at the meeting was mostly on the grounds that the project would disrupt SNCC's operations, leaving behind a shell at the end of the summer when the white volunteers returned to their campuses. Moses reverted generally to his silent self; but he also temporized by attempting at once to argue for the project and present the concerns of the radical minority in COFO. An originator of the plan, he nonetheless refused to state whether he favored or opposed it. Moses acknowledged the doubts he and others had, worrying that the scheme could start "the threatened bloodbath and have violent consequences we cannot handle."[88] But he was committed to a vision of blacks and whites standing together against an injustice. In an interview years later, Moses more vividly described the issue:

> We were split. I mean we met for months over this question. By and large most of the staff did not want to do it.... You had the staff on the one hand and the people that we were working with on the other. The people by and large wanted the students to come back. Mrs. Hamer, and excellent case in point. She wanted the students to come back and so we were at loggerheads.[89]

Moses' position was a delicate one. How do you help poor, black, uneducated people develop leaders within their own ranks by bringing in hundreds of affluent, white, college students? Ultimately SNCC warily adopted the plan for increased numbers of whites and allowed those supporting it—including Marion Barry, James Forman, and John Lewis—to travel with Moses to persuade the dissenting COFO staff to acquiesce.[90]

The debate stretched across the weeks in typical movement fashion until a discussion in Hattiesburg, Mississippi, in mid-January 1964 was interrupted by news of the death of Louis Allen, the man who had asked Moses for federal protection to testify on the Herbert Lee case.[91] Allen's death may have been the catalyst to the decision on the part of the fragile COFO coalition to accept the Freedom Summer project and its plans to use white volunteers. Moses later explained:

> We got a telephone call that Lewis Allen had been murdered on his front lawn in Liberty. And I went over there to speak to his wife.... And ... thinking through this, ... I had to step in and make my weight felt in

terms of this decision about the summer project.... We couldn't guarantee ... the safety of the people we were working with.... I had to step in between this loggerhead between the staff on the one hand and the people that we were working with. And so that's how the decision was made to actually invite the students down for the summer of 64.[92]

This was the turning point for Moses: with this evidence of federal betrayal he began to assume leadership.

It was also a turning point in the democracy of participation and action that was being born in Mississippi. Freedom Summer required organization, a degree of impersonality, the enlistment of skill, and purpose across the country. It meant that whatever community was to form would have to be not of local people—sharing race and custom and oppression—but of strangers—differing in race, class, and region— joined by choice.

SEVEN

FREEDOM SUMMER

The Freedom Vote in the fall of 1963 was one victory for Robert Moses and his co-workers. The movement needed whatever victories it could get. Registration of blacks by mid-1963 was about three percent of all voters in the state; of all eligible blacks, only six percent were registered.[1] The state was intransigent, the federal presence negligible. Nationally visible figures like Martin Luther King were not at the Mississippi battlefront to lend voice and publicity. "It was clear," Moses has remarked, "that the NAACP and SCLC and CORE, none of them were really willing to put a major drive into Mississippi.... They called for working in other parts of the South first.... And NAACP's whole policy was work all around the state."[2] SNCC's customary methods were not cracking Mississippi. In November 1963 VEP director Wiley Branton had cut off funds to COFO's operation in Mississippi, announcing that the organization would continue to offer minimal support for the Greenwood office from December through March and explaining that the funds already allocated to Mississippi exceeded those given to any other state. In a letter sent jointly to Henry and Moses, he added: "Of almost equal importance to our decision is the fact that the Justice Department has failed to get any meaningful decrees from any of the voter registration suits which have been filed.... We are also very concerned about the failure of the federal government to protect the people who have sought to register and vote or who are working actively in getting others to register."[3]

The historian Clayborne Carson describes the 1964 Mississippi Freedom Summer project as an "expression of SNCC's increasing militancy" to force a confrontation between Washington and the state.[4] Acknowledging the possible dangers in mounting a large-scale summer event, in January 1964 Moses declared, "The Federal Government must take action even if it means the imposition of federal troops or the occupation of a town or particular locality."[5] SNCC was growing combative toward the federal government. It was a paradoxical radicalism, an angry desire for the established institutions to be more visibly present. And SNCC's method of baiting the government was to pursue the eminently respectable activity of registering citizens for the vote. The enlistment that summer of about one thousand Northern white volunteers, and SNCC's cooperation with more mainstream rights groups under COFO, put the organization more into line with coalition liberalism than had its previous efforts to build indigenous movements of blacks within small communities.

Yet the COFO group still was led by a small group of dedicated SNCC workers. At a convention held in early February, Moses outlined in detail the various programs planned for the summer project. The Freedom Registration plan was discussed in detail, and debate ensued over whether people should be required to sign their own names, because reprisal was possible should the registrants' names fall into the wrong hands. Typically, a vote was taken among the nearly one hundred people attending. At this session Al Lowenstein spoke of the philosophy behind a massive summer project and noted that the goals were to help the black community, not simply to cause trouble, and to convince local whites that change was inevitable.[6]

The spring of 1964 was spent publicizing and building support for the summer project among sympathetic Northern liberals in the Democratic party. A SNCC news release on March 20 following a COFO conference in Atlanta outlined a plan to bring two thousand civil rights workers to Mississippi to "conduct voter registration and political education programs." Prominently featured were the candidacies of Fannie Lou Hamer and the Reverend John Cameron for the congressional seats of incumbents.[7] The *Student Voice* announced a "Peace Corps type operation for Mississippi" to aid in the voter registration campaign along with programs that would foster research projects, establish freedom schools, and develop community centers.[8] Moses wrote a memorandum to "Friends of Freedom in Mississippi," enlisting their help in securing a hearing with the presi-

dent before the onset of the summer project. He urged
them to send a letter to Johnson asking for a meeting
with the group and gave instructions for publicizing
the event, if held. Among the recipients were Harry
Belafonte, James Baldwin, Dick Gregory, and Marlon
Brando, and the leaders of all the civil rights groups.[9]
And on May 25, Moses, Aaron Henry, and Dave Dennis
jointly signed a letter to President Johnson, explaining
the summer project plans and requesting a meeting
with COFO and representatives from other civil rights
groups, as well as the National Council of Churches.[10]
In early June, SNCC was building a list of "committed
faculty people who would receive material oriented
specifically for them."[11] A number of officials of the
United Federation of Teachers, including Albert
Shanker, were sent detailed letters describing the special educational programs planned for the summer in
Mississippi and asking for volunteers, observers, and
funding.[12]

Freedom Summer was a massive undertaking. Planning was centered in the COFO office in Jackson. Outside the state people worked diligently to organize the
effort, including the national SNCC office in Atlanta,
Stanford University volunteers, and, as Ed King puts it,
"wherever Al Lowenstein happened to be."[13] A May
27 SNCC news release announced that recruiting was
taking place at "Freedom Centers" on Northern and
Southern college campuses as well as by mail from
protest groups in the South.[14] The students initially
recruited in 1963 for the Freedom Vote had come
chiefly from the Ivy League. Lowenstein, who galva-
nized that effort, was their source of information and
encouragement; they had little knowledge of Moses or

SNCC and COFO offices. Despite the reservations of many SNCC staffers, once again Lowenstein characteristically plunged ahead, assuming that agreement for the project from Moses, Aaron Henry, and SNCC chairman John Lewis meant support from everyone. And Moses, at least, believed Lowenstein critical to the success of the project. In a handwritten note written in late February or early March, Moses alludes to the resentment of others toward Lowenstein but urges:

> If you pull out it won't reduce any tensions absolutely, it will merely be an exchange of one set for another. You know yourself that nothing political and significant can be done without public tension—it stands to reason they won't be done without private ones also. You not only have to stay—you *must* if at all possible, come to the March 15 COFO meeting. We have invited Farmer, Forman, Wilkins, and King. We are just beginning to open up the Pandora of inter-civil rights organizational tensions. You have got to help us iron them out. If we lose dialogue then we will be lost.[15]

At a West Coast freedom rally, Lewis announced that the project's aim was to "saturate" the state with volunteers so that "the Federal Government will have to take over."[16]

All the civil rights groups participated in the project; many liberal organizations also sent money and other support. During the first three months of 1964, SNCC raised nearly $100,000.[17] The Medical Committee for Human Rights was established specifically to help in the enterprise. The Committee on Religion and Race of the National Council of Churches financed the orientation program for volunteers and sent to Mississippi its own staff of clergy and lawyers under the auspices of its Delta Ministry.[18] But the white churches of Mississippi literally and morally closed their doors to any kind of accommodation to the rights of blacks. Ed King calls the white church in Mississippi "the guardian of the soul of the Closed Society."[19] Ministers who tried to integrate their churches were removed from their pulpits by their congregations. A black woman from Tougaloo in Jackson who, with other students, was barred from entering a white church to worship asked a white man, "But what would Jesus do?" The response: "Leave Christ out of this. What does He have to do with it?" Often such attempts ended with the arrest and jailing of the integrationist students and ministers, white and black.[20]

SNCC raised funds by reprinting descriptive articles on its efforts that appeared in national magazines such as *The Saturday Evening Post, Look, Newsweek,* and *The Nation.* After each reprint was an outline of recent arrests and harassment of blacks and civil rights workers, urging interested readers to write or call SNCC headquarters in Atlanta.[21] Another device was a direct appeal from a celebrity. James Baldwin signed a letter mailed soon after the disappearance of the three civil rights workers, noting that over one thousand volunteers—"teachers, nurses, technicians, college students, legal advisors both Negro and white"— from all over the country were working to support Freedom Schools and voter registration drives.[22]

Much of the money for the various programs within the summer project came late, at the same time as the volunteers' arrival in June. Ed King recalls that in May the office in Jackson lacked money to buy stationery to send out mailings; response to applications from volunteers was slow. When King arrived at the Lynch Street office he found about eight people working on a mailing and discovered they had not eaten all day; they had been living on sardine sandwiches for the past few days. He offered all the cash he had—about five dollars— and the group agreed to spend most of that on stamps. Moses left the office, bought a loaf of bread and a jar of peanut butter, and returned to pass out the food.[23]

COFO accepted assistance from the National Lawyers Guild, which like the Southern Christian Education Fund had long been accused of communist associations. Its participation might have endangered the standing of COFO with liberals. Instead, the effect was fortunate: for counterbalance, the liberals sent additional lawyers.

SNCC had come a long way from the time in 1960 when the Atlanta students demanded that Martin Luther King call Moses into his office to interrogate him about possible subversive connections. Now the organization was criticizing King for firing Jack O'Dell, an employee who had been linked to the Communist party.[24] Believing O'Dell to be no longer a party member, King had decided that he nonetheless could not take the risk of having SCLC called "communist inspired." King's basic concern, so far from that of Moses, was that he always be perceived as working within the compass of national politics and institutions. But whereas SNCC as a whole had come to scorn red-baiting, Moses was contending that SNCC should avoid contact with anyone potentially damaging to the movement who was not a proven member of SNCC. The disagreement, as he defined it, was "between a princi-

pled position that political association is never relevant
even when it causes turmoil, and a pragmatic one that
it would have occasional relevance." What SNCC
needed was "a criterion of flexibility without a flat
statement one way or the other."[25] It was an uncharacteristic attempt on the part of Moses to stake out practical liberal ground at a certain cost in ethical purity.
Like King much earlier, he had come to understand
the long-term consequences of antagonizing those who
would support you.

Red-hounding by white supremacists, at any rate,
was a recurrent threat. As early as September 1962,
newspapers in the South had carried articles connect-
ing the citizenship and voter registration classes with
an attempt by communists to enroll blacks in the party.
And once again, segregationists raised the name of Carl
Braden of the Southern Conference Education Fund. A
series of articles in the *Jackson Daily News*, picked up
by other papers through wire services, linked Moses
with Braden.[26] Moses reacted at first to the series with
some thought of filing a libel suit. According to Braden,
Moses and Bill Higgs, a Jackson attorney who had
worked with SNCC, called Braden about filing a suit
against the newspapers and officials of the Citizens'
Council. The plan was first to present in federal court a
formal request for a retraction under Mississippi's honest libel law.[27] Part of this apparent overreaction to the
charge of communist affiliation was the threat to others; for example, David Lollis, who ran the Mount Beulah Christian Center, the site of a planning session with
Braden and Moses for an Adult Education Workshop.
The publicity that raised accusations of communist
sympathies was about to cost Lollis his job. SCEF coun-

seled against any such action, and in a letter jointly to
Moses and Higgs, Braden gently explains: "Most people
are already aware of the use of Redbaiting to try to
discredit the integration movement.... It is quite a
shock when it first happens to you, but the effect soon
wears off.... The best way to fight these attacks is to
continue to work as we have."[28]

The incident created tensions between Moses and the
Bradens. SCEF hoped to assist those who lost jobs or
homes because of civil rights activities through their
program called "Operation Freedom." An article about
Braden's trip to Mississippi in the September issue of
SCEF's magazine, *Southern Patriot*, however, led Moses
to suggest that Braden was taking credit for the voter
registration workshops. This, coupled with the Red
Scare attacks resulting from Braden's visit to Mississippi, led Wiley Branton of the VEP to suggest to the
Bradens that they and SCEF withdraw from activity in
the South. This elicited a thirteen-page rebuttal and
response from Anne Braden: "You are saying . . . that
when a person or an organization is attacked with the
label 'red,' he should . . . withdraw from social activity.
. . . This is the social price of McCarthyism—that many
people with creative contributions to make have been
driven out of useful activity . . . and I think this is especially true in the South." Surely the affair, at last in
retrospect, must have given Moses pause and brought
him dangerously close to what he most wanted to
avoid: the victim become the executioner. In a note to
Anne Braden in late October, Moses remarked, "I did
get a copy of the memo you sent to Wiley [Branton];
you did a beautiful job, I'm just sorry we all had to be
so cruddy about it all."[29]

In February 1963 Moses suggested to Fay Bennett, executive secretary of the National Sharecroppers Fund, that if she could "find an official government representative who can vouch for the Sharecroppers fund and the Government's official and unofficial interest in these programs [training programs for Southern Negro farm people] it will serve to dissolve the ever present communist anxieties and save weeks of letter writing and procrastination."[30] This negotiating on the part of Moses between his craving for purity and his practical obligation to achieve some measure of his goals in a world stubbornly impure was a foreshadowing of his equally dichotomous state of mind in 1964: increasing radicalization coupled with increasing determination to call upon the practical aid of the political and governmental establishment. And he would be betrayed.

While concentrating on the summer project, Moses found time to work on other registration campaigns. The Justice Department, acting with uncharacteristic aggressiveness, had obtained a federal injunction requiring the registrar at Hattiesburg, Mississippi, to enforce registration laws strictly without regard to race.[31] On January 6, 1964, the Supreme Court refused to consider an appeal against the injunction. The movement had won a victory at least in the courts.[32] And so it was Hattiesburg that civil rights groups chose as a site of a Freedom Day that anticipated the massive project that summer. The event included multiple community drives for food and welfare in addition to voter registration. On Freedom Day, COFO brought rights leaders from all over the state for the mass demonstration. COFO also cooperated with the National Council of

Churches to bring a white clerical presence to the effort. Over 50 white clergymen stood by as 150 Southern blacks tried to register. While Moses was arrested for "obstructing a sidewalk," integrated groups were permitted to picket the courthouse. This was the first demonstration, Moses has observed, "where people were not arrested wholesale. So we began to inch away at the whole right to picket and to demonstrate around the voting." The real breakthrough, according to Moses, was the impact that Mississippi had on people from outside the state, who went back to their home communities and began to get others involved.[33] A month later ministers continued to come from the North, a steady flow each week, to picket the county courthouse and assist in voter registration activities. In addition, these religious leaders fed information to the Justice Department that helped to put pressure on the administration.[34] Freedom days were organized in other Mississippi communities as well.[35]

Responding to this rekindled enthusiasm among blacks for registration projects, SNCC started the "Freedom Registration" campaign to register blacks outside the Democratic party, because the party in Mississippi was effectively closed to blacks.[36] It was a logical extension of the successful Freedom Vote inaugurated the previous fall. Moses, at an early February COFO convention, explained that its ultimate object would be the creation of a viable party organization that would be recognizable as legitimate in the state. At this stage, plans were formulated to register blacks on mock polling lists and to hold a parallel primary during the state's June 2 Democratic primary. Included in the outline was the plan to challenge the seating of

Mississippi congressmen on the floor of the House of
Representatives on the grounds that the exclusion of
black citizens from the vote had tainted the elections.[37]

The idea of establishing an organization to mount
campaigns for black candidates evolved slowly. Mendy
Samstein comments:

> We all had a sense that what we're organizing has to be
> built into some kind of political organization.... we
> were organizing people not only to register, but to work
> politically.... You have to build up an indigenous
> group [which] has strong enough people that would
> want to put up the candidate from their own midst.[38]

The vehicle for this far-reaching effort came to be called
the Mississippi Freedom Democratic party (MFDP). The
new party, officially founded in April 1964 at a meeting
in Jackson, was intended to compete with the regular
Democratic party in Mississippi, to document the will
among Southern blacks to vote, and to challenge the
seating in Congress of white representatives from Mississippi.[39] Accordingly, the group ran one Senate and
three House candidates including Fannie Lou Hamer,
for the June primaries.[40] The MFDP also planned to
contest the legitimacy of the regular Democratic slate
at the party's August national convention in Atlantic
City, New Jersey. The scheme was in the liberal tradition of pluralism and equitable representation that Al
Lowenstein had urged the group to pursue the previous
summer. It evoked memories of an earlier generation of
American revolutionaries who had seized power from a
British government that refused to give them a voice.

Although some in SNCC wanted the MFDP to be a

permanent institution for black interests, Moses saw it as a temporary instrument. His desire to build small, indigenous movements had accommodated itself to a different tactic: if Mississippi blacks could not be integrated into the national Democratic party, the MFDP could establish local power that would come to affect national politics. The earlier Freedom Vote had taken politics to the people "where they were." And its significance was that it paved the way for a statewide organization.[41] Once that happened, blacks would enter the mainstream political party. At this point, the objective of establishing a momentarily separate party within the state did not contradict SNCC's movement toward alliance with liberals in the national Democratic party, and was not a thrust toward black separatism. The MFDP was open to both races, and its intention was to become, in place of white racist Mississippi Democrats, the state's representative within the national party. That purpose had been clear from the beginning. Moses had proposed the Freedom Democratic party idea on March 20, 1964, to Joseph Rauh, counsel for the United Auto Workers, a union with great influence within the Democratic coalition. At the time Rauh was speaking as chairman of a panel on direct action sponsored by the National Civil Liberties Clearinghouse, a meeting that James Forman and Moses attended. Bill Higgs, also present, recalls that in answer to Moses' question, "Should the Democratic Party tolerate the Democratic delegation from Mississippi at its national convention?" Rauh responded: "I promise you if the Mississippi delegation is challenged, they will be unseated." Moses, Higgs says, replied, "Well, Mr. Rauh, I want to inform you that they will be challenged. And we're going to hold you to your promise."[42] In Rauh's later account, "That's where I first saw Bob Moses. I liked him, he liked me. And we started in partnership there for the August fight."[43]

Rauh naively believed there would be little difficulty persuading his party to give the MFDP strong support.[44] Passage of the Civil Rights Act in June 1964, and the emergence of Goldwater as the Republican frontrunner, would stunt those expectations; but at the time Rauh was thinking like a good liberal, seeking a workable and mutually beneficial connection between a moral issue and a political gain. The logical, practical solution to the problem, as he saw it, was to seat both delegations. The scheme soon seemed to be working. California and Massachusetts convention delegates became early supporters of the new party within the party, and by convention time about ten delegations favored its seating. The job of Ella Baker and her staff in Washington was to raise funds as well as provide political support for the MFDP.[45] Americans for Democratic Action, of which Rauh was vice president, was one of several liberal groups to offer support.

Meanwhile, in Mississippi, plans were being put into place to implement Freedom Summer, which intended the MFDP to be, among other things, an attraction to black voters and thereby an instrument for increasing their number. In early June, a document entitled "The 'Freedom Ballot' in Mississippi" was mailed to SNCC supporters not only as part of a fund-raising effort, but also to notify supporters of the MFDP and its planned challenge. The appeal ends with a summary depicting the current environment in Mississippi:

This is roughly where we stand in the summer of 1964. The State Legislature is in a panic; it has just passed what is probably the biggest batch of clearly unconstitutional laws in the history of this country. The Citizens Council is stronger than it has ever been. The Klu [sic] Klux Klan has revived in the southwestern part of the state, and burning crosses are spreading eastward and northward. The Hederman papers have managed, in a few short months, to foster a climate of panic and fear in the white community that has spread throughout the state. It is in this climate that COFO political workers must continue and intensify present registration drives, begin as many new drives as our numbers will permit, and aid Negro communities in the formation of purposeful indigenous leadership. The danger now is greater than it has ever been—and so is our hope.[46]

At the SNCC staff meeting in Atlanta on June 10, less than a week before student volunteers were to begin their training for the Project, members of SNCC raised a complaint against COFO. They purported that civil rights groups such as the NAACP, which did little in Mississippi, were simply using the summer program to raise money. The one rights group to be recalcitrant about contributing people and money was the national office of the NAACP. SNCC's participatory democracy was focused on the silent majority of blacks who were farmers, sharecroppers, and the unemployed, not the property owners, businessmen, or professionals who composed the national constituency of the NAACP.[47] As always, Moses kept his sight on the larger purpose, patiently explaining the reasons why any funds— whether raised by SNCC, NAACP, or SCLC—were important to the COFO coffers. Some staffers questioned

Moses' loyalty to SNCC and accused him of placing COFO's interests ahead of those of SNCC. Moses answered that his commitment was "basically as a SNCC person. The energy that makes COFO positive comes from SNCC; and SNCC is committed to the development of this kind of a group because we need coordination."[48] This questioning, as Mary King points out, was probably a result of lingering anger over the coming influx of white volunteers. Moses had a distinctive way of talking about sensitive issues: he stated facts without embroidery and with an almost toneless flatness; as a purist, he would often bring a controversial or moral issue into the open, dispelling illusion and rationalization. The issue of white volunteers came up later in the meeting, and Moses observed:

> In discussing whites, we have always tried to locate positive elements in the white community to speak out—not to infiltrate segregationist White Citizens Councils to try and change them. The people who're being invited to work with us this summer were not asked to do that nor were they recruited for that purpose. . . . There's a tiny trickle beginning to flow that could expand as a result of the Mississippi Summer Project with teachers working with teachers and ministers working with ministers—counterparts to counterparts.[49]

It had been and it would continue to be the central question within SNCC. And it was not only a question of whether Northern middle-class whites were by their very nature extraneous to the Mississippi effort. Their recruitment and use involved a bringing of order and structure to a group that had prided itself on a kind of conducted anarchy. Moses, the best-known exponent of leaderless direction, of common decision making centered in small-scale communities, was of necessity depending on Al Lowenstein, who embodied centralized direction and leadership. Lowenstein, with connections to the National Student Association and possessed of charismatic speaking ability and personal magnetism, was the activist most capable of attracting and galvanizing upper-middle-class white college students. He soon withdrew from Freedom Summer and became increasingly concerned about the "radical" bent of SNCC. Convinced that the organization was becoming infiltrated by communist influences, Lowenstein actively worked, some COFO staff believed, to undercut Freedom Summer.[50]

SNCC now, however, had a network of "Friends of SNCC" on college campuses across the country, ready and willing to work in Mississippi. A memorandum outlined the administrative structure for the Jackson office, which was to coordinate the summer project. The functions varied from communications, security, and finances, to research, housing, and personnel. Two people were placed in charge of orientations during the summer; screening of volunteers was to be undertaken initially by field staff. Precautions were taken so that each of the approximately fourteen project directors would know the name of each volunteer in advance; "anyone arriving on a project whose name has not been given the project director in advance should be checked out with Jackson." A personnel committee was given the task of handling "cases where people do not work out on a project . . . [and] cases where people must be sent home." Finally, "Bob Moses, Dave Dennis and others will constitute an appeal board for decisions about which people feel the need of advice or about which there is disagreement."[51]

COFO actively recruited faculty on college campuses across the country, sending detailed letters of invitation that outlined the various projects and tasks that informed and committed academicians could undertake, ranging from economic and political research or political campaign managing for the Freedom candidates to conducting staff seminars.[52] Nearly one thousand volunteers worked on various projects.[53] Not all these volunteers were college students, on whom the publicity was fixed. Other participants were lawyers, clergy, doctors, high school and college teachers—all were recruited and volunteered for periods of one week to an entire summer.[54]

The SNCC staff also discussed nonviolence at the June 10 meeting. Many advocated arming SNCC members in self-defense, much like the local blacks. Sam Block, who had worked with Moses in McComb, charged:

> No one here has lived the life of Gandhi. Amzie Moore has reported that vigilantes will kill Fannie Lou Hamer, Bob Moses, Aaron Henry, Dave Dennis and himself. Bob's too valuable to be killed in Mississippi, because there's nothing in Mississippi worth dying for! I'm not going to carry a gun but if someone else is going to protect himself, then let him protect me as well![55]

Moses believed that SNCC workers should remain nonviolent. But he would not tell local Mississippians what they could or could not do:

I don't know if anyone in Mississippi preached to local
Negroes that they shouldn't defend themselves. Probably the closest is when I asked Mr. E. W. Steptoe not to
carry guns when we go together at night. So, instead, he
just hides his gun, and then I find out later. Self-defense
is so deeply ingrained in rural southern America that
we as a small group can't affect it. It's not contradictory
for a farmer to say he's nonviolent and also to pledge to
shoot a marauder's head off. The difference is that we on
the staff have committed ourselves not to carry guns.[56]

Moses was placed in a familiar wedge. Intent on making a fragile yet critical coalition work, he had to deal
with conflicts among the various organizations making
up COFO as well as rivalries within SNCC itself.

By May, when applications began to tumble in, publicity for Freedom Summer was heavy. Two separate
articles appeared in the Sunday May 17 New York
Times, one describing the aims of the project, the other
concentrating on the student volunteers with a headline, "600 Students Join Mississippi Drive."[57] The Reporter, featuring an article predicting "a hot summer in
Mississippi," noted in describing the freedom schools
that the National Council of Churches planned to establish a number of its own centers "at an estimated cost
of $50,000." State officials were gearing for the summer
with increased police force and newly passed repressive
laws.[58] A Wall Street Journal reporter noted that the
state Senate had a bill pending that would require li-
censing of all schools by the local county school super-
intendent—a direct hit at the freedom schools. The proposed penalty for violation was in typical Mississippi
style: six months in jail and a $600 fine.[59] Newsweek's
story centered on Jackson, describing Mayor Allen

Thompson's planned defenses against demonstrations and voter registration as an invasion, barely second to that of Normandy in World War II. The article cited his budget of over $2 million, a good chunk of which he used to buy a thirteen-thousand pound tank built to specification and accommodating twelve men. The reporter noted that when the tank was put to its first test—putting down a demonstration at Jackson State College—a tear-gas shell had gone off inside it.[60] Despite all of this publicity predicting an explosive situation, the White House remained deaf to Moses' and others' pleas for recognition and prevention. Moses again wrote to the president about a week before the summer volunteers were due to begin orientation sessions. Once more he asked for federal protection for blacks and volunteers from the Justice Department, the FBI, and federal marshals. He concluded, "I hope this is not asking too much of our country."[61]

In June the first group of student volunteers showed up for the Freedom Summer training sessions conducted by SNCC and COFO staff on the campus of Western College for Women in Oxford, Ohio. Almost all were educated, middle-class white students. "These students," Moses said, "bring the rest of the country with them. They're from good schools and their parents are influential. The interest of the country is awakened, and when that happens, the Government responds to that interest."[62] John Lewis, SNCC chairman, recruited white college students throughout the Midwest and Far West because "they didn't have to spend the summer working hard to get back to their college."[63] Dave Dennis, second in command to Moses, expressed this reasoning in a more calculated way. He pointed out that the slaughter of one thousand blacks would not mean anything, while whites would be protected, particularly if the volunteers were the sons and daughters of influential people, such as young Jerry Brown.[64]

Many black SNCC workers overlooked that these volunteers were self-supporting, committed to paying their own expenses without summer jobs. A SNCC news release announced that "students are selected on the basis of the skills they have to offer."[65] The students had been chosen in part for their emotional stability and were required to have parental consent if under twenty-one; eighteen was the minimum age for participation. Dorothy Zellner, interviewing for SNCC in Cambridge, Massachusetts, in early spring gives a good indication of what SNCC was not looking for when writing an evaluation of one applicant:

> I think she's arrogant. I explained about running Mrs. Hamer and that many people would raise eyebrows because she is an ex-sharecropper. She said, "Well, why are you running her?" Later she asked why we were running a *woman* for office.... She also said she wouldn't want to participate in anything to which she was opposed.... When I asked her if she had taken part in any of the civil rights activities here ... she said no, she was writing her term thesis.... [She] says that a reporter from *Life* approached her about doing a picture story during the summer—All-American Girl in Mississippi Freedom School sort of thing.[66]

Moses was consulted about dealing with such applicants, and in this report is a note: "Just spoke with Bob Moses, and he told me to pick the willing ones (i.e., willing to do anything) and the *non*-rugged individualists."[67]

In addition, applicants were asked to bring $150 with them and a list of people to call who would be willing to pay as much as $500 bail money should they be arrested.[68] The issue was not economic but emotional and psychological, and it continued to fester after the arrival of the volunteers. Many of the black students withdrew from the whites they met, perhaps because some of the whites exhibited a conception of the South based on *Gone With the Wind*.[69] Racial attitudes worked in both directions, and blacks whose lifelong experiences had taught them to distrust, fear, and even hate whites found it difficult to reverse their feelings simply because of the presence of willing workers.[70] Moses himself, however, had a magical effect on the impressionable white college students. Among them, he was a cultural hero.[71]

Training during the first week was geared toward those volunteers who would be working on voter registration; the second week's training was for those who would teach in the Freedom Schools. Whether thousands during Freedom Summer would be enrolled as voters or as members of MFDP, whether the hundreds of children and adults for whom the Freedom Schools were to be established would attend, or whether local blacks would use the community centers: no one knew if these goals would be accomplished. But for Moses some basic and seemingly small gestures, such as the right of a black person to have white people in his home, would be a breakthrough.[72] And despite the conflict within COFO over the white students' presence in the project, the reaction in the black communities was slowly if fitfully receptive. As a white SNCC worker remarked, "One of the amazing things about the Summer Project was that thousands of Negro homes were open to white people.. . . This means that you're willing to open up the possibility of your house being bombed or you being fired, . . . [which is] a real indication that they wanted the Summer Project."[73] Others in SNCC had more far-reaching goals: to move beyond simple direct-action integration, to distance themselves from a strict reliance on nonviolence as a founding principle, and to heighten public awareness of the race issue through the presence of white students in black communities.[74] Doubtless, though, the orientation program was not going to be able, nor would it have the need, to impart to the recruits the diversity of the project's objectives. Like the whole Mississippi enterprise from the beginning, like the politics to which SNCC was introducing black Mississippians, like the concept of participatory democracy that was soon to seize the imagination of the left, for the volunteers Freedom Summer was to be a continuing event in which act and learning were inseparable.

On June 14, the opening night of the training session, Moses addressed the first group of about three hundred student volunteers. He presented the task in hard, modest terms: "No administration in this country is going to commit political suicide over the rights of Negroes."[75] He explained that the task of the volunteers was to force action through public pressure and spur the federal government to take action. Finally, he warned,

Don't come to Mississippi this summer to save the Mississippi Negro. Only come if you understand, really understand, that his freedom and yours are one.. . . Maybe

we're not going to get very many people registered this
summer. Maybe, even, we're not going to get very many
people into freedom schools. Maybe all we're going to
do is live through this summer. In Mississippi, that will
be so much![76]

On June 21, Moses was talking to the second group of
students, once more setting tough, measured purposes:
he equated the guerilla warfare in Vietnam with the
battle for civil rights in Mississippi. He again remarked
that achievements would come in ways as modest as
simply talking with black residents in their homes,
showing a presence and concern:

> You are not going down there to try to be heroes. You
> are heroes enough just going into the state. This is not a
> Freedom Ride. The point is to stay out of jail if you
> possibly can, and don't put yourself in any unnecessar-
> ily dangerous situation. You have a job to do. If each of
> you can leave behind you three people who are stronger
> than before, this will be 3000 more people we will have
> to work with next year. This is your job.[77]

Mississippi, he noted, had been called "the closed society," but he believed the vote could open it. And he
devoted the rest of his talk to the physical dangers
that awaited the recruits: risk of arrest for no apparent
reason, the everpresent "voice" of shotguns, lack of
funds and supplies.[78] The volunteers were told to shave
their beards, never to travel alone or in integrated
groups, and not to go anywhere at night. This was basic
and elementary advice. This description by Ed King,
the candidate for lieutenant governor in the Freedom
Vote, recounts his feelings after years of being followed
and sometimes attacked:

> There was one time that I did drive alone ... and
> thought I might get out of Jackson without being seen
> in the dawn hours. But the long trip across the city was
> thirty minutes of terror.... I stayed on back streets....
> I worried that my car might stall.... A cab driver stared
> at me—I was sure he would radio news of my presence
> to the police. The white driver of a garbage truck sig-
> nalled me to pass him—I would not do it, certain that
> some trap lay ahead.[79]

As Moses paused to choose his next words carefully, a
staffer whispered in his ear that three COFO workers—
James Chaney, Andrew Goodman, and Michael
Schwerner—had disappeared the day before. Moses
continued: "Yesterday morning, three of our people left
Meridian, Mississippi, to investigate a church-burning
in Neshoba County. They haven't come back, and we
haven't had any word from them."[80] The three had
been picked up, jailed, and then released by the Neshoba County deputy sheriff, Cecil Price. Goodman, a
twenty-one-year-old white college student from New
York, was a summer project volunteer. Chaney, also
twenty-one, was a native black Mississippian and
CORE volunteer who worked with Schwerner, the head
of the CORE office in Meridian. Schwerner, by training
a social worker, came from New York.[81]

John Doar, representing the Department of Justice,
had also come to the Ohio training session to talk to
the students about the role of the federal government.
Before Doar spoke, Moses cautioned the students not to
take out on him their frustration and concern about the
missing workers: "A year ago this week Medgar Evers
was buried. It was a near riot situation, and Doar was
sent in to prevent worse. He has helped us."[82] Yet Doar

simply repeated the worn excuses the government had used throughout the entire movement: "There is no possible way that anyone can be completely protected from violence." Asked why the government was working to protect the Vietnamese from the Viet Cong but not the black people of Mississippi from the white community, he replied, "Maintaining law and order is a state responsibility."[83] Even after all the evasions and broken promises of the Justice Department, in his need for a federal presence in Mississippi Moses was still speaking of Doar as an ally.

The fate of the three rights workers at the beginning of the project weighed heavily on Moses. The tragedy must have been particularly bitter for him to handle. He had tried for months to alert the federal government to the danger faced by native black Mississippians and civil rights volunteers. In the words of Ed King, Moses "would not, almost could not, talk about Neshoba" in the first days after the disappearance.[84] On June 25 he delivered his closing words to the volunteers.

> There is a weariness . . . from constant attention to the things you are doing, the struggle of good against evil.
> The kids are dead. . . . There may be more deaths. . . . The way some people characterize this project is that it is an attempt to get some people killed so the federal government will move into Mississippi. And the way some of us feel about it is that in our country we have some real evil, and the attempt to do something about it involves enormous effort . . . and therefore tremendous risks. . . . And all I can say really is . . . be patient with the kids, and with Mississippi. Because there is a distinction between being slow and being stupid. And the kids in Mississippi are very, very . . . very slow.[85]

In an internal SNCC publication, Moses talked of the effect of fear on civil rights workers, noting that it often created a paralysis of inactivity and resulted in disillusionment or even cynicism. He concluded, "If anything what we're trying to do, or have to do, is to see how you can move even though you are afraid."[86] One white volunteer remarked that Moses, "starts, one thinks, from a position that he is living on borrowed time."[87] Perhaps that was the only way to survive psychologically.

Yet despite all this, Moses managed to project the same calm equanimity, the same leadership of example. As Casey Hayden relates:

> After the beginning of the Freedom Summer project, those of us who had been working in that crowded, filthy, hot, hectic, tense place in planning for the summer and then going through the initial impact of the murders were a bit at loose ends, the work being mostly done, and we were wondering what to do next and asking around if anyone had seen Bob. I went to use the restroom and there was Bob on his hands and knees, scrubbing out the toilet.[88]

In the frenetic days that followed the disappearance of the COFO workers, the COFO staff and volunteers did all they could to prompt federal action.[89] Moses explained to the volunteers that FBI intervention was necessary because local authorities were "psychologically incapable" of carrying on such investigations. In addition, a federal presence would set the stage for volunteers to accomplish their tasks and prepare local blacks to continue on their own after the summer.[90] Within days Moses issued a memorandum to all "Mis-

sissippi Summer Project Contacts." It warned that unless the federal government acted immediately, all participants would be in danger. A letter to parents of all
volunteers assessed the situation, explained precautions that were being taken, and suggested ways in
which the government could extend protection.[91]

The disappearance of the three men prompted SNCC
groups in Washington, Chicago, and elsewhere to organize demonstrations. Yet Moses opposed these, still believing that such actions would embarrass the federal
government into retreat from whatever activity the
movement might otherwise coax out of it. Meanwhile,
the Northern offices of SNCC were flooded by calls from
people determined to head south in the wake of the
violence.[92] On June 27, Moses made a plea to the people
of good will who were thinking of coming down to
Mississippi on their own to refrain from doing so. He
cautioned that "untrained, and unoriented" volunteers
would pose additional problems of supervision, housing, and, above all, protection from violence.[93] During
the days when the whereabouts of the three workers
was unknown, and then after the discovery on August 4
of their bodies buried in a large earthen dam on a farm
outside of Philadelphia, Mississippi, the national media
followed events closely.[94] Lawrence Guyot has remarked that had all three of the COFO victims been
black, the thundering national repercussions would not
have occurred; so far during the decade at least sixty-
three people, all black, had been killed in issues involving the vote in Mississippi.[95]

Despite his rhetoric about the possible need for federal troops, Moses had hoped that alerting the nation
and the government about the possible dangers

awaiting volunteers participating in Freedom Summer
would make unnecessary the kind of armed troop intervention that had occurred in Little Rock and at Ole
Miss. He had counted on the status of white college
students to prevent Mississippi authorities from acting
as they might have toward blacks.[96] Less than a month
later when events in Mississippi had brought Representatives William Fitts Ryan of New York and Philip Bur-
ton of California to view the situation during a weeklong stay, Moses rejected charges that the purpose of
the project was to get people killed: "We ourselves have
been risking our lives for the last three years."[97]

In the wake of the killings, the government did move
into Mississippi. As a result, the level of violence during
the summer turned out to be lower than some SNCC
workers had expected. To be sure, there were bombings
of "freedom houses" and COFO headquarters, and
many burnings of black homes and churches, but mi-
raculously there were no additional deaths of volunteers. Media pressure, the presence of nearly one thousand white volunteers, and the federal police
intervention that followed the disappearance of the
three volunteers worked to frighten off some potential
assailants. Attorney General Kennedy sent in a seven-
man team of Justice Department lawyers headed by
Walter Sheridan, the man who had indicted Teamsters
president Jimmy Hoffa on a charge of tampering with
a federal jury.[98] There also evolved a growing black
militancy that subdued the racists. Some SNCC workers believed the relative restraint among white Mississippians was due to a new determination among blacks
not to allow themselves to be victims. But on July 22,
Martin Luther King spoke to a rally of three thousand

at the Masonic Temple in Jackson and reiterated the
need to remain nonviolent and to register with the
MFDP. The *Mississippi Free Press* commented, "The
King had finally come to darkest America to be among
the people."[99]

Nonviolence, the cornerstone of the SCLC, came to
be used more and more only as a tactic within SNCC,
and the principle itself rapidly lost adherents in Mississippi. At an August 4 meeting—after the bodies of
Goodman, Schwerner, and Chaney had been discovered—Stokely Carmichael captured the angry mood of
the crowd in Greenwood:

> From now on we're gonna check on niggers who ain't
> doing right! . . . I talk a lot of nonviolence to the white
> folk, but let me catch a black man doin' us wrong. . . .
> Cause just as soon as I'd tell a white man to go to hell,
> I'd shoot a black man. . . . Another thing. We're not goin'
> to stick with this nonviolence forever. We don't go
> shooting up *their* houses. It's not *us* who does that.[100]

In a discussion later that night SNCC staffers debated
whether to sponsor local protests designed to test the
1964 Civil Rights Act, actions SNCC leaders knew
might end in violence. When one worker announced
that "the first thing [the Greenwood protesters] want is
to kill white people," Carmichael announced, "We can
only control them by joining them. I'm not thinking
how to justify it to the community; I'm thinking how to
justify it to COFO." He then left the room "to get the
mandate from Bob" in Jackson. When he returned
later, his attitude and demeanor had changed; he said
simply, "What I think we ought to do is work harder on
freedom registration forms."[101] The heated discussion

that took place over the issue of using arms for self-defense foreshadowed the militant turn SNCC would later take under Carmichael. But at this point, he, like most others, was under Moses' influence. SNCC confronted white racism not with a warning of counterviolence, but with a steady, unrelenting attack on the social and psychological bases of Jim Crow. That fall at a western conference of SNCC, Moses brought the larger issue of violence to a national level:

> The Neshoba County murders [of the three civil rights workers] raise the whole question of what does our society do where the law doesn't function at all to protect people.... Where are the recourses in our society? ... It seems to me that the country is simply not willing to face up to that. The justice department of this administration says it can't be a police force.... But what if the local police force is not a police force? What if it's part Klu [sic] Klux Klan and part white citizens council? And in on the planning with the terrorists? Then what does the society do in that situation? ... The federal government is more willing to sacrifice the lives of Negroes in those situations than it is to tamper with the structure of the government.[102]

And workers in the summer project had continued to be harassed. Much of the harassment was a matter of arbitrary arrest or nonlethal violence. Some of the tormentors contemplated murder. In a three-day period COFO totaled these events in Mississippi:

JUNE 21
Brandon: Molotov cocktail explodes in basement of Sweet Rest Church of Christ Holiness. Fire; minor damage.

McComb: Homes of two civil rights workers planning to house summer volunteers bombed. One damaged extensively. Seven dynamite sticks left on lawn of third home with no civil rights ties.

Meridian: Three civil rights workers missing after a short trip to Philadelphia [Goodman, Schwerner, and Chaney].

JUNE 22

Clarksdale: Four volunteers arrested on vagrancy charges while engaged in voter registration work. Held 3-1/2 hours, released.

Brandon: Negro youth killed in hit-and-run accident.

JUNE 23

Philadelphia: Missing car found burned; no sign of three workers. Car was on list circulated statewide by Canton White Citizens Council.

Jackson: Shots fired at home of Rev. R.L.T. Smith. White man escapes on foot, reportedly picked up by a city truck. (Smith's home is under 24-hour guard.)

Moss Point: Knights of Pythias Hall firebombed. Arson attempt on side of building. Damage slight. Used for voter rallies.

Moss Point: Two summer volunteers picked up as they leave cafe, relax on private lawn. Taken by police at 85 m.p.h. without lights at night to Pascagoula jail. Held in "protective custody" overnight, then released.

Jackson: Civil rights worker held eight hours after receiving $5 change for a $20 bill.

Jackson: White car fires shot at Henderson's cafe. Negroes pursue. Three shots fired, hitting one Negro in head twice.

Clarksdale: Local pastor, a civil rights leader, arrested for reckless and drunk driving. He is a total abstainer.

State-wide: Negroes try to attend Democratic Party county conventions. Participation systematically discouraged.

Ruleville: Look, Time reporters covering voter rally at Williams chapel, chased out of town by car at speeds up

to 85 m.p.h. Early next morning, nine Negro homes hit
by bottles thrown from similar car.[103]

SNCC did not take the violence without response.
Moses worked with the National Lawyers' Guild to file
a broad-based lawsuit, *COFO v. Rainey*, against the
county sheriffs in Mississippi, particularly Sheriff
Rainey of Philadelphia, whose jurisdiction covered the
case of the three missing workers. Rainey would later
be accused of being one of the assailants. Many volunteer lawyers worked to compile an extensive brief docu-
menting the tactics of the white power structure in the
South. The suit itself never advanced past the Southern judges.[104]

Among the most important achievements of the summer project of 1964 was to fix the nation's attention
and arouse its conscience on Southern racism. Moses
himself hoped "to force the rest of the country to take a
look at Mississippi.... We knew Mississippi couldn't
stand a hard look."[105] "The Project's triumph," one
commentator observed, "may be measured in column
inches of newsprint and running feet of video tape. Easily the most spectacular and sustained single event in
recent civil rights history, it provided summer-long,
nationwide exposure of the iniquities of white supremacy in the deepest of the Deep South states."[106] Other
results included the development of the Mississippi
Student Union to link black high school and college
students active in the civil rights movement, an adult
membership of seventy-five thousand in the MFDP, and
establishment of statewide political organizations with
local leaders who had seen a national political convention.[107] Mendy Samstein declared with satisfaction:

Cracks were finally made in the Mississippi iceberg. For the first time in the state there were literally hundreds of local people who no longer feared to become active workers—not just passive supporters—of the movement.... From eight projects and fifty workers before the summer, the movement started the fall with over thirty projects and more than 300 workers.[108]

Years later Aaron Henry, the titular head of COFO and a long-time NAACP leader, would call Freedom Summer "the greatest sociological experiment the nation has ever pulled off," noting that the goal was the "freeing of the minds of blacks . . . [who] began to look upon themselves as somebody.... There was the opportunity of people to learn . . . about each other. You can read about me all you want . . . but until you sleep in that bed and I sleep in that bed, and we use the same bathroom in the morning . . . the human relations aspect . . . was the greatest thing we accomplished."[109]

If success is calculated by whether the project forced the federal government to send troops to Mississippi, then it fell short. But the murders of Chaney, Schwerner, and Goodman did bring a massive federal presence to Mississippi not only to search for the bodies, but also to infiltrate the Ku Klux Klan. J. Edgar Hoover flew to Jackson to open the largest branch of the FBI in the nation, a symbolic act that must not have gone unnoticed among Southern conservatives. And the 210 navy men sent by President Johnson to search for the missing rights workers also found the bodies of some blacks; E. W. Steptoe, the rural black leader of Amite County's NAACP, has noted that they "would disappear down there into those swamps and be killed, and nothing was ever done about it."[110]

The federal government did make an attempt. But, from the start, the intervention was timid, legalistic, and clearly expressive of a wish that the whole business would go sedately away. Allen Dulles, the retired CIA chief who flew to Mississippi as a special emissary of the president in the wake of the disappearance of the three workers, had met with COFO leaders, including Moses. He made it clear that "we want this mess cleaned up." When asked to what he referred, he indicated that the various demonstrations should be stopped.[111] John Doar, the Justice Department attorney most closely connected with Moses and his voter registration work in Mississippi, has suggested that the FBI finally got serious and systematic in its investigations only after events forced it to act. These events included the increasing violence in the state, the resurgence of the Ku Klux Klan, the disappearance of the three rights workers, and Dulles's trip to Mississippi. By the end of the year, the FBI had interviewed over one thousand people, including nearly five hundred Klan members, in its investigation of the killings of the civil rights workers.[112]

Despite pronouncements to the contrary, FBI agents could have intervened in the violence of whites toward blacks. After the three civil rights workers vanished, Moses asked COFO attorneys William Kunstler and Arthur Kinoy to search the legal statutes for help. Kinoy found in federal Reconstruction statutes a provision for appointing special federal commissioners with full legal powers, including arrest, in areas where local law enforcement officials were ineffective in preventing the violation of the civil rights of U.S. citizens.[113] But the federal government satisfied itself with a temporary and, then as long as possible, largely symbolic presence. Neither the FBI nor the Justice Department—both citing respect for the constitutional limits of federal authority—maintained day-to-day protection of civil rights workers. For his part, J. Edgar Hoover stated emphatically that the FBI "most certainly would *not* give special protection to the summer volunteers."[114] The summer's statistics were staggering: six killed, eighty beaten, one thousand arrested, thirty-seven black churches and thirty-one black homes burned or dynamited.[115] Only in numbers of deaths did the summer end better than its beginnings had presaged. But that only suggests how much better things might have been had Washington acted with its full authority, and done so from the start.

EIGHT

"TO BRING
MORALITY INTO
OUR POLITICS"

The initial phase of the Freedom Summer—voter registration drives, Freedom Schools, and the like—had failed to bring Washington to the Mississippi battle lines. SNCC workers hoped that the next phase, the attempt to seat Mississippi Freedom Democratic party delegates at the Democratic National Convention in Atlantic City, would at last empower the state's black citizens. The MFDP was first rebuffed by the regular Mississippi Democratic Party. Whites would simply cancel the local caucuses where the MFDP was expected to intrude, or move their location. On June 19 from Oxford, Ohio, on June 19 Moses issued a COFO press release announcing that a federal complaint had been filed in Greenville, Mississippi, challenging the election procedures for Mississippi delegates to the Democratic National Convention. The charge cited violation of the Constitution through the systematic disenfranchisement of black voters. The suit asked for a judicial panel to review present procedures and referred to an earlier suit filed on June 2 in Jackson that successfully squelched a poll tax statute that violated the Twenty-fourth Amendment.[1]

The MFDP then held its own state convention on August 6 in a black Masonic Temple in Jackson to select its delegates while COFO worked on building a coalition to support the new party's aims among out-of-state liberals. The *Mississippi Free Press* printed a special report just before the state convention on the origins and agenda of the MFDP and reproduced a "Freedom Registration Form," which contrasted in its simplicity to the voter registration questionnaire encountered by blacks throughout the state.[2] Joe Rauh, legal counsel for the party, gave a workshop to the MFDP executive committee on procedures to be followed later that month at the convention.[3]

Spirits were high, and many MFDP delegates trusted that their appeals to the outside world would be answered.[4] They further assumed that their support for Johnson's programs, while the regular Mississippi delegation was openly for Goldwater, would strengthen their position at Atlantic City.[5] And initial support for their cause did come from diverse liberal organizations. Twenty-five members of Congress had by August expressed support for the challenge along with nine state delegations that passed resolutions endorsing the insurgent party before the Democratic National Convention.[6]

But it was also clear by that time that President Lyndon Johnson had made up his mind not to seat the MFDP.[7] Johnson would not permit the MFDP's challenge to alienate white voters anywhere. The white Mississippi delegation, angered by the passage of the Civil Rights Act on July 2 that banned discrimination in public accommodations and voting, was threatening a walk-out on this issue alone. Johnson so badly wanted no one to disturb his placid pool of support that he had the FBI wire MFDP activists' rooms as well as the Atlantic City hotel room of Martin Luther King.[8] The Mississippi delegation, joined by other Southerners, had walked out in 1948 over a civil rights plank, and he was determined that it would not happen again if he could help it. As early as June a national committee counsel, Harold Leventhal, sent out a series of letters to various leaders, including the chairs of the credentials committee and the party, which suggested ways to prevent any unpleasantness the MFDP challenge might stir up.

An early August strategy session by Johnson campaign advisers considered how to avoid a floor fight over the issue.[9] On August 12 the president assured the governor of Mississippi that the MFDP would not be seated.[10] On August 19, just five days before the Democratic Convention, the president arranged a meeting with black leaders; King was persuaded by his advisor Bayard Rustin not to go. Rustin had been the subject of a bitter debate in late July over the way SCLC support would be handled for the MFDP at the Democratic Con-

vention. Asked to coordinate a mass demonstration outside the convention hall, Rustin agreed only on the
condition that he be in charge of handling all activity
connected with garnering MFDP support from individual delegates and state delegations—something Ella
Baker in Washington had been working on for some
months.[11] Now Rustin was continuing to try to ensure
his control over tactical details. Joe Rauh, the MFDP
counsel, had hoped that King would attend the meeting
with the president and suggest seating both delegations, a compromise not without precedent.[12] In fact,
the twenty-minute "meeting" turned out to be a lecture
by LBJ about the white backlash, a display complete
with dozens of charts, graphs, and figures.[13]

At the beginning of the convention, the MFDP hoped
for a backing of ten percent of the credentials committee membership; as few as eleven members who believed that the MFDP had a valid case could force the
issue to the floor. There, if the insurgent party won the
vote of eight delegations, the minority report stating
the case of the MFDP would receive a roll call vote
shown on national television. One early slick maneuver
of the administration was to get Governor Carl Sanders
of Georgia, chair of the rules committee, to change the
rules so that only state delegations could request a roll
call: the MFDP had counted among its supporters
Puerto Rico, Guam, and the Virgin Islands—none representing states.[14] The MFDP publicly fought to be recognized as the only legal, open delegation from Mississippi. Privately, however, Joe Rauh pushed for seating
both delegations. Then, if the white Mississippi delegation left in protest as expected, the MFDP would get
all of the seats. "When you're bargaining," goes his

retrospective explanation, "you never take publicly your private position." As early as August 14, Rauh, after meeting in Washington with the liberal Senator Hubert Humphrey and the chair of the Credentials Committee, had believed that he had an agreement with them. Their only problem seemed to be who would tell the President; it was determined that John Bailey, the national party chairman, would do so.[15]

Arriving at the segregated Gem Motel in Atlantic City on Friday, August 21, the sixty-eight Mississippi delegates for the MFDP began, like a conventional party interest group, fervently to lobby liberals and moderates at the convention.[16] The group had prepared "information worksheets" on each state's delegates and credentials committee members, if any. Beside each name, comments summarized whether the individual was a supporter of the MFDP. The worksheet for Michigan listed seven delegates, including Charles Diggs, with the comment "definite supporter" and "strong supporter" on the credentials committee. A handwritten remark was added next to Diggs's name: "sold us out."[17]

Al Lowenstein was part of a five-man legal team acting as MFDP's counsel to the credentials committee, but "his real role was that of a lobbyist ... [with] connections throughout the main elements of the Democratic Party. These connections were both the reason the MFDP needed Allard and the reason they would end up accusing him [and Joe Rauh] of betrayal."[18] Rauh would remember that "the delegates themselves were magnificent advocates for their position. So was Bob Moses."[19] Arthur Waskow comments on Moses' "insistence on open party processes and his insistence that the constituents in Mississippi be remembered.... An excellent politician who can manipulate when necessary but . . . who (it seems to me) himself avoids manipulation on many occasions when he could easily use it."[20]

On August 22, two days before the convention officially was to open, the MFDP presented its case to the credentials committee with an impassioned and now legendary speech by Fannie Lou Hamer. This forty-six-year-old wife of a Ruleville sharecropper had become a field worker for SNCC in December 1962. Soon afterward she lost her job of checker and time keeper in charge of paying the cotton pickers.[21] She vividly recounted what life was like for a black Mississippian. She recalled her first arrest for civil rights activities:

> [The Policeman] said, "You bitch, you, we gon' make you wish you was dead." I heard the highway patrolman tell the black man [a prisoner], said, "If you don't beat her, you *know* what we'll do to you." The first Negro began to beat, and I was beat until I was exhausted.... After the first Negro . . . was exhausted, the State Highway Patrolman ordered the second Negro to take a blackjack. The second Negro began to beat.... I began to scream, and one white man got up and began to beat me on my head and tell me to "hush."
>
> One white man—my dress had worked up high—he walked over and pulled my dress and he pulled my dress up, back up.... All of this is on account we want to register, to become first-class citizens, and if the Freedom Democratic Party is not seated now, I question America.[22]

Part of the speech was televised, exposing millions of ordinary Americans for the first time to the essence of the white supremacy in the South, and conveying to the broad public something of the issue before the convention.[23] By calling for a live news conference during Mrs. Hamer's remarks, President Johnson tried to deflect attention from some of the most gripping words ever uttered at a national political convention. He then proceeded to talk about his dog to a group of governors visiting Washington.[24] His attempt to change the subject failed dismally. Mrs. Hamer's speech was rebroadcast during prime time that night. The President was informed that 416 telegrams had been received on that day in support of the MFDP—and one in support of the regular Mississippi delegates.[25] Soon after, twelve members of the credentials committee announced they would support the MFDP challenge.[26]

Johnson disregarded suggestions that the recent registration drives for black voters in the South might even help the Democratic ticket win some closely contested Southern states.[27] The president's support in as many as four Southern states was jeopardized when the Alabama delegates refused to take a pledge to support the presidential ticket. The Mississippi regular delegates refused as well, and the delegations from Arkansas and Louisiana were urged to walk out in sympathy.[28] Johnson, unable to distract the public and the media and to quiet his liberal supporters, was forced to shape some sort of compromise.

The next day, on August 23, after meeting for over three hours and resolving the Alabama issue by requiring its delegates to sign a pledge of loyalty to the party's nominee and platform, the credentials committee declared a recess to figure out what to do about the Mississippi challenge. It appointed a special subcommittee, charged with finding a compromise. Its chair was Walter Mondale, attorney general of Minnesota and a protégé of Humphrey who would later succeed him in the Senate. Johnson, exercising his complete control of the convention, packed the new subcommittee with administration stalwarts: Charles C. Diggs, Jr., of Michigan; Irving Kalter of Georgia; former Governor Price Daniel of Texas; and Sherwin Markham of Iowa.[29] Reporters asked credentials committee Chairman David Lawrence whether the MFDP delegates could take the place of the regular Mississippi delegates who had refused to sign the loyalty pledge; Lawrence ignored the question. As James Reston remarked, "Lyndon Johnson is in complete charge of this convention over the telephone. . . . Meanwhile, the Credentials Committee worries along about what to do about the squabbling and rebellious Alabama and Mississippi delegations, with constant guidance from the White House."[30]

One of the MFDP lobbyists, Mendy Samstein, put it bluntly: "The whole way the press projects it and the way it's interpreted is that here is this Credentials Committee sitting, this august body deliberating the legal points of this Challenge. Well, this is nonsense. It was a pure power thing. It was a pure political thing. And nothing was happening in that Credentials Committee. Everything was happening outside of it."[31] On that Sunday, the credentials committee did discuss the Mississippi issue and the motion was made to allow the MFDP delegates admittance as observers only. By Rauh's account, he was not allowed to speak in opposition; the chair would not recognize him. And then, in what must have been an orchestrated move, another delegate member, who was supposed to be a MFDP supporter, proposed to amend the motion by adding that the MFDP receive two at-large delegates.[32] Aaron Henry, at a news conference with Martin Luther King, argued that the proposal to admit MFDP people to the convention floor as observers was tantamount to a "back-of-the-bus compromise." King suggested that the "natural reaction" of black voters would be to go fishing on election day.[33]

That Sunday night a group of MFDP delegates and supporters held a caucus at King's suite. There is a great deal of inconsistency among the major participants as to what happened at this meeting. Lowenstein, Rauh, and Edwin King gave differing accounts.[34] According to Mendy Samstein, Moses tried throughout to discuss alternatives and various compromises.[35] In Rauh's rendering, the "real" meeting took place in the bedroom of the suite, and he was not part of that group. His information came from Al Lowenstein—whose version is that Moses, Ed King, and others agreed to accept the two at-large delegates if nothing else could be gained.[36] Ella Baker, part of the Sunday evening inner room meeting, emphatically disagrees: "Never, never, I'm sure that never was Bob's position.... We were mostly supporting . . . [the idea that] . . . those who took the loyalty oath would be seated. And if this meant that so many of the regulars took it that there was only room for two of MFDP, then we would consider that. That's entirely different from a courtesy seating of two without power of any sort."[37] Lowenstein later remained relatively silent about this meeting. In a March 1967 interview, he "requested that the tape recorder be turned off when the interview began to touch on events in 1964."[38] One of the MFDP delegates, Mrs. Annie Devine, recalls:

> Bob did not want FDP to accept the compromise. No compromise period. He didn't advise us. He sat back and watched and waited.... He did not tell FDP anything. He talked to people, he spoke to people but Bob did not say, you know, this is the compromise, let's do this and let's do that. There was not one time that he said let's do this, or you do this or you don't do that. It wasn't his nature anyway.[39]

The credentials committee was scheduled to meet at 2:00 P.M. on monday, August 24, some six hours before the official opening of the convention. At the Pageant Motel an hour before the meeting, Hubert Humphrey met with Moses, Rauh, Aaron Henry, Fannie Lou Hamer, Ed King, Edith Green, Martin Luther King, and MFDP supporters on the credentials committee in an attempt to reach an acceptable compromise. Nothing was accomplished and the meeting was rescheduled for that night. Arthur Waskow called this "a major secret meeting" that was "evidently a most upsetting occasion. Moses came down from it looking like death itself."[40] Because it appeared that the MFDP had the required eight state delegations and eleven members of the credentials committee for a minority report, the administration had the meeting and any decision postponed until Tuesday to avoid a floor fight on the opening night of the convention.[41]

Subcommittee chair Mondale subsequently notified Rauh of a compromise proposal: the delegates would continue as designated guests of the convention and the

Johnson forces further promised that any state delegation that discriminated against blacks would be barred from the 1968 convention. On behalf of MFDP, Rauh rejected the proposal outright.[42] He was warned that his role in the challenge would injure Senator Humphrey, a close friend and ally, who has written of the experience, "Johnson was testing me one more time."[43] Commenting later at a SNCC conference on the promise offered by the Democratic party to the MFDP, Moses was to remark:

> The Compromise . . . that precinct meetings be open to registered voters regardless of race . . . doesn't help us. Cause we can't register people. So we asked Humphrey in a closed session: "Okay, the precinct meetings are open to registered voters. How many voters do you guarantee us in Mississippi in the next four years? 400,000? 100,000? Any?" And he said, "We can't guarantee you any because the Democratic Party doesn't run the administration."[44]

Rauh, as a good liberal and loyal attorney for his MFDP client, continued his quest, futile from the outset, for an arrangement acceptable to the MFDP. He proposed to the credentials committee and the Democratic party chairs that both delegations be seated. This counterproposal originated with Representative Edith Green of Oregon, who believed that every member of both delegations who signed the loyalty pledge should be seated; Mississippi's vote in the convention would then be divided proportionately among the seated delegates.[45] Johnson rejected this compromise, which would rend his inherited coalition. Southerners would be certain to leave the convention if such a bargain were struck. "If those baboons walk onto the convention floor," Texas Governor John Connally told Johnson, "we walk out."[46]

John Stewart, an attorney then serving on Hubert Humphrey's staff, explained the technical maneuver used by the administration to appear unable to accept Edith Green's compromise: "It really boiled down to the fact that regardless of the morality of the issue involved, there was a problem of the call to the Convention in '64 [that] did not provide a basis for excluding the white Mississippi delegates ... [and] ... there was a serious legal problem about the seating of ... the FDP people ... who had not met the requirements of their state as a third party in some instances." According to Stewart, a delegation could not be unseated unless it did not meet the terms of the "call to convention," and the Mississippi white delegation did meet the terms. Humphrey had undergone a rather "heated" session with people from the MFDP, including Moses, who "expressed himself quite articulately and quite forcefully."[47] Moses' response to Stewart's position was stated after the convention in a talk in New York:

> They say we can't be seated for legal reasons. I mean, *legally* we can't be seated.... That's exactly how to miss the whole issue.... You say we're not legal because we don't abide by Mississippi's laws, but the laws of Mississippi are illegal.... They don't abide by the laws of the U.S. In fact your Attorney General has just said so. He filed a suit which is now before the Supreme Court which says that Mississippi laws are unconstitutional across the board.[48]

On Tuesday, August 25, the MFDP met in its Atlantic City church headquarters. Rauh addressed the dele-

gates, pleading for tolerance of party liberals, especially
his close friend Humphrey—and implicitly for consid-
eration of the compromise. Rauh would remember that
Ella Baker proceeded to "cut me up" for being part of
the liberal establishment and not caring about poor
Mississippians.[49] Rauh then went to the two o'clock
meeting of the credentials committee, where Michigan
Congressman Diggs told him to call Walter Reuther,
head of the United Auto Workers and Rauh's boss. President Johnson had requested that Reuther fly in to put
pressure on delegations such as Michigan's to withdraw
support from the MFDP.[50] Rauh got a temporary postponement of the meeting to make the call. Reuther
essentially reiterated the administration's "compromise" and told him to go ahead to the credentials committee and accept it.[51] Rauh responded that he would
not accept anything without talking with Aaron Henry.
Rauh knew well enough that the administration had
made a mistake in appointing Aaron Henry and Edwin
King as the two delegates. Neither Rauh nor Aaron
Henry could make decisions for a committedly democratic group like the MFDP. The very existence of the
MFDP dramatized the principle of one man, one vote—
the selection by black Mississippians of their own representatives. The administration and the party in this
critical juncture lay bare their inability to understand
not only the moral premise on which the creation of
the MFDP rested but also the very real and dangerous
physical battle the delegates had fought to be there.

   Rauh's description of his last-ditch efforts to seek a
vote in the credentials committee that would bring the
issue to the floor of the convention indicates that Mondale agreed to his request for a postponement of the

credentials committee meeting. Then another member of the subcommittee, Sherwin Markham, announced, "A decision has been made. There will be no further delay." Mondale concluded, "Well, I guess that's it, Joe."[52] Accounts by Mendy Samstein and Walter Tillow agree that the idea of Rauh's consulting with Henry was contrary to the expressed will of the MFDP delegates. At a three-hour meeting held on Tuesday morning before the afternoon credentials committee session, the MFDP delegates had made it clear that no condition or compromise would be acceptable other than Edith Green's proposal to seat those from both delegations who took the loyalty oath. At the credentials committee meeting Rauh was at the Credentials Committee meeting faced with the administration's compromise for two at-large delegates, and suddenly had to check with the MFDP—as though its mandate had not been clear enough.[53] When Rauh asked the committee for a postponement, he was shouted down; his request for a roll call was ignored. Mondale then announced the Johnson compromise and asked for an oral vote; sympathizers with the MFDP could not garner against it the necessary eleven votes.[54]

At the same time, Moses, Henry, Edwin King, Martin Luther King, Ralph Abernathy, Andrew Young, Bayard Rustin, and Walter Reuther were conferring in Hubert Humphrey's rooms far from the credentials committee meeting. Suddenly someone shouted, "It's all over. It was unanimous for the compromise." In Rauh's words, "Bob Moses lost his cool. It was like hitting him with a whip, like a white man hitting him with a whip, everybody had ratted on him. It wasn't true, of course."[55] Humphrey, according to Edwin King's recollection, explained to SNCC that Johnson "will not let that illiterate woman [Fannie Lou Hamer] speak on the floor of the Democratic Convention." Moses shouted at Humphrey, calling him a racist.[56] An aide to Humphrey then wheeled in a television set, and the gathering would hear an announcer say that the MFDP had accepted the Johnson compromise. That was enough. "You cheated!" exclaimed Moses.[57] What other words would have been adequate? Moses strode away, enraged at the apparent alliance between the Northern liberals and the Southern racists within the Democratic party.[58] Ed King maintains that the announcement was as much as surprise to Humphrey as it was to the MFDP people, and believes the maneuvering was Mondale's doing—a sort of political domino in which Humphrey's Senate seat would go to Mondale when Humphrey became vice president. Moses thought otherwise: Humphrey was simply stalling and preoccupying the MFDP group while Mondale engineered the compromise pressed by the credentials committee and the administration.[59]

The MFDP quickly called an emergency meeting to discuss the credentials committee vote, in which Rauh had been among the defeated supporters of the MFDP plan. Black leaders who had supported the Johnson compromise were prohibited from speaking, as was Al Lowenstein.[60] Moses expressed his resentment at the compromise's being imposed on the MFDP, and at the Democratic party's telling the MFDP which two delegates it would seat.[61]

Johnson was determined that the regular Mississippi delegates would subscribe to the loyalty pledge before being seated. Beyond their own proposal, the Johnson troops would not go and they could not be outmaneuvered. While they were working up their plan, they had ensured that no other would be acceptable, using all the means available to them through the federal patronage system to shape the thinking of the members of the credentials committee. The administration mobilized black elected officials to lobby the insurgents to accept the compromise. Courtland Cox, SNCC's program director, has related one maneuver on the part of a black congressman:

> We had a list of delegates we thought were solid. The Negro congressman asked us for the list, and Bob [Moses] did not want to give it to him. I said to Bob, "Do you think this man is going to steal this list of names?" And the Congressman said, "Yes, I want to give this list to credentials committee chairman David] Lawrence, to show him we have the strength to pull a minority vote on the floor." In my ignorance, I pressed Bob to give him the list so that he could show that we had some clout. Bob gave the list reluctantly, and what happened next was unbelievable. Every person on that list, every member of that credentials committee who was going to vote for the minority, got a call. They said, "Your husband is up for a judgeship, and if you don't shape up, he won't get it."[62]

President Johnson used this information and "pulled every string, enlisted every ally, and used all the forces at his command, including the FBI, to defeat the MFDP challenge."[63] Rauh would remember, "There were so many hatchet men that you had to stand with your back to the wall all the time because of the hatchet men."[64]

On Wednesday morning, August 26, Rauh met with the MFDP delegates to discuss their options. He informed the Mississippians of Johnson's pressure tactics and of the slide in liberal support; he assured them that they had already been successful in dramatizing before the country the issue of racial discrimination in Southern politics. They would get no more from the administration or the convention.[65] Moses let the delegates discuss their options among themselves.[66] Lawrence Guyot notes that "Bob's personal position was that the people should reject the compromise.... [His] position, basically was the decision to be made by the MFDP."[67] It appears that a group of eight delegates had met with Rauh and agreed not to file a minority report,[68] but at the Wednesday morning meeting Moses pointed out that the MFDP had been willing to accept the compromise of Congresswoman Edith Green that both the regular delegation and the MFDP sign a loyalty pledge and the seats be divided between the two groups.[69] And SNCC organizer Mendy Samstein recounts the "anger of the Mississippi group, which I identified with and which was articulated by Bob [Moses]. The press knew his influence. He was the key man; he was calling the shots."[70] And so did the Johnson administration. Humphrey told Moses, "Now look, Moses, anything you tell those people they're bound to do, so like I know you're the boss of that delegation."[71] The Green compromise was a little closer to the wishes of the Freedom Democrats than to those of Johnson, and their willingness, however reluctant, to accept it demonstrates that the insurgent delegates were something other than ideologues. But in the end, nothing could close the gap between the Freedom Democrats and the Johnson forces. The MFDP voted that morning to reject the administration compromise.

During the day, many liberals and black leaders spoke to the MFDP delegates in an attempt to change their minds. Bayard Rustin and Martin Luther King, each reasoning from his own premises, tried to explain the art of liberal compromise. But their remarks to the rural poor, who made up most of the MFDP membership, seemed condescending. King spoke to the MFDP of "the need of pragmatism even in the most idealistic of situations."[72] Economic improvement for blacks, King was convinced, could come only from federal programs passed by a coalition that would include unions, white liberals, blacks. A shift by white Southerners to the Republican party, he believed, would strengthen the liberal, labor, black coalition in the Democratic party.[73] The NAACP under Roy Wilkins's leadership had never supported the MFDP or Freedom Summer in any tangible way. Indicative of his position is his remark to Fannie Lou Hamer at the convention: "You people have put your point across. You don't know anything, you're ignorant, you don't know anything about politics. I been in the business over twenty years.... Now why don't you pack up and go home?"[74] Edwin King would recall that Martin Luther King was ambivalent about the proposal. As a leader who liked to work through the political establishment, he wanted the MFDP to accept the compromise. But he also said that if he were a Mississippi black, "I would vote against it."[75] The National Council of Churches, represented at the Wednesday deliberations, intimated that it would cut off funding for MFDP and COFO programs if the Freedom Democrats did not go along. Bill Higgs, the white Mississippi activist lawyer, remembers the stormy Wednesday:

Moses got up and spoke. It was really like listening to
the Lord, I tell you it was! King had just finished some
wishy-washy speech, you know. Moses could have been
Socrates or Aristotle, somebody like that, you know. I
mean he tore King up. He said, "This reasoning that
you've been giving here is inaccurate. We're not here to
bring politics into our morality but to bring morality
into our politics." And as Moses was finishing, King and
everybody knew the jig was up.[76]

Perhaps this best illustrates Moses' purity acted out. He
wanted to clothe action with meaning; practical politics must have moral direction.

Ed King, in a later interview, paints SNCC as frightened of Martin Luther King's magnetism and its possible effect on unsophisticated Mississippi farmers.[77] It
may have been Martin Luther King's ambivalence that
prevented the administration's compromise from ever
seriously becoming an option: later he would admit
that Fannie Lou Hamer had been right not to accept it.
At the end of the MFDP caucus, the delegates again
voted to reject the Johnson compromise.

On television that evening Rauh remarked that
whereas the compromise, as he saw it, was in fact a
victory for the MFDP, the insurgent party would continue the fight. Though he was official counsel for the
group, Rauh in effect sided with Johnson by announcing that he and other liberals who had supported the
MFDP would now support the administration compromise. The MFDP delegates refused to go along.[78] Moses
and others in the MFDP staged a sit-in on the convention floor the day before Johnson's nomination. The day
following that event they sat on the floor as convention
aides filled the regular Mississippi delegation's vacant

chairs. Other Southern Democrats were perplexed and mystified; one announced, "The old niggers in our area like us. They like the old guard."[79]

"You cannot trust the political system," Moses remarked, "I will have nothing to do with the political system any longer."[80] He has observed that at Atlantic City the Freedom Democrats declared:

> Here are your sharecroppers, who have empowered themselves in the political process.... Are you ready and able to incorporate them into the Democratic Party? And the response, in essence, was, no, they have to be trained in the university, they have to go through the credentialing process . . . in order to become part of that process. And that was one of the great losses . . . [rejecting] an answer to the problems that later erupted as the [urban] rebellion. Because that event posed a political way to handle what was happening in the cities.[81]

And in an interview given in 1989, Moses pointed out that the Democratic party had lost the moral cutting edge in politics that during the following decade could have channeled the explosion in urban cities into political solutions.[82]

Once again, the federal government and the liberals had failed to support the rights of blacks at a critical moment. In setting aside an immediate moral issue for the sake of a practical politics, they would claim to be acting in the eventual interests of the moral good. President Johnson thought he had been treated badly; he believed he had shown support for the MFDP and considered himself a friend of Southern blacks, having recently forced the Civil Rights Act of 1964 through Congress. And in a six-month period laws were to be passed providing urban mass transit, a food stamp program, and new provisions for health and education along with the establishment of the Office of Economic Opportunity.[83] But Moses and Fannie Lou Hamer perceived the process of compromise as sullying, as both inherently immoral and belonging to a past in which justice had been compromised out of existence.[84] In a television interview Moses was asked why he opposed the compromise soon after the MFDP voted to reject it. He responded in exasperation: "We are here for the people.... They don't want symbolic votes. They want to vote for themselves."[85] Johnson's supporters regarded what the MFDP perceived as adherence to principle as arrogant and ill-mannered ingratitude. A year later an article in the *Saturday Evening Post* reiterated that the rejection by the MFDP of the compromise— "even though the plan had been thought up by Lyndon Johnson"—annoyed the president, "and ever since then the Administration has been quietly creating roadblocks in F.D.P.'s path."[86] Years later Aaron Henry explained:

> Lyndon made the typical white man's mistake: Not only did he say "You've got two votes"—which was too little, but he told us to whom the two votes would go.... He didn't realize that sixty-four of us came up from Mississippi on a Greyhound bus, eating cheese and crackers and bologna all the way there.... What kind of fool am I, or what kind of fool would Ed [King] have been to accept? ... Ed and Aaron can get in but the other sixty-two can't. This is typical white man picking Black folks' leaders, and that day is gone.[87]

It would have taken a lifetime for either group to learn to talk to the other. Each made a moral claim, and the two claims were exclusive.

A study in differing concepts of moral rightness, the fight at the convention along with the civil rights movement as a whole also manifested contrasts in courage. Moses' refusal to compromise was an example of the kind of stubborn courage that he had demonstrated in Mississippi; and if there is anything a social movement craves it is courage. But Martin Luther King, Jr., himself, a leader of a broad coalition and therefore a compromiser, had carried the burden of leadership since the mid-1950s, facing physical danger while undertaking the complex tasks of holding alliances and negotiating with governments. In the question of the delegates he took a special sort of risk, that of inviting the scorn of believers in a simpler virtue: and the scorn was forthcoming, perhaps deservedly. At the moment, Moses' courage had to contend with his disillusionment, which was to attend him long afterwards.

The Freedom Democrats under Fannie Lou Hamer and Lawrence Guyot kept trying to work within the Democratic party. Even after the convention debacle, the MFDP held a parallel general election in which sixty-three thousand votes were cast for Johnson and Humphrey.[88] Mississippi continued its efforts to squelch the fledgling party. Before the convention the state had filed an injunction against anyone's using the name or operating in any way with the MFDP. A few weeks after, all delegates were handed subpoenas to appear in Chancery Court in Jackson to hear the case of *Mississippi v. Edwin King*; the group filed a counterinjunction with the federal district court, claiming that the state injunction violated both the First and the Fifteenth Amendments.[89]

Aaron Henry returned to ally himself with the NAACP when in 1965 that organization elected to separate its own voter registration activities from that of SNCC. "Our volunteers will be well-dressed," Henry was quoted as saying, "This is the dignified, American way."[90] But others in SNCC agreed with Moses. Atlantic City, one of them said, "indicated to some of us that you cannot get too close to the power structure and expect to change it. So that's why some of us are guarding against being absorbed by the Establishment. We want to be outside the Establishment. We speak from that vantage point."[91] Compromise with established reality was not what the black Mississippi MFDP delegates—who were challenged by Klansmen even on their way to the Democratic Convention and stayed in a segregated motel in Atlantic City—had been about. As Moses has observed, he was looking for one person within the party who could say, "No. Here's what's right . . . not only in this situation but for the country."[92] But he could not find that person. Many years later during an interview for the civil rights television series, *Eyes on the Prize*, Moses remarked, "I think the issue was a moral issue. . . . What is ironic is that we were told that morality doesn't enter into politics . . . because we are now twenty years later in an era in which politics is defined by what is morally correct."[93]

After the 1964 election the MFDP formally announced a challenge to the seating of the Mississippi congressional delegation on grounds that the November vote had been illegal and unconstitutional.[94] Moses had no expectation of success, for he had learned the

ways of the federal government. He assumed the Johnson administration would use this new challenge in
the same way it had used the last. At the August 1964
convention, the insurgents had served the administration in its ultimately failed quest for a loyalty pledge
from the Mississippi delegation. Moses believed the administration would not support this new congressional
challenge; it would merely employ the threat of it to
push Great Society legislation through Southern Democrats in positions of seniority.[95] Lee C. White, assistant
special counsel to the president, wrote in a briefing
memorandum to Johnson prior to a meeting with Martin Luther King that there was "cause for concern"
about a statement King had made concerning the
MFDP challenge.[96] Moses was accurate, at least, in ex-
pecting that the congressional establishment would not
back up the MFDP maneuver. At issue was power that
the white liberal elite was not prepared to share, at
least not with activists like Moses. The Democrats also
feared losing white moderates in the South. The government argued that the freedom delegation was illegal
because it had not abided by Mississippi's laws; at the
same time the Justice Department was filing suit
against the state on the grounds that its voting laws
were unconstitutional.[97]

After the Atlantic City convention Moses was no
longer the engaged militant who six months earlier had
announced, "We intend to challenge whether the country will permit people to be elected from districts where
Negroes are not allowed to vote."[98] His optimism was
limited to a temporary internal dynamic: "Why can't
we set up our own [state] government? So that in 1967,
if we get organized enough between now and then, we

can . . . declare the other one no good. And say the federal government should recognize us."[99] Several years later he reflected:

Well, I don't think that the Democratic Party to this day has confronted the issue of bringing into its ranks the kind of people that were represented by the MFDP. That is the real underclass of this country. The Democratic Party primarily has organized around the middle class. And we were challenging them not only on the racial grounds . . . but we were challenging them on the existence of a whole group of people who are the underclass of this country, white and black, who are not represented.[100]

Moses realized that SNCC would be at a disadvantage without liberal help, but he had concluded that it could no longer work within the system: "We've been hated for a long time in the South, but we could always go to the North and be heroes. Now we may find ourselves isolated and destroyed in the North. We have to prepare ourselves for that. Somebody may have to be ploughed under. But, after all, that's what a revolution means."[101] Redemption, Moses now seemed to believe more than ever, lay in communal democracy, intimate in scale:

What we have begun to learn and are trying to explore about people is how they can come together in groups . . . , and talk to each other and make decisions about basic things, about their lives. . . . People . . . first think that in order to . . . get them together, they would have to have something for them to talk about. . . . A program to carry to them or . . . something to organize them around. But it doesn't turn out to be true, from our experience. You could in the North, in the ghettos, get together 10 or 20 people and out of their getting together and giving them a chance to talk about their main problem would come programs that they themselves decided on.... If that happened and began to happen around the country, that would be the key to spreading some of the things that have happened in the South to the rest of the country.[102]

Hostility to liberalism among SNCC workers was growing apace with the hostility, already emergent before Freedom Summer, to the small bands far at the left flank of conventional liberalism, the white summer volunteers. As a group they doubtless were liberal in much of the way that word was soon to be understood by black militants—privileged, morally earnest in a middle-class and collegiate way. But it was in this capacity that they had inevitably brought to Freedom Summer the attention from the public, the press, and the government that the white North would not have bestowed on black civil rights workers. And like it or not, Freedom Summer needed that attention. It is unjust that black activists could not have drawn a like notice. And it is an injustice to the volunteers that, in the very fact of their success in drawing publicity, they symbolized the inequality. But both the black SNCC workers and the summer volunteers were committed to fighting injustices longer and broader than these. Before Freedom Summer Moses, perhaps thinking of the injunction of Camus against being either victim or executioner, had recognized the plight of the white students:

We're going through a big thing right now even in terms of attitudes of the Negro staff towards the white staff.

... The white students [are] ... now made the victims. You know it's a process mainly of cleansing, but the problem is whether you ... can move Negro people from the place where they are now the victims of this kind of hatred, to a place where they don't in turn perpetuate this hatred.... Neither do [we] want to integrate into the middle-class white culture, since that seems to be at this point in vital need of some kind of renewal.[103]

The one person whom the more militant SNCC workers came especially to identify with white liberalism was Allard Lowenstein, the activist-politician who had been so instrumental in bringing the Northern white college volunteers by the hundreds to work in Mississippi. It was typical of his liberalism still to fear the presence of subversion within the radical wing of the civil rights movement—and in any event Moses' whole point was that it would not have mattered: this 1950s style of thinking was now irrelevant. Lowenstein's liberal politics operated on the experience of the labor fights of past years, when communist infiltration of unions had been real. But extensive FBI investigations reveal no communist inroads into SNCC or the rights movement.[104] And yet as late as December 1964 the FBI apparently was still investigating both SNCC and the MFDP. A memorandum from the Washington MFDP office to Moses, Forman, Guyot, and others tells of "a source very close to the White House" who disclosed memos written about the "Communist infiltration of SNCC." In this memorandum Moses was listed with the notation that "Attorney General Kennedy has named him as a communist," presumably because Moses had spoken in November at a fund-raising dinner for the

National Guardian and because he had "led the fight against the LBJ compromise at Atlantic City."[105]

But the New Leftists came in time to suspect Lowenstein of affiliation with another kind of subversive force, the CIA. By the late sixties it had become public that for over a decade the CIA had subsidized the National Student Association, the organization Lowenstein had once headed.[106] Lowenstein believed in structure and leadership in the traditional power-broker American business hierarchy. One SNCC worker, a Yale recruit, has explained:

> SNCC broke with Lowenstein on political grounds.... What SNCC *said* was that Lowenstein didn't belong, Lowenstein was a New Deal liberal recruiting black votes for the Democratic power structure. What this country needed was revolution. You had to understand that black people wanted no part of white imperialist capitalist America, fighting a racist war in Vietnam and murdering black people here at home.... The Movement wasn't out there courting broken heads for the right to sit at a lunch counter; ... Lowenstein believed in the system ... which meant Lowenstein was the enemy.[107]

And this man who had come to the South in the grand tradition of the perpetual organizer and manager of great social projects later rejected the summer project for having an ideology and organization that were alien to his liberal but elitist ideals.

As Moses reflects, "The [summer] project was very delicate in terms of getting off the ground at all. Mississippi was the only place where all the civil rights organizations got together. People were skeptical of everybody's motives and who was trying to take over."[108] Lowenstein was an object of that skepticism. Ed King describes what both Lowenstein and Moses offered in their contrasting understandings of what the movement needed: "The leadership offered by Lowenstein was to respond to his brilliance.... Moses ... gave us total acceptance.... He offered understanding, not just analysis. Lowenstein knew where he stood; it was encouraging to stand with him. Moses hardly even knew where he was going; but it was inspiring to be near him."[109]

Negotiation of the sort that Rauh conducted between the Freedom Democrats and the administration was in a tradition of a liberalism that 1950s McCarthyites had despised precisely for its habit of compromise and its suspicion of an absolutist morality. The maintenance of that tradition in the face of the 1950s redbaiting meant the preservation of civil, intelligent public discourse, which includes discourse in defense of racial justice. Now it turned out that liberalism of that sort was to be under attack from its own left flank. Yet for several years, and especially after liberals in exact faithfulness to their cold war commitments escalated the fighting in Vietnam, they and the radicals were to face each other with a hostility more openly bitter than that between either group and the conservatives. Rauh would never again work for the MFDP; Moses would never again seek such aid.

SNCC's quarrel with the convention liberals was an event in the unfolding advocacy of participatory democracy. Moses observes:

The FDP delegates were the only people at that whole
convention who were free in any meaningful use of the
term. The President told everybody else . . . what to do.
All I cared about was the insides of those 68 delegates
and the future of the FDP in Mississippi. It wasn't my
responsibility to care about Humphrey or the backlash.
We couldn't let others single out two people and ap-
point them our spokesmen. The whole point of the FDP
is to teach the lowest sharecropper that he knows better
than the biggest leader what is required to make a
decent life for himself.[110]

To the thinking of Charles Sherrod, a SNCC field secretary long active in both sit-ins and voter registration
work, accepting the Johnson plan

would have said to blacks across the nation and the
world that we share the power, and that is a lie! The
"liberals" would have felt great relief for a job well
done. The Democrats would have laughed again at the
segregationist Republicans and smiled that their own
"Negroes" were satisfied. That is a lie! We are a country
of racists with a racist heritage, a racist economy, a
racist language, a racist religion, a racist philosophy of
living, and we need a naked confrontation with ourselves.[111]

More broadly, in giving compromise a bad name the
maneuvering of the liberals at Atlantic City must have
contributed to a mentality, increasingly aggressive in
the years that followed, that purity is to be measured
by how many people the pure refuse to cooperate with.
To compromise means to blur, to deny the truth, which
demands to be seen in absolute clarity; to befriend and
compromise is to endorse the enemy. What had begun
as a break with the NAACP practice of tempered legal-

ism grew to be contempt of law and temperance. And a participatory democracy that is intent on limiting the number of participants ends by being a contradiction in terms. Even within the deliberating in the MFDP during the convention was a possible hint of the ruthless chastity of the later politics of the most disaffected left. One analysis suggests that the "real Purists," the black voteless Mississippians in the delegation, were not given time to discuss the compromise but were told by the "so-called Purists" such as Moses and other SNCC leaders what to decide.[112] Yet Jack Minnis, writing in the spring of 1965, attested to the democratic nature of the MFDP delegation: "A clear majority were 'of the people,' and were representative in the sense that they thought and acted like those whom they represented."[113] Purity of a sort, at any rate, was now ascendant within SNCC. It was purity of a sort that has since come to define the later sixties, at once fortifying and destructive.

NINE

DISILLUSION AND RENEWAL

Beginning in the fall of 1964 Moses increasingly distanced himself from the organizational and policy discussions within SNCC. James Forman, SNCC's executive director, attributes this to the "almost Jesus-like aura that he [Moses] and his name had acquired."[1] Yet Moses worked with Forman to shape a plan for the following summer that they called the Black Belt Program. It was projected to carry farther the work of Freedom Summer, using black student volunteers.[2] An internal document entitled "COFO Program (Winter 1964–Spring 1965)" announced the limited continuation of a number of summer projects, including voter registration and Freedom Schools.[3] One worker, John Harris, noted in a year-end field report on Sunflower

County that local participation in voter registration, Freedom Schools, and the MFDP was strong. He wrote of plans to hold mock elections in January 1965 for county and local offices. At the same time, of the 400 who attempted to register to vote over nearly six months, only ten were accepted.[4]

In September Moses left the United States on a three-week tour of Africa with Fannie Lou Hamer, James Forman, and others.[5] There Moses learned that the U.S. government had distributed farcical propaganda about the favorable status of blacks in this country. At a meeting with Guinea's head of Ministry of Information and Tourism, the group discovered misconceptions about the benefits that black Americans were going to receive from the coming elections. Moses, speaking in French, informed the minister that most blacks in the South were denied the right to vote. The minister explained that his information had come from some journals and some speeches of Martin Luther King.[6] Moses returned further disillusioned. In his absence, a group of civil rights representatives had met with Courtland Cox, SNCC's program director. The meeting further frayed the weakened COFO coalition, and SNCC emerged too radical for the more moderate SCLC and NAACP organizations.

Clayborne Carson has suggested that the retreat of the organization held during early November 1964 in Waveland, Mississippi, became a turning point toward the black nationalist direction that SNCC was to take under Stokely Carmichael. A series of "position papers"—many unsigned, written for discussion—bespeaks the tensions inherent in an interracial organization. The papers indicate that the overriding issues were leadership and the problems with white participation. One unnamed writer said:

> The lack of adequate leadership and serious workers in the past was not an immediate concern, because the organization was small, but the sudden overnight growth (remember I said SNCC will spend close to a million dollars this year) into a major organization with a national image that is both recognized and appreciated (whether positively or negatively) has made it necessary for us to begin to deal with the problem.... We don't have direction because we first of all can't really say whether we are organizers, agitators or demonstrators.... And don't fool yourself by saying it's not a question of either-or, because it *has* to be one or the other.[7]

The local community workers, most of them black, increasingly demanded more influence in making decisions in a group that gradually had become centralized under college-educated volunteers.[8] A draft article written in early November for the *Southern Patriot* refers to the growing complexity of COFO as a result of the continuation of several summer project initiatives— Freedom Schools, libraries, community centers, food and clothing drives. There was a need for coordination of the various activities from the Jackson headquarters:

> Advocates ... say the increasing centralization will increase efficiency.... Others feel the spirit of the early movement pioneered by SNCC field secretaries, is being lost. As project staff are supplemented by professionals—doctors, nurses, teachers, ministers, lawyers—the projects tend to lose the close ties within the staff that allowed for innovation and decisions by consensus.[9]

Some of the written papers were signed, and one in particular voices leadership concerns:

> My basic criticism seems to be the lack of efficient, *democratic* structure in which COFO can operate. I am afraid that now we will adopt a very efficient structure that won't be as democratic as possible.... Selection of the top staff . . . should be done by the staff as a whole. . . . As to project director, I think he should be a *Negro*, but one who is willing to listen and learn.... Also, we should concern ourselves with two basic concepts of policy: are we primarily a service organization and only secondarily a political organization or vice versa? . . . As for the last problem, it is the most serious. How to organize successfully and still remain only an organizer and not a boss.[10]

Another statement is even more telling of the indigenous blacks' feelings:

> I started working for the SNCC on the 18th of March, 1963 . . . in Greenwood, Mississippi. I was living on the Runnymede Plantation at the time . . . a day hand.... After I started working with the movement, I was asked to leave the plantation.... I was put on the staff by Bob Moses . . . making $10 a week.... On June 18th I was put in jail in Itta Bena for seeking police protection after the Hopewell Baptist was bombed with tear gas. I stayed in jail 58 days for nothing at all. I worked in the first Freedom Vote? . . . Then about March, 1964, I was cut off the staff.... If Bob Moses hired me, he should be the one to put me off the staff.... I could get closer to the people here than the people from the North. I have picked cotton for two dollars a hundred just like other people on plantations. I don't want my children picking and chopping for the same thing. That is one of the reasons that I want to work in the movement.[11]

A few weeks after returning from his extended trip to Africa and fund-raising in the North, SNCC chairman John Lewis sent a memorandum to all SNCC staff. He recounted rumors of an alleged coup in SNCC leadership and persisting redbaiting. He exhorted the staffers to "reassure our friends, supporters, and the American public that we are a unified, effective, strong, and vital force on the American scene for social, economic, and political change."[12] But SNCC was falling into groupings, ranging from hardliners, who stayed in Mississippi working for COFO or the MFDP, to floaters given to lofty discourse.[13] One writer defines two factions; the hardliners urging more structure, the floaters distrusting "centralized organization and top-down leadership."[14] Lewis later described Moses as the leader of a group of Northern blacks and Northern whites who promoted an attitude that came to be called "Freedom High." They encouraged people to do whatever they wanted to do without being responsible to anyone. Moses had a "tremendous impact . . . not just in Mississippi" and his followers made him "the all-perfect and all-holy and all-wise leader, and I think that's one of the reasons he changed his name."[15]

At the end of November 1964, Moses was in New York City for an awards dinner sponsored by the *National Guardian*. Jack Newfield of the *Village Voice* interviewed him on this occasion and described Moses as "direct yet self-effacing . . . and carrying a dog-eared copy of Camus' 'Resistance, Rebellion, and Death.'"[16] The article, which appeared in the newspaper on December 3, 1964, compared Moses to the biblical hero, saying that the present-day Moses had been "trying to draw justice from the stone of Mississippi," using as his inspiration "the housemaids, cotton pickers, and tenant farmers of Mississippi." In the interview, Moses voices his disillusion with a traditional Left that could talk only of coalitions and leaders from the top:

> But it is the little people on the bottom who must learn about themselves and organize their own organizations that fulfill their own needs.... The people don't need spokesmen or decision-makers, just the confidence to try to represent themselves? . . . This nourishment from the bottom of society is something the national leaders don't know anything about . . . These people . . . know what is needed to make a decent life for themselves, not the national leaders who know how to solve every problem the country faces except how to live on $30 a week.[17]

As if to underscore his disillusionment, in December 1964 Moses announced he was dropping his surname and would use only his own middle name (and his mother's maiden name), Parris. He had become fed up with the media's viewing him as a leader, he explained, and this was his way of avoiding an assigned role.[18] Soon he also resigned as head of COFO, saying that "my position there was too strong, too central, so that people who did not need to, began to lean on me, to use me as a crutch."[19] As Amzie Moore expressed it: "Well, I think everybody knows . . . that Bob Moses was the leader.... He didn't project leadership. He didn't say 'I'm the man, you do this, that, and the other.' He didn't even argue with you on a point except where people were involved. He was always on the side of the people. Always."[20] He had been in Mississippi to assist local people to develop their own leadership.

A few months later Moses, apparently speaking of the country's white majority, expressed a surprisingly hopeful view: "I don't happen to believe that they, if they were presented with real information about people and how they live, if they weren't forced to live under myths about themselves and other people, that they would consciously choose to isolate other people. To force them into ghettos. To restrict their participation in society. Now that's just a faith principle."[21]

In the aftermath of Atlantic City Moses was finding new ways of articulating his concept of personal and communal liberation. SNCC was still trying to rediscover direction. At the April 1965 SNCC executive committee meeting, Forman lamented the serious problem of leadership, the poor morale, and the lack of programs in Mississippi. The response was, "You have a riff [sic] between project programs and state oriented programs. When Moses left, there was a vacum [sic]. People use[d] to be able to go to him about their problems, now they have no one."[22] It would seem that under Moses, the leader who rejected leadership, the organization had possessed a greater coherence than conventional wisdom would have expected. Moses was "like an Apostle who makes his circles, and he goes to this mission and that mission and the other mission, to straighten them out on anything that they might be confused about. And then he makes the circuit. But they have the responsibility of carrying out . . . their particular mission."[23]

Much has been written about SNCC's lack of hierarchy and the amorphous organizational structure within the group even in the years when Moses was actively directing voter registration programs. Lowenstein, in an interview given in 1967, remarks that "Bob's forte was never organizing, structuring.... Bob was very much opposed to structure. But ... he was very much in favor of the summer project which was in a sense structure."[24] Moses was an organized *person*, purposeful and centered in pursuit of a difficult goal, and in that capacity more able to organize projects than Lowenstein has given him credit for.

Among the abundant correspondence with volunteers and SNCC workers throughout these years that illustrate Moses' organizational skills is a December 1962 letter to Joan Trumpauer, then a student at Tougaloo, about plans for a statewide conference in February 1963. A former freedom rider, she had served a stint in Parchman Prison as a result and was one of the first two white students admitted to Tougaloo in the fall of 1961. Moses' letter contains eighteen items to be attended to, ranging from the number of staff and students and whom to contact for lists of participants to such details as the need for attendees to bring their own linen. For the conference program, he suggests not only what but how: a session on nonviolence, based on discussion rather than lecture, possibly with a film; the Freedom Singers' song-writing workshop. The overall purpose of the conference, he stressed, should be "to motivate some of the Mississippi students to take the summer off and work in direct action projects in the Mid-South where they can get first hand experience in organizing a project, facing the MAN, etc."[25] While preparing for this conference, he was suggesting ways such students could use their experience with COFO for college credit and was instrumental in securing funds from the Field Foundation for a work study project.[26]

In his organizational work on the Freedom Summer project, Moses sent a letter to students accepted for it along with materials to read and a book list that included W. E. B. Du Bois' *Souls of Black Folk*, Michael Harrington's *The Other America*, and Lillian Smith's *Killers of the Dream*.[27] And although Moses did not coordinate the Freedom Schools, he had begun the year before to concern himself with the education of illiterates. Detailed planning preceding the curricular conferences held in the spring of 1964 included daily schedules for the schools, a listing of school sites, and a rationale for each suggestion. From his earlier research on programmed instruction, Moses was directly involved in providing possible contributors to the curriculum.[28] So successful were the Freedom Schools that the number of sites expanded from a projected twenty-five to forty-one; nearly twenty-five hundred blacks, ranging in age from preschool to seventy years, attended classes.[29]

A detailed memorandum that Moses issued to all COFO workers on August 11, 1964, called for a general staff meeting at Tougaloo on August 17, and is indicative of his thoroughness and penchant for detail within a strict attendance to the larger goal. It includes a list of what must be done in preparation for the meeting, suggests that each project meet separately with its staff and volunteers, and names all those expected to attend. No detail had been overlooked. Each project was to give a report. Staff cars were to be brought because arrangements had been made for them to be serviced at Tougaloo. The medical committee was prepared to provide free checkups for staff as well. In all, the memorandum lists sixteen separate projects, including the

Freedom Democratic party, the Freedom Schools, federal programs, libraries, community centers, and the food and clothing operation.[30]

Perhaps the best example of Moses' ability to coordinate and galvanize people through his own organizational skills is an "emergency memorandum" dated July 19, 1964, sent by Moses and the MFDP coordinators to all field staff and voter registration volunteers. The memorandum stresses the work to be done to bring about the challenge of the MFDP at the Democratic National Convention in August: "If we are to have any degree of success *everyone* who is not working in Freedom Schools or community centers *must* devote all their time to organizing for the convention challenge." The document then gives a detailed analysis of the number of blacks registered in each county and the number needed in each to achieve the goal of two hundred thousand freedom registrants. It ends with a recapitulation of the various projects under way to publicize the freedom registration and an outline of the status of the MFDP organization in each of the five congressional districts.[31] Yet Moses was often viewed as the leader of the floaters who wanted to break free of all centralized structures.[32] Cleveland Sellers describes one incident that took place in Atlanta when he was at a SNCC meeting and joined a group of floaters holding a rump meeting in a nearby apartment:

> The three of us—me, Rap [Brown], and Ivanhoe [Donaldson] took [the "floaters"] to the cleaners. . . . It was five in the morning before we were finished. A very important thing happened during the course of the night, however. Bob Moses withdrew from the discussion. He didn't withdraw because we were winning or

because he was tired. He did so because he realized that those aligned with him, the Floaters, were incapable of pursuing his ideas as well as he.... I have always believed that Bob Moses began a gradual withdrawal from SNCC that night.[33]

The floaters, at any rate, represented an element in an organization seeking a new purpose. And by Forman's account they were suspected of connections that enemies and wellwishers of SNCC had thought to detect there. In September 1964 the syndicated columnists Rowland Evans and Robert Novak called Moses "dangerously oblivious to the Communist menace to the rights movement and so militant in his championship of Negro rights that at times he approaches black nationalism."[34] For some time SNCC's use of the legal services of the National Lawyer's Guild had brought complaints because some members were suspected Communists; Joe Rauh considered it "immoral" to accept their help.[35] The reaction of Moses and others to such criticisms—and Moses believed it was because of this that Al Lowenstein had separated himself from SNCC's activities during the previous summer[36]—was to ignore the redbaiting simply because it deflected attention from the main goals of COFO.[37] And writers in such national magazines as *The New Republic* helped to discount the suspicions and allegations. A leader of the National Council of Churches, Dr. Robert Spike, insisted that the SNCC "has no relation to the Communist Party apparatus.... Unfortunately, in this country if you're a radical you're a Communist."[38]

In February 1965 SNCC's program director Courtland Cox was replaced by Cleveland Sellers, a pragmatic, veteran civil rights activist whose approach was political rather than philosophical. He had little patience with floaters, less with moral consistency; growing up in the rural South, Sellers represented black activists who had become convinced that a hard, militant, aggressive organization was the only way to deal with racism.[39] In part, the drive for organization and structure within SNCC may have been the pressure of a success-oriented culture that could not understand a will, as Moses phrased it, to "put energy into something and to make something that's meaningful to yourself." Moses reflected on this attitude: "How many people come up to the SNCC people and say, 'Well when are you going back to work?' And they mean, 'When are you going to fit into society?' "[40] Yet the direction SNCC activists were to take would put them at odds with society even as they used its organizational tools.

Two months later at a SNCC executive committee meeting, it was proposed that all floaters be ordered to join a project or leave the movement. Stokely Carmichael remarked: "I'm at the point where I feel we need discipline concerning programs. You see, how can we question others when people like Moses and Cox get away with a lot of things and are never questioned about them?" At this time, Moses and his wife were working in Birmingham, Alabama, although notes in the report on the state's personnel indicate "No contact with Bob Parris and Dona Richards." Remarking that "Bob says he just wants to see what it is like to organize in a city," someone suggested that the group should find out what he and his wife were doing. Marion Barry added, "If it was anybody else, we'd be raising hell." During this entire discussion, Carmichael defended Moses, and finally the group agreed to get in touch with him about attending staff meetings. "All should be subject to discipline," Forman argued. "If Bob is above discipline, he should be project director." The consensus of the executive committee seemed to be for establishing concrete programs; the reason floaters existed was that the organization had, in Carmichael's words, "no *radical* programs." Although the original proposal was voted down, the committee did decide to draw up a list of "problem people."[41]

Moses meanwhile held to his original concept of SNCC as an organization devoted to building local structures native to the region and letting them flourish without further out-of-state intervention. At a SNCC staff meeting on April 23, 1965, Moses (now using the name Parris) still stressed the need to have the organizer become part of the group, not its focal point. At this discussion he urged:

> We need a people conference. If FDP is to survive, they must either hook up with the rest of the south, and the south in turn with the rest of the country or be absorbed into the Democratic party. The only people willing and able to help them are SNCC and SDS [Students for a Democratic Society].... To get people in motion, first call them together.... Most political movements depend on a few people who work very hard; we want maximum participation of the people. [M. L.] King doesn't put people in motion. He has separate campaigns.[42]

He was against Forman's attempts to build a larger, tightly organized SNCC: "Do we build a SNCC machine or do we organize people?"[43] Moses was living a set of convictions of a kind that Gene Roberts, in an article in the *New York Times*, had disparagingly assigned to SNCC: "It was a must that you be able to quote Camus, especially *The Rebel*, and distrust all organizations, including SNCC." Moses was urging SNCC workers to "go where the spirit says go, and do what the spirit says do."[44]

Late in 1964 Moses announced that several hundred Freedom Summer volunteers would stay on to work in Mississippi. Moses, however, never resumed his role in the state. He had helped put black people there in touch with one another, and he had drawn the attention of the country to the state. He had initiated new forms of participatory democracy and grass roots politics. It seems he had no more to do.[45]

Soon after, Tom Hayden, working with Students for a Democratic Society (SDS), invited Moses to speak at a mid-April rally planned in connection with a march on Washington to protest the Vietnam War. Moses was shifting his concerns from the civil rights to the antiwar movement. "Negroes," he believed, "better than anyone else are in a position to question the war—not because they understand the war better, but because they better understand the United States." Like other radicals, he began to identify the country with its foreign policy:

> Most liberals think of Mississippi as a cancer, as a distortion of America. But we think Mississippi is an accurate reflection of America's values and morality. Why else can't the people who killed Andrew, James and Mickey be brought to justice, unless a majority of the community condones murder. Sheriff Rainey is not a

freak; he reflects the majority. And what he did is related to the napalm bombing of "objects" in Vietnam.[46]

Another remark typical of Moses and much of the antiwar movement is recorded in a 1965 interview:

> The rationale this nation uses to justify the war in Viet-
> nam turns out to be amazingly similar to the rationale
> that has been used by the white South to justify its
> opposition to the freedom movement. For the racist
> white Southerner, there is a logic in this parallel. He
> condones murder in Vietnam for the same reason he
> condones it at home—he sees a threat to his civili-
> zation.[47]

Moses spent the spring and summer of 1965 enlisting
the support of civil rights workers against the Vietnam
War. By the end of the summer, Moses, Cox, and Carmichael, along with Staughton Lynd and other pacifists,
had opened an office in Washington to enlist "students,
poor people, and intellectuals" to protest the war in
Vietnam.[48] One of the events in which Moses took part
was an "Assembly of Unrepresented People" who gathered at the White House in silent vigil to protest their
opposition to war. In late September Moses and his
wife, Dona Richards, attended a meeting at the Institute for Policy Studies in Washington to discuss ways
to merge the civil rights and antiwar movements.[49] The
merger was consistent with Moses' identification of
American blacks with repressed third-world people everywhere.[50] But, after delivering some talks against the
Vietnam War in 1965, he took a leave of absence from
SNCC, perhaps because of criticism that his antiwar

activities were diverting attention from the rights movement.[51]

The movement, however, had achieved some of its major goals. On August 6 President Johnson signed the Civil Rights Act, authorizing federal examiners to register qualified voters and suspending literacy tests as a condition for eligibility to vote. And the Twenty-Third Amendment, outlawing the poll tax in all elections and ratified the year before, would result in an increase in black registered voters from seven percent in 1964 to fifty-nine percent in 1968.[52]

Moses agreed to be a guest speaker in the summer of 1965 at a six-week training session for student leaders, the "Encampment for Citizenship," sponsored by the Ethical Culture Society and under the direction of Al Lowenstein. Held on the campus of the Fieldston School in Riverdale, New York, the camp featured a diverse group of eminent speakers—including Moses, William Sloane Coffin, William F. Buckley, Jr., Tom Hayden, Norman Thomas, James Wechsler, and the Republican candidate for mayor of New York, John Lindsay.[53]

That fall Moses again traveled to Africa. He returned to the United States in the spring of 1966. This trip, according to SNCC staff worker Stanley Wise, convinced Moses that blacks must work alone. The propaganda spread by the U.S. Information Agency about the status of American blacks so antagonized him that for a time he broke off all relations with whites, believing that blacks had to withdraw into themselves to develop their own identity and survival. "They were people he cut away in one fell swoop," recalled Stanley Wise.[54] Lawrence Guyot, who had worked closely with Moses in Mississippi, suggests that Moses abandoned relations with whites because he had come to question the seriousness of their commitment to blacks.[55] Amzie Moore recounted that Moses had come to see him after his return from Africa and "stayed about four months, or five months. And we discussed ... how to go about building an economy and getting folks ready." At this time, Moore characterized Moses as "very careful, didn't speak to anybody hardly, seemed to have been out of touch with whites.... He was more withdrawn."[56] Back in the United States, Moses organized an exclusive meeting in New Orleans black SNCC and CORE field secretaries.

In May 1966, Stokely Carmichael took over as chairman of SNCC. After graduation from college in 1964, Carmichael had worked first for the Nonviolent Action Group (NAG) at Howard University and then for SNCC full time. His experiences in Selma, Alabama, in the march and demonstrations made famous by Martin Luther King prompted Carmichael to organize rural blacks in Lowndes County, Alabama. He formed the Lowndes County Freedom Organization with its symbol of a snarling black panther.

At a fall 1966 SNCC staff conference, the group listed "Assumptions Made by SNCC." Included in this list was the observation that the "first break in our desire to integrate came when Bob Moses started developing parallel structures in Mississippi. The MFDP asked the question: was there any room for Negroes in the Democratic Party. The answer was: 'There is room for two, but the rest must sit in the balcony.' "[57] At this session organizational changes were made, including a requirement that only southern blacks would serve on the coordinating council.[58] And in December 1966, a group of separatists in SNCC narrowly succeeded in voting out all whites as workers and participants in the organization, with the ban to go into effect the next year.[59] The ideal of civil rights had become transmuted into racial separatism. Yet most of the New Left radicals who fostered the antiwar movement were themselves whites or Northern blacks.[60] Moses' work belongs to the important shift that soon expanded the struggle for black civil rights in the United States to the white liberal protest against the war in Vietnam.[61]

In the Sputnik era of the late 1950s, when the nation in its fear of falling behind the Soviet Union gave favored status to teachers of mathematics and science, Moses had received draft deferrals. Before leaving for Atlanta in 1960 he had applied but was rejected for conscientious objector classification. And in June 1961, he appealed his 1-A status, explaining that he would be working in Atlanta "this summer and throughout the coming year" on a voter registration project in Mississippi. He suggests that this would be appropriate alternative service.[62] In July the Selective Service System in New York notified him that although his case would not be reopened, he could meet with a government appeals agent later that month. The following May he received from the Department of Justice notice of a hearing on his claim to conscientious objector status. Moses requested that the hearing, scheduled for June, be delayed until July when he would be in New York. In preparation, a detailed inquiry was made into his background and submitted to the U.S. attorney's office in New York on March 21, 1962. It embraced interviews with neighbors and relatives, including his father, and information from schools attended and fellow workers: a typical government investigation. The report included facts that were germane, such as his work abroad with the American Friends Service Committee in college, and trivial details, among them the comment of a former Hamilton College instructor for whom Moses occasionally did some babysitting. His father noted that Moses' brothers had served in the army, one for two years and the other was currently in Europe.[63] Now, in July 1966, he received a draft notice. In an interview with Kenneth O'Reilly, the author of *Racial Matters*, Moses speculated that the FBI had something to do with his new draft status.[64] The radical direction of the civil rights movement and his own participation in the resistance to the war may have been the cause. Moses considered resisting the government and going to jail, but he had already spent too much time in jail. He did not want to make himself an example in this case as he had done throughout the civil rights movement.[65] He had earned a rest.

Many SNCC workers had endured great physical and psychological stress. Ivanhoe Donaldson, who had worked closely with Moses in SNCC, has commented on the emotional costs:

> It wiped out half the people who got involved. I think you kind of had to be a little philosophical about life to survive.... Some people freaked out from the violence. Some people were battle-weary.... They went into shock? ... I think there was a heavy toll in that generation, people who were active. It's not to be romantic. I think the evidence is just there.[66]

Connie Curry's early work in Mississippi with Moses through her affiliation with the NSA and continuing

involvement in the civil rights movement enabled her
to observe the drain on Moses:

> I remember watching the changes in Bob Moses....
> Nonviolence as a way of life was good as an ideal, but it
> was something that was absolutely alien to all of our
> backgrounds.... Being beaten and thrown into jail and
> trying to love everybody while they did it to you ... was
> bound to mess you up.... Those early ... SNCC people
> ... really believed that they were going to win.... I
> don't think that anybody ever envisioned the long years
> of struggle and violence and everything—anguish....
> Look what it did to Bob Moses.... He used to get hurt
> every time anybody would look mean at him, literally. I
> mean, he would feel it, and you could imagine that kind
> of sensitivity in Mississippi where people wanted to kill
> him.[67]

The effect on Moses' personal life continued beyond
his years of voter registration. His wife, Dona Richards,
who was directly involved in the struggles in Mississippi, apparently broke with him over the antiwar participation. She did not endorse the idea that SNCC officially should take a position on the nation's
involvement in Vietnam, because she feared it would
lead to additional charges of communist infiltration
within the organization and cripple efforts to raise
funds.[68] But in a November 1965 staff meeting of SNCC
the group agreed to draft an antiwar statement; at this
time Moses was in Africa.[69] And on January 6, 1966,
SNCC issued at a press conference a "Statement on
Vietnam" that declared "16% of the draftees from this
country are Negro, called on to stifle the liberation of
Vietnam, to preserve a 'democracy' which does not exist for them at home."[70]

Rather than report to the New York City draft board on August 1, which would have involved another conflict with authority—and this one with no benefit to the black or any other community—Moses borrowed money from his brother Gregory to "go away"; he fled to Canada at the end of July and worked for some two years at odd jobs—night watchman, janitor, telephone salesman, cook preparing airline meals.[71] He remarried, to Janet Jemmott, who had worked as a SNCC field secretary in Natchez, Mississippi.[72] In the spring of 1968, they traveled to Africa, making their way to Tanzania in 1969, where several former SNCC members were working for the local government. During the next several years Moses and his wife taught mathematics and English, respectively, at the same secondary school; they began to raise a family. For Moses, this was a long restorative period of meditation, seclusion, and immersion in a markedly different culture. His absence added to his mythological stature in the U.S. civil rights organization. This flight from adulation only served to increase his reputation of intellectual and moral leader.

Moses and his wife returned to the United States after President Carter's amnesty program in 1977 and settled in Cambridge, Massachusetts. He became involved in his children's education in the public schools, troubled that the children of minorities were not expected to become high achievers in mathematics. In 1982, when his eldest daughter entered the eighth grade, he began teaching as a volunteer through the Open Program in the school to develop community participation in the education of minority students. Awarded a five-year "genius" grant from the MacArthur

Foundation of Chicago, Moses used his funds to establish and develop the Algebra Project in the Boston public schools to teach mathematics to inner-city youth. Its workings are not far removed from the methodology he employed in Mississippi.

As he remarks in an article describing the project, he used "an older, yet less well known, 'community organizing tradition' " that contrasted with the massive marches and demonstrations organized by Martin Luther King.[73] The essentials of the Mississippi organizing tradition have their likeness in this new project: families put to the work of organizing; the empowerment of local people and their recruitment for leadership; and finally, a concept that had gotten an earlier articulation from Booker T. Washington. That rights leader—now out of fashion among radicals—had urged black people to "cast down your bucket where you are," draw on the resources of your own community, and deal with its particular needs and issues. Moses attributes his modernization of the technique to Ella Baker.

"The Computer Revolution that we are going through now," Moses told newspaper editors in 1990 at their Atlanta convention,

> is that this new math and literacy requirement is going to affect who is and who is not to be a citizen.... There are things that must be done if we are not going to have a generation of people who function as serfs in our inner cities, just as the people that we worked with in the '60s on the plantations in Mississippi were serfs in society then.... The voting efforts that took place in the '60s and centered around the question of empowerment, and particularly empowering black people so they could

participate in the political arrangements, now has a new dimension.[74]

His work in educating children in mathematics has taken him around the country and once again to Mississippi. He calls the Algebra Project "our version of Civil Rights 1992."[75] Moses still demonstrates how critical the work of organizing on an intimate scale is to those who would hope to effect lasting social and educational change in the world.[76] And his comparison of Ella Baker with Martin Luther King shows Moses to be faithful to his idea of leadership:

> There was always within the movement a tension between organizing and leading, or organizing and mobilizing.... You can trace in the movement the tension in people between their roles as organizers and as leaders, and try to get a sense of what that meant. I think of Ella Baker. She was a great organizer, and she was a leader, too. But one of the characteristics of organizers is that their work emerges, and they themselves subside....
>
> It never occurred to me to think about the movement in terms of King. I lived and breathed the *movement*.... The other question seems to me more important. Not the emergence and success of an individual, but the emergence and the success of, the failure and repression of the movement as a whole, the study of its false starts as well as its successes, its failures as well as its victories.[77]

One author has remarked that the visual impact of the television series "Eyes on the Prize" "only begins to catch the genius, the frustration, and the power of community organizing under such circumstances."[78] And, in his new project, Moses continues another revolution, modestly presented. At the same 1990 conference the reporter Charlayne Hunter-Gault nicely caught the elusive hero of the civil rights movement: "the legendary Bob Moses, whom nobody ever sees, but whose work is always in evidence."[79]

NOTES

Introduction

1. Quoted in James Forman, *The Making of Black Revolutionaries* (New York: Macmillan, 1972), 286. Moses describes this incident on a tape he made in the fall of 1962 describing SNCC's work in Mississippi. It was later transcribed and published with the title "Mississippi: 1961–1962" in *Liberation* 14 (January 1970): 6–17, with an introduction by Staughton Lynd.
2. Mary King, *Freedom Song* (New York: William Morrow, 1987), 146.
3. Cleveland Sellers, *The River of No Return* (New York: William Morrow, 1973), 83.
4. Sally Belfrage, *Freedom Summer* (New York: Viking Press, 1965), 74.
5. Transcript of tape made by Edwin King at the funeral of Amzie Moore, Edwin King personal papers, in the possession of the author.
6. Interview by Michael Garvey, March 29, 1977, Cleveland, Miss., in Oral History Program of the University of Southern Mississippi 184 (1981): 65.
7. Quoted in Robert Penn Warren, "Two for SNCC," *Commentary* 39 (April 1965): 41.
8. Germaine Bree, *Camus, rev. ed.* (New Brunswick, N.J.: Rutgers

225

University Press, 1964), 36ff., 118. More recent studies of Camus that consider some of the same issues are Anthony Rizzuto, *Camus' Imperial Vision* (Carbondale: Southern Illinois University Press, 1981); Harold Bloom, ed., *Albert Camus: Modern Critical Views* (New York: Chelsea House, 1988); Patrick McCarthy, *Camus: A Critical Study of His Life and Work* (London: Hamish Hamilton, 1982).

Notes to Chapter One

1. Robert Moses' uncle, William Henry Moses, Jr., could trace his ancestors as far back as a female household slave named Julia Trent, the daughter of a white plantation owner's son named Peter Trent, who had been wounded in the Civil War. The Trent family owned a plantation of some one thousand acres near Cumberland, Virginia. William Henry Moses, Jr., interview with author, June 30, 1991, Newport News, Va.
2. William H. Moses, *5 Commandments of Jesus* (n.p.: National Baptist Convention, n.d.).
3. Gregory Moses, Jr., interview with the author, June 2, 1993, Detroit, Mich.
4. Quoted in Nicholas Lemann, *The Promised Land: The Great Black Migration and How it Changed America* (New York: Alfred A. Knopf, 1991), 99. See also Moses' comments about his father in an interview conducted by Robert Penn Warren in February 1964 and published in Warren's *Who Speaks for the Negro?* (New York: Random House, 1965), 90–91.
5. Quoted in Seth Cagin and Philip Dray, *We Are Not Afraid: The Story of Chaney, Schwerner and Chaney and the Civil Rights Campaign in Mississippi* (New York: Macmillan, 1988), 87.
6. A teacher at Stuyvesant has recalled Moses as being "quiet, reserved, soft spoken and a good athlete." Quoted in "Resumé of the Inquiry Re: Robert Parris Moses, Conscientious Objector," March 21, 1962, U.S. Department of Justice, Southern District of New York, 1. Copy in the Mississippi Department of Archives and History, Jackson, Miss.
7. Robert Moses, interview by Taylor Branch, in *Parting the Waters: America in the King Years, 1954–63* (New York: Simon and Schuster, 1988), 325.
8. William H. Moses, Jr., interview with author, June 30, 1991, Newport News, Va.
9. Moses was granted a $900 scholarship and an opportunity to

earn an additional $200 each year by working in the Commons (dining hall). "Resumé of the Inquiry," 1–2.

10. Letter from W. Robert Connor to the author, n.d. [Fall 1990].
11. Fellow basketball players remark that his selection as varsity co-captain in his senior year owed more to his "natural quality for leadership" than his skill as a player. Letters from William F. Fivaz, September 28, 1990, and Thomas A. Fagan, November 10, 1990, to the author; Gregory Moses, Jr.,interview with author, June 2, 1993, Detroit, Mich.
12. Letter from Richard J. Miller to the author, October 9, 1990.
13. Letter from Richard P. Canuteson to the author, n.d. [Fall 1990].
14. Letter from Alfred P. Ingegno, Jr., to the author, September 28, 1990.
15. Letter from Dr. Jonathan G. Greenwald to the author, October 10, 1990.
16. The *Hamilton College Spectator,* September 1952 to May 1956, *passim*; SNCC biography sheet of Robert Moses, Mississippi Freedom Democratic Party Collection, Martin Luther King, Jr., Center for Non-Violent Social Change, Atlanta, Ga. See also "Resumé of the Inquiry," 9.
17. "Resumé of the Inquiry," 10.
18. Letter from James E. Schade to the author, n.d. [Fall 1990].
19. *Spectator,* November 11, 1955, 4.
20. Letter from Michael G. Sundell to the author, February 23, 1993.
21. *New York Times,* February 12, 1956, 17.
22. Letter from Emerson Brown, Jr., to the author, June 19, 1993.
23. Letter from Wayne Mahood to the author, October 14, 1990.
24. Letter from Michael G. Sundell to the author, February 23, 1993.
25. This paragraph is based on accounts of a talk Moses gave to the International Relations Club on October 24 in the fall of his senior year at Hamilton. *Spectator,* October 19 and 26, 1956.
26. American Friends' Service Committee Records, Peace Collection, Swarthmore College.
27. Quoted in Warren, *Who Speaks for the Negro?,* 98–99.
28. Letter from Gordon S. Hall to the author, September 29, 1990. The then-president, Richard T. Field, recalls that such a stand was "heretical," but the decision was influenced by the "favorable impression that Bob (and others) made on us all." Letter from Field to the author, n.d. [Fall 1990].

29. In 1991, having rejected several overtures from Hamilton for the conferring of an honorary degree, Moses would finally accept one.
30. "Resumé of the Inquiry," 3.
31. Mary King, *Freedom Song* (New York: William Morrow, 1987), 145.
32. William H. Moses, Jr., interview with author, June 30, 1991, Newport News, Va.
33. "Resumé of the Inquiry," 6.
34. William H. Moses, Jr., interview with author, June 30, 1991, Newport News, Va.
35. Interview with Robert Moses by Lemann in *The Promised Land*, 99.
36. Quoted in Lemann, *The Promised Land*, 99.
37. Robert Moses, "Commentary," in *We Shall Overcome*, ed. Peter J. Albert and Ronald Hoffman (New York: Pantheon, 1990), 69–76.
38. William H. Moses, Jr., interview with author, June 30, 1991, Newport News, Va.
39. Quoted in Ben H. Bagdikian, "Negro Youth's New March on Dixie," *The Saturday Evening Post* 235 (September 8, 1962), 16.
40. Interview with Robert Moses in Cagin and Dray, *We Are Not Afraid*, 86.
41. Quoted in Branch, *Parting the Waters*, 300. (Walker would soon become executive director of SCLC, replacing Ella Baker.)
42. Letter to "Fellow American" with attached detailed petition, dated March 31, 1943, William Henry Moses, Jr., Papers, the Amistad Research Center, Tulane University, New Orleans. William Moses had distinguished himself as a young man in 1930 by refusing to accept lower wages than whites in an integrated production of *Green Pastures* in New York City. William Henry Moses, Jr., Papers, Box 1. After retiring from teaching, William Moses was a syndicated columnist for several African-American weeklies; he wrote a feature entitled "From the Dark Side" that ran from 1969 to 1984. Letter from Andy Simons, Reference Archivist, December 18, 1991, the Amistad Research Center, Tulane University, New Orleans.
43. Quoted in Warren, *Who Speaks for the Negro?*, 90.
44. Moses gives this version in an interview on May 19, 1986, for "Eyes on the Prize," a fourteen-part television series, produced by Blackside, Inc., Boston, Mass. Transcript (partially edited) SR 1, CR 405, show 5, team B. See also Cagin and Dray, *We Are*

Not Afraid, 86–87. After the visit to Virginia, Moses worked for the King Legal Defense Fund; Bayard Rustin was organizing a King rally at the armory where Moses' father worked. Other sources report that Moses was already working in New York for the Committee to Defend Martin Luther King, Jr. See, for example, Clayborne Carson, *In Struggle: SNCC and the Black Awakening of the 1960s* (Cambridge, Mass.: Harvard University Press, 1981), 46. Carson notes that Moses had worked with Rustin in 1959 on the second Youth March for Integrated Schools.

45. Milton Viorst, *Fire in the Streets* (New York: Simon and Schuster, 1979), 244–45.

Notes to Chapter Two

1. Interview with Julian Bond in Howell Raines, ed., *My Soul Is Rested* (New York: G. P. Putnam, 1977), 101.

2. Ella Baker, interview by Anne Romaine, March 25, 1967, New York City, in "The Mississippi Freedom Democratic Party Through August, 1964" (Master's thesis, University of Virginia, 1970), 370 (hereafter referred to as Interview by Romaine).

3. John Lewis, interview in Raines, *My Soul Is Rested*, 102n.

4. Julian Bond, interview in Raines, *My Soul Is Rested*, 101–2.

5. Ella Baker, interview by Ellen Cantarow, in *Moving the Mountain: Women Working for Social Change* (New York: Feminist Press, 1980), 84.

6. Cleveland Sellers, *The River of No Return* (New York: William Morrow, 1973), 41.

7. Clayborne Carson, *In Struggle: SNCC and the Black Awakening of the 1960s* (Cambridge, Mass.: Harvard University Press, 1981), 26.

8. Connie Curry, interview in Raines, *My Soul Is Rested*, 104–5, 107. She, along with Ella Baker, was elected as a nonstudent advisor to SNCC at its organizational meeting, the only white member of its executive committee at that time.

9. Mary King, *Freedom Song* (New York: William Morrow, 1987), 145.

10. Quoted in Raines, *My Soul Is Rested*, 105n.

11. Minutes of SNCC July 1961 Meeting, item 7, 2, Civil Rights Collection, Social Action Vertical File, MSS 577, State Historical Society of Wisconsin, Madison (hereafter referred to as CR Collection, SHSW). See also Irwin Klibaner, "The Southern

Conference Education Fund: A History" (Ph.D. diss., University of Pennsylvania, 1963).

12. Taylor Branch, *Parting the Waters: America in the King Years, 1954–63* (New York: Simon and Schuster, 1988), 328.

13. Calvin Trillin, "Letter from Jackson," *New Yorker* 40, (August 29, 1964): 93.

14. Carson, *In Struggle*, 13.

15. Carson, *In Struggle*, 17.

16. Sellers, *The River of No Return*, 42.

17. Branch, *Parting the Waters*, 328.

18. Seth Cagin and Philip Dray, *We Are Not Afraid: The Story of Goodman, Schwerner and Chaney and the Civil Rights Campaign in Mississippi* (New York: Macmillan, 1988), 88.

19. James C. Cobb, *The Most Southern Place on Earth: The Mississippi Delta and the Roots of Regional Identity* (New York: Oxford University Press, 1992), 231.

20. "Life on the Delta," SNCC Publication, n.d., Mississippi Department of Archives and History, Jackson, Miss.

21. Cantarow, *Moving the Mountain*, 89.

22. Robert Moses to Jane Stembridge, "Friday Morning" [probably August 19, 1960], SNCC Papers, series IV (Executive Secretary Files), box 17, folder 7, Martin Luther King Center for Non-Violent Social Change, Atlanta, Ga. (hereafter cited as MLK Center).

23. Tape made by Moore, in the Carl and Anne Braden Papers, Social Action Collection, MSS 6, State Historical Society of Wisconsin.

24. Interview with Robert Moses in "Eyes on the Prize," transcript (partially edited) SR 1, CR 405, show 5, team B. Blackside, Inc., Boston, Mass.

25. Amzie Moore, interview, in Raines, *My Soul Is Rested*, 235.

26. Membership in the Citizens' Councils of Mississippi rose from the original group of fourteen men in the summer of 1954 to about 85,000 members four years later. Hodding Carter, *The South Strikes Back* (Garden City: Doubleday, 1959), 18, 105.

27. Quoted in Steven F. Lawson, *Running for Freedom: Civil Rights and Black Politics in America Since 1941* (Philadelphia: Temple University Press, 1991), 87.

28. Quoted in Trillin, "Letter from Jackson," 94.

29. Interview with Lawrence Guyot in Raines, *My Soul Is Rested*, 239.

30. Moses to Stembridge, n.d., SNCC Papers, series IV, box 17, folder 7, MLK Center.
31. Interview by Romaine, September 3, 1966, Knoxville, Tenn. Moore recalled several years later that "our discussion then did not deal in politics. . . . We talked about the bare necessities of life that people just didn't have." Interview by Michael Garvey, March 29, 1977, Cleveland, Miss., in Oral History Program of the University of Southern Mississippi 184 (1981).
32. Letter from the Reverend Edwin King to the author, July 20, 1991.
33. Stembridge to Moses, August 25, 1960, SNCC Papers, series IV, box 17, folder 7, MLK Center.
34. Stembridge to Moses, August 25, 1960, SNCC Papers, MLK center.
35. Emily Stoper, *The Student Nonviolent Coordinating Committee: The Growth of Radicalism in a Civil Rights Organization* (Brooklyn, N.Y.: Carlson Publishing, 1989), 21.

Notes to Chapter Three

1. Drew Jubera, "This Moses Leads Blacks in New Age Civil Rights," *Atlanta Constitution*, June 8, 1989, D4.
2. James Farmer, *Lay Bare the Heart: An Autobiography of the Civil Rights Movement* (New York: Arbor House, 1985), 2–3, chap. 17 passim; August Meier and Elliott Rudwick, *CORE: A Study in the Civil Rights Movement 1942–1968* (New York: Oxford University Press, 1973); Neil R. McMillen, "Black Enfranchisement in Mississippi: Federal Enforcement and Black Protest in the 1960s," *Journal of Southern History* 53, no. 3 (August 1977): 358–59.
3. Ella Baker, interview by Anne Romaine, March 25, 1967, New York City, in "The Mississippi Freedom Democratic Party Through August, 1964" (Master's thesis, University of Virginia, 1970) 366–67 (hereafter referred to as Interview by Romaine).
4. Timothy Jenkins, interview in Howell Raines, ed., *My Soul Is Rested* (New York: G. P. Putnam, 1977), 227–28.
5. An additional forty whites were lynched in Mississippi during this period—making the total 578. See Table 1, "Lynchings by State and Race: 1882–1962," in *The Negro Almanac: A Reference Work on the Afro-American*, 4th ed., comp. and ed. Harry A. Ploski and James Williams (New York: John Wiley, 1983), 247.

6. Bob Moses, interview in Nicholas Lemann, *The Promised Land: The Great Black Migration and How it Changed America* (New York: Alfred A. Knopf, 1991), 179–80.
7. Ella Baker, Interview by Romaine, 367.
8. Lonnie King, interview in Raines, *My Soul Is Rested*, 229.
9. Taylor Branch, *Parting the Waters: America in the King Years, 1954–63* (New York: Simon and Schuster, 1988), 486.
10. Bob Moses, "Mississippi: 1961–1962," *Liberation* 14 (January 1970): 8.
11. Clayborne Carson, *In Struggle: SNCC and the Black Awakening of the 1960s* (Cambridge, Mass.: Harvard University Press, 1981), 46; Harold Hampton and Steve Fayer, eds. *Voices of Freedom: An Oral History of the Civil Rights Movement from the 1950s through the 1980s* (New York: Bantam Books, 1990), 141.
12. Claude Sitton, interview in Raines, *My Soul Is Rested*, 379.
13. "The Southern Freedom Movement," *Monthly Review* 17 (July–August 1965): 38.
14. Minutes, SNCC Meeting, July 14–16, 1961, Baltimore, Md., 2,4. Civil Rights Collection, Social Action Vertical File, MSS 577, State Historical Society of Wisconsin, Madison (hereafter referred to as CR Collection, SHSW).
15. In the July 14–16, 1961, minutes of the SNCC meeting is the note that Walker of SCLC remarked that the main thing was to get the job done and SNCC was free to do it whatever way seemed best. SNCC Minutes, July 1961, CR Collection, SHSW.
16. Bob Moses to Wyatt Tee Walker, August 3, 1961, SNCC Collection, Mississippi Department of Archives and History (hereafter referred to as MDAH).
17. Letter from John Doar to Bob Moses, July 17, 1961, SNCC Collection, MDAH. From July 1960 to December 1967, Doar served as a trial lawyer and first assistant in the Civil Rights Division within the Department of Justice. See John Doar and Dorothy Landsberg, "The Performance of the FBI in Investigating Violations of Federal Laws Protecting the Right to Vote— 1960–1967" (unpublished essay, 1971). Copy in John F. Kennedy Presidential Library, Dorcester, Mass. (hereafter cited as JFK Library).
18. Branch, *Parting the Waters*, 493.
19. "Sworn Written Application for Registration" facsimile, April 18, 1955, Edwin King Memoirs, in the possession of the author. The preamble to this twenty-one-question application begins:

"By reason of the provisions of Section 244 of the Constitution of Mississippi and House Bill No. 95, approved March 24, 1955, the applicant for registration, if not physically disabled, is required to fill in this form in his own handwriting in the presence of the registrar and without assistance or suggestion of any other person or memorandum."

20. Lawrence Guyot, November 23, 1966, Jackson, Miss., Interview by Romaine, 80.

21. Report to the Voter Education Project of the Southern Regional Council from Moses, December 1962, series VI, Voter Education Project, Southern Regional Council Papers, reel 177, Civil Rights Microfilm Collection, Woodruff Library, Atlanta University, Atlanta (hereafter cited as SRC Papers, Atlanta University).

22. Charles Stewart, "Report on Mississippi Summer Project—1964," September 1964, Civil Rights Workers, Miscellaneous Small Collections, SC 3095, State Historical Society of Wisconsin (hereafter referred to as SC, SHSW).

23. Raines, *My Soul Is Rested*, 396; see also John M. Glen, *Highlander, No Ordinary School, 1932–1962* (Lexington: University Press of Kentucky, 1988).

24. Interview by Romaine, 79, 80.

25. Moses, "Mississippi: 1961–1962," 8.

26. Fred Halstead, "Trying to Vote in the Delta Takes Nerve," interview with Travis Britt in *The Militant* 26 (February 26, 1962): 3. Although Britt may have been exaggerating, the young people were not economically dependent on whites for survival yet.

27. Branch, *Parting the Waters*, 493; Carson, *In Struggle*, 48.

28. *U.S. Commission of Civil Rights, Hearings*, Jackson, Miss., 1965 (Washington, D.C.: Government Printing Office), 1: 212.

29. Mendy Samstein, September 4, 1966, Knoxville, Tenn., Interview by Romaine, 149–50.

30. Tom Hayden, *Revolution in Mississippi* (New York: Students for a Democratic Society, 1962), 3.

31. Moses, "Mississippi: 1961–1962," 9.

32. John Doar to Robert Moses, August 14, 1961, CR Collection, SHSW.

33. Barbara Carter, "The Fifteenth Amendment Comes to Mississippi," *The Reporter* 28 (January 17, 1963): 25.

34. Moses, "Mississippi: 1961–1962," 9.

35. Halstead, "Trying to Vote in the Delta," 3. Other sources quote the police officer in variant words.

36. Moses, "Mississippi: 1961–1962," 9.

37. Moses, "Mississippi: 1961–1962," 9–10. Also see Doar and Landsberg, "The Performance of the FBI," 32–34.

38. Interview with John Doar in Hampton and Fayer, *Voices of Freedom*, 148–49.

39. Carter, "The Fifteenth Amendment Comes to Mississippi," 23.

40. Jenkins, interview in Raines, *My Soul Is Rested*, 231.

41. Gilbert, "John F. Kennedy and Civil Rights for Black Americans," *Presidential Studies Quarterly* 12, no. 3 (Summer 1982): 389–90.

42. Seth Cagin and Philip Dray, *We Are Not Afraid: The Story of Goodman, Schwerner and Chaney and the Civil Rights Campaign in Mississippi* (New York: Macmillan, 1988), 308–9. Cox was given an "Extremely Well Qualified" rating by the American Bar Association, yet he became "one of the most malignant judicial obstructionists of civil rights, actually referring to Blacks in open courtroom as 'niggers' and 'chimpanzees.'" Gilbert, "John F. Kennedy and Civil Rights," *Presidential Studies Quarterly*, 390.

43. The Justice Department under Kennedy brought thirty-seven voter registration suits in the South by mid-1963, most filed in Mississippi. Gilbert, "John F. Kennedy and Civil Rights," 391–92.

44. Emily Stoper, *The Student Nonviolent Coordinating Committee: The Growth of Radicalism in a Civil Rights Organization* (Brooklyn, N.Y.: Carlson Publishing, 1989), 40, 310. Jones is unclear about whether this rumor circulated at this particular time; but the period was the summer of 1961.

45. Cagin and Dray, *We Are Not Afraid*, 144. Moses, according to his recollection, was given a ninety-day suspended sentence, and an appeal was later dropped. Moses, "Mississippi: 1961–1962," 10.

46. "Resume of the Inquiry Re: Robert Parris Moses, Conscientious Objector," March 21, 1961, U.S. Department of Justice, Southern District of New York, 7, MDAH.

47. Carter, "The Fifteenth Amendment Comes to Mississippi," 23.

48. Typically Moses sought to compensate the heroism of individuals like Steptoe. A little over a year later a handwritten note from Moses, dated October 2 [1962], to the SNCC Atlanta headquarters, requested that Steptoe be given a secondhand car because "he's interested in becoming active in voter registration" and noted that he would work under COFO. CR Collection, SHSW.

49. SNCC fund-raising handbill, "Facts . . . McComb, Mississippi," n.d., CR Collection, SHSW.

50. Federal Bureau of Investigation: files 44–1348, 44–18167, U.S. Department of Justice, Washington, D.C.

51. Moses, "Mississippi: 1961–1962," 10. Moses' recollection of the experience years later was somewhat more philosophical. He remembered leaving his body, watching his beating with detached concern from a comfortable distance in the air. Jubera, "This Moses Leads Blacks," D4.

52. *Civil Rights Hearings before Subcommittee No. 5 of the Committee on the Judiciary, House of Representatives*, serial no. 4, pt. 2 (Washington, D.C.: U.S. Government Printing Office, 1963): May 28, 1963, 1,249 (hereafter referred to as *CR Hearings*, House Judiciary).

53. I. F. Stone, *In a Time of Torment* (New York: Random House, 1964), 361.

54. *McComb Enterprise Journal*, August 30, 1961.

55. *McComb Enterprise Journal*, August 30, 1961.

56. Quoted in Halstead, "Trying to Vote in the Delta," 3.

57. Carter, "The Fifteenth Amendment Comes to Mississippi," *23*.

58. Jack Minnis, ed., "A Chronology of Violence and Intimidation in Mississippi Since 1961," SNCC Publication, 5, CR Collection, SHSW; Moses, "Mississippi: 1961–1962," 11.

59. Mary King, *Freedom Song* (New York: William Morrow and Co., 1987), 146. Moses in 1965 would drop his surname and use Robert Parris only. Carson, *In Struggle*, 156.

60. "Resumé of the Inquiry," 11.

61. Interview by Emily Stoper in *The Student Nonviolent Coordinating Committee*, 291.

62. Letter from Miriam Cohen Glickman to the author, March 1993; Cleveland Sellers quoted in Doug McAdam, *Freedom Summer* (New York: Oxford University Press, 1988), 142.

63. Lawrence Guyot, interview in Raines, *My Soul Is Rested*, 239.

64. Len W. Holt, "A Southern Lawyer Speaks of Freedom," *Freedomways* 2, no. 2 (Spring 1962): 179.

65. Carson, *In Struggle*, 48.

66. Doar and Landsberg, "The Performance of the FBI," 32–33, 35. See also Moses' account of this incident in "Mississippi: 1961–1962," 11.

67. Minnis, "A Chronology of Violence," 5; see also Carter, "The Fifteenth Amendment Comes to Mississippi," 22; Janet Feagans, "Voting, Violence and Walkout in McComb," *New South* 16

(October 1961): 3; SNCC untitled summary of events in Mississippi, MDAH.

68. Branch, *Parting the Waters*, 508.
69. Moses, "Mississippi: 1961–1962," 11. Nearly a year later, on August 28, 1962, the Justice Department filed suit against Mississippi officials who had failed to register black voters in *United States v. Mississippi*. Doar later noted that the evidence collected for this case and several others in Mississippi during this period was important in gaining support in Congress for the voting rights legislation passed in 1965. Doar and Landsberg, "The Performance of the FBI," 28 n. 19.
70. Doar and Landsberg, "The Performance of the FBI," 33 n. 32.
71. Quoted in Kenneth O'Reilly, *"Racial Matters": The FBI's Secret File on Black America, 1960–1972* (New York: Free Press, 1989), 68. Moses noted that during September, the Justice Department began to investigate voting complaints, interviewing people and gathering affidavits over a two-week period. "Mississippi: 1961–1962," 12.
72. Carter, "The Fifteenth Amendment Comes to Mississippi," 21.
73. Branch, *Parting the Waters*, 510.
74. Moses describes this incident in some detail in "Mississippi: 1961–1962," 12–13. He remarks, "It's one thing to get beat up and its another thing to be responsible, or to participate in some way in a killing" (12).
75. See John Doar's evaluation of the investigation in "The Performance of the FBI," 36–39.
76. Moses, "Mississippi: 1961–1962," 12.
77. SNCC fund-raising handbill, "Facts . . . McComb, Mississippi."
78. *CR Hearings*, House Judiciary, May 28, 1963, 1,249.
79. Quoted in SNCC news release 50, dateline Natchez, May 16, 1964, CR Collection, SHSW.
80. SNCC news release dated about August 2, 1962, CR Collection, SHSW.
81. Moses, "Mississippi: 1961–1962," 13.
82. Under date of January 31, 1964, a SNCC publication notes: "Liberty, Amite County: Louis Allen, Route 5, Liberty, was found dead in his front yard. He had been shot three times with a shotgun." Minnis, "A Chronology of Violence," 18.
83. SNCC news release dated December 6, 1991, CR Collection, SHSW.
84. Bob Zellner interview in Hampton and Fayer, *Voices of Freedom*, 146.

85. SNCC fund-raising handbill, "Facts . . . McComb, Mississippi."
86. Moses, "Mississippi: 1961–1962," 14.
87. Charles McDew, Oral History Reminiscence, Civil Rights Documentation Project, Moorland-Spingarn Research Center, Howard University, Washington, D.C. Charles Jones refers to textbooks used in Mississippi that called the Civil War the "war of Northern aggression." Interview by Emily Stoper in *The Student Nonviolent Coordinating Committee*, 196.
88. SNCC "News," December 6, 1961, CR Collection, SHSW. SNCC also persuaded the federal government to file a lawsuit to force desegregation of the McComb bus terminal.
89. James Forman, *The Making of Black Revolutionaries* (New York: Macmillan, 1972), 235.
90. Branch, *Parting the Waters*, 518.
91. Branch, *Parting the Waters*, 234–37.
92. Moses, "Letter from Magnolia," in Hayden, *Revolution in Mississippi*, 1; Cleveland Sellers, *The River of No Return* (New York: William Morrow, 1973), 52–53. Also reprinted in Joanne Grant, ed., *Black Protest: History, Documents, and Analyses, 1619 to the Present*, 2nd ed. (New York: Fawcett World Library, 1968), 303.
93. Hayden, *Revolution in Mississippi*, 2.
94. Moses, "Mississippi: 1961–1962," 13.
95. Doar, in his unpublished essay written with Landsberg, explains that "b-suits" applied to "anyone, public official or private citizen, who interfered with registration or voting by threat, intimidation, or coercion by any means." These "b" cases, or Section (b) of the 1957 Civil Rights Act, involved intimidation or interference. See "The Performance of the FBI," 1–2 n. 1.
96. The crux of this legal difficulty was the need to prove that inflicting physical harm (even including murder) on an individual was the result of an intent to prevent the person attacked from seeking to register to vote. The *Screws* conviction was overturned by an appeal before the Supreme Court because the prosecution, while proving that Claude Screws had intended to kill Robert Hall, had not proved Screws's intention to interfere with Hall's civil rights.
97. Doar and Landsberg, "The Performance of the FBI," 8.
98. Doar and Landsberg, "The Performance of the FBI," 25 n. 16.
99. Doar and Landsberg, "The Performance of the FBI," 16–17.
100. The lackluster performance of the FBI in its investigation of

voter intimidation cases between 1961 and 1963 Doar attributes to the sparseness of the FBI operation in Mississippi as well as the attitude of some of the resident agents. "The Performance of the FBI," 39.

101. *Jet* 19 (October 19, 1961): 4–5; (November 2, 1961): 20. Bryant later withdrew his support of the voter registration project.

102. Carson, *In Struggle*, 49–50.

103. Lucia Guest, "Their Dream Is Not to Be Nervous," *Mademoiselle* 60 (November 1964): 164, reports Moses as saying "Mississippi is unreal when you are not there, and the rest of the country is unreal when you are."

104. Moses, "Letter from Magnolia," printed in Hayden, *Revolution in Mississippi*, 1–2.

105. SNCC news release dated December 6, 1961, CR Collection, SHSW. Presumably SNCC was working to raise bail funds. Jim Forman, executive director of SNCC, wrote to Moses on November 10: "I assure you that we are working very hard and are urging people to write to you. . . . Be of good cheer; we shall overcome." CR Collection, SHSW.

106. William Higgs, January 12, 1967, Washington, D.C., Interview by Romaine, 282–83.

107. See William Higgs's explanation, Interview by Romaine, 283–84.

108. Carter, "The Fifteenth Amendment Comes to Mississippi," 24. Bill Higgs got in touch with Eleanor Roosevelt, who managed to induce President Kennedy to get the FCC to threaten to revoke the stations' licenses. Interview by Romaine, 284.

109. Moses, "Mississippi: 1961–1962," 14–15.

110. Interview by Romaine, 55–56.

111. Stoper, *The Student Nonviolent Coordinating Committee*, 83.

112. Howard Zinn, *SNCC: The New Abolitionists* (Boston: Beacon Press, 1964), 79.

Notes to Chapter Four

1. A statistical outline of counties in Mississippi as of 1960 compiled for a SNCC report in the spring of 1963 listed the percent of farmed land owned by whites in three Delta counties: LeFlore, Sunflower, and Washington. In LeFlore, ninety percent of farmed land was under white ownership, yet ninety-two percent of farmers in the country were tenants; in Sun-

flower, whites owned eighty-eight percent of farmed land, and eighty percent of the farmers were tenants; in Washington, the figures were ninety-two and seventy-two percent, respectively. "Survey: Current Fieldwork," series VI, Voter Education Project, Southern Regional Council Papers, reel 173, Civil Rights Microfilm Collection, Woodruff Library, Atlanta University, Atlanta, Ga. (hereafter cited as SRC Papers, Atlanta University). This information was submitted as part of the documentation for the *Civil Rights Hearings before Subcommittee No. 5 of the Committee on the Judiciary, House of Representatives*, serial No. 4, pt. 2 (Washington, D.C.: U.S. Government Printing Office, 1963), May 28, 1963, 1,279 (hereafter cited as *CR Hearings, House Judiciary*).

2. That spring Curtis Hayes and Hollis Watkins, the two McComb high school students who had worked and demonstrated with Moses the summer before, had started voter registration drives in the city of Hattiesburg, about sixty-five miles east of McComb. Bob Moses, "Mississippi: 1961–1962," *Liberation* 14 (January 1970): 15.

3. Quoted in Calvin Trillin, "Letter from Jackson," *New Yorker* 40 (August 29, 1964): 92.

4. Bernice Robinson to Moses, July 19, 1962, and report by Robinson dated July 19, 1962, Papers of the Highlander Research and Education Center, Social Action Collection, State Historical Society of Wisconsin, Madison (hereafter cited as SHSW). By the summer of 1961 the "Citizenship Schools" previously handled entirely by Highlander staff had been taken over by the SCLC and were coordinated at Dorchester Center in Georgia with a grant from the Field Foundation administered by Highlander. John M. Glen, *Highlander, No Ordinary School, 1932–1962* (Lexington: University Press of Kentucky, 1988), 162, 169–70, 210–12.

5. Mississippi Adult Education Program, Civil Rights Collection, Social Action Vertical File, MSS 577, SHSW. See also Bernice Robinson, "Mississippi Voter-Education Report," July 19, 1962, Papers of the Highlander Research and Education Center, SHSW. Braden, in a report to SCEF, described a weeklong trip spanning July 13 to 19, in which he traveled throughout the state with Moses; the two had met with Mt. Beulah's director, David Lollis, to plan the workshop. Braden to Jim Dombrowski, SCEF, July 23, 1962, Carl and Anne Braden Papers, MSS 6, box 20, folder 3, SHSW.

6. And during the winter and spring of 1961–62 SNCC "helped the *Mississippi Free Press* for the first two or three months of its existence." Moses, Memo to SNCC executive committee on the SNCC Mississippi Project, undated but about fall 1963 (the memorandum makes reference to the election of Paul Johnson as governor of Mississippi), SNCC Papers, series XV, State Project Files, 1960–68, box 104, Martin Luther King, Jr. Center for Non-Violent Social Change, Atlanta, Ga. (hereafter cited as MLK Center). Medgar Evers and others established this weekly paper to give the civil rights movement a voice.

7. Quoted in Trillin, "Letter from Jackson," 100.

8. [Horace] Julian Bond, "The Southern Youth Movement," *Freedomways* 2, no. 3 (Summer 1962): 310.

9. Moses, "Mississippi: 1961–1962," 15.

10. "Voter Registration Continues in Ruleville Despite Threats," *Mississippi Free Press* 1, no. 39 (August 8, 1962): 1.

11. Moses memorandum to "the press and others," n.d., CR Collection, SHSW.

12. Moses, "Mississippi: 1961–1962," 15.

13. Lawrence Guyot, interview by Anne Romaine, November 23, 1966, Jackson, Miss., in "The Mississippi Freedom Democratic Party Through August, 1964" (Master's thesis, University of Virginia, 1970), 81 (hereafter cited as Interview by Romaine).

14. Moses, "Mississippi: 1961–1962," 16. LeFlore County was the scene in 1955 of the trial of Emmett Till, a visiting fifteen-year-old black boy from Chicago who had made a modest pass at a white woman in the hamlet of Money and was then murdered in nearby Tallahatchie County (his self-confessed murderers were still free).

15. CBS presented in early October an hour-long documentary entitled "Mississippi and the 15th Amendment," which featured the Ruleville voting attempts during the summer; the *Mississippi Free Press* reported that "white Mississippi blacked out the hour-long CBS program." 1, no. 43 (October 6, 1962): 1.

16. Seth Cagin and Philip Dray, *We Are Not Afraid: The Story of Goodman, Schwerner, and Chaney and the Civil Rights Campaign in Mississippi* (New York: Macmillan Publishing Co., 1988), 184–85. See also Howell Raines, ed., *My Soul Is Rested* (New York: G. P. Putnam, 1977), 244–45, for Charles Cobb's and Lawrence Guyot's descriptions of the incident.

17. See Moses' description in "Mississippi: 1961–1962," 16–17. He notes that he drove to Greenwood with Willie Peacock, arriving

there at 3:30 or 4:00 A.M. (17). On tensions in Greenwood, see *New York Times*, August 18, 1962, 12.

18. Ivanhoe Donaldson, "Field Report," SNCC Papers, series IV, box 17, folder 1, MLK Center. Donaldson's report appears as "Notes from Southern Diaries," in *Freedomways* 4, no. 1 (Winter 1964): 141.

19. Lawrence Guyot, interview in Raines, *My Soul Is Rested*, 241.

20. Allard Lowenstein, March 4, 1967, Charlottesville, Va., Interview by Romaine, 126.

21. Lawrence Guyot, interview in Raines, *My Soul Is Rested*, 288.

22. Bob Moses, September 3, 1966, Knoxville, Tenn., Interview by Romaine, 57–58. Dave Dennis has said that in practice he and Moses co-directed the COFO coalition: "Once the organization was formed, we sort of merged everybody in to call ourselves COFO workers. The national offices of CORE and SNCC didn't like that, but that's the way we felt we could keep from having any real competition among the organizations." Harold Hampton and Steve Fayer, *Voices of Freedom: An Oral History of the Civil Rights Movement from the 1950s through the 1980s* (New York: Bantam Books, 1990), 148.

23. Moses, Interview by Romaine, 59–60.

24. Jack Minnis, ed., "A Chronology of Violence and Intimidation in Mississippi Since 1961," SNCC Publication 9, CR Collection, SHSW. See also Moses, "Mississippi: 1961–1962," 17.

25. Carl Braden to Jim Dombrowski, July 23, 1962, Braden Papers, box 20, folder 3, SHSW.

26. *Mississippi Free Press* 1, no. 39 (September 8, 1962): 1. The story, first published in the *Jackson Daily News* on Friday, August 31, was picked up by the Associated Press and appeared in the Louisville, Ky., *Courier-Journal* on September 1, 1962, and in the Montgomery, Ala., *Advertiser* on September 2, 1962.

27. Sunflower County, Senator James Eastland's home area, had a population that was seventy-four percent black. See James Atwater, "If We Can Crack Mississippi," *Saturday Evening Post* 237 (July 25–August 1, 1964): 16.

28. Fannie Lou Hamer, interview in Raines, *My Soul Is Rested*, 249–50.

29. Howard Zinn, *SNCC: The New Abolitionists* (Boston: Beacon Press, 1964), 93–94.

30. *Mississippi Free Press* 1, no. 35 (August 8, 1962): 1. A SNCC news release, dateline Ruleville, September 17, 1962, summarizes a field report written by Moses describing this incident and other

economic reprisals and pressures directed at blacks and SNCC workers. CR Collection, SHSW.

31. *New York Times*, September 10, 1962, 1.; September 11, 1960, 12. The *Mississippi Free Press* reported that the girls had been en route to register at Jackson State College and that one was the granddaughter of a local voter registration activist. 1, no. 40 (September 15, 1962): 1.

32. Around September 10, Moses would recall, he was in Jackson when Charles Cobb called him about the shooting; Moses immediately telephoned the Justice Department and went to Ruleville the next morning. Cobb had been arrested and accused of the shootings as an attempt to generate publicity. "Mississippi: 1961–1962," 17. See also Charles Cobb, interview in Raines, *My Soul Is Rested*, 246–47; *New York Times*, September 11, 1962, 20.

33. "Mississippi: 1961–1962," 17.

34. SNCC news release, dateline Ruleville, September 17, 1962. CR Collection, SHSW. On the voter education classes in Ruleville, see Bernice Robinson to Myles Horton, July 30, 1962, Papers of the Highlander Research and Education Center, SHSW.

35. Detailed report by Moses to the Voter Education Project of the Southern Regional Council, December 1962, series VI, Voter Education Project, reel 177, SRC Papers, Atlanta University. See also Carl Brauer, *John F. Kennedy and the Second Reconstruction* (New York: Columbia University Press, 1977}, 165.

36. John Doar and Dorothy Landsberg, "The Performance of the FBI in Investigating Violations of Federal Laws Protecting the Right to Vote—1960–1967," (unpublished essay, 1971), 17a–18. Copy in the John F. Kennedy Presidential Library, Dorcester, Mass. (hereafter cited as JFK Library). See also Guyot, interview by Romaine, 83. Guyot argued that winning this case would have eliminated the need for the MFDP and later congressional challenges. The case, of course, was held up in the federal district courts of Mississippi, ultimately losing in a two-to-one decision.

37. Moses, "Mississippi: 1961–1962," 17.

38. Moses, "To the Chicago Friends of S.N.C.C.," February 27, 1963, series VI, Voter Education Project, reel 177, SRC Papers, Atlanta University. Reprinted as "Letter to Northern Supporters," in *Black Protest: History, Documents, and Analyses, 1619 to the Present*, 2nd ed., ed. Joanne Grant (New York: Fawcett World Library, 1968), 300.

39. Vol. 1, no. 49 (November 17, 1962): 1, 4.

40. Moses to SRC Council, December 1962, series VI, Voter Education Project, reel 177, SRC Papers, Atlanta University.
41. Robert E. Gilbert, "John F. Kennedy and Civil Rights for Black Americans," *Presidential Studies Quarterly* 12, no. 3 (Summer 1982): 392.
42. Mary King, *Freedom Song* (New York: William Morrow, 1987), 146.
43. *New York Times*, September 14, 1962, 1, 12.
44. Moses to SRC Council, SRC Papers, Atlanta University. In this report Moses notes that the blacks who attempted to register "for the entire program" was a bit over 1,100.
45. The County Board of Supervisors voted forty to twenty-nine to suspend the program. The *Mississippi Free Press* attributed the decision to the voter registration work in the county. 1, no. 49 (November 17, 1962): 1.
46. Moses, "To the Chicago Friends of S.N.C.C."
47. SNCC news release, dateline Clarksdale, January 4, CR Collection, SHSW; *Mississippi Free Press* 2, no. 4 (January 5, 1963): 1. See also Ivanhoe Donaldson, interview in Raines, *My Soul Is Rested*, 256–58. Donaldson had been working in Louisville for the Student Nonviolent Action Committee, affiliated with the Atlanta office of SNCC, on the food collection drives.
48. Lawrence Guyot, interview in Raines, *My Soul Is Rested*, 242. Typical is a letter to Moses dated October 4, 1963, from people in the San Jose, Calif., area: "In the past two weeks we have sent off 270 pounds of good used clothing." The donors report that at a recent "Birmingham Memorial Rally" they had raised $750, which would go to SNCC, CORE, and the NAACP. CR Collection, SHSW.
49. Moses to John W. Blyth (The Diebold Group), February 22, 1963, from Greenville, CR Collection, SHSW.
50. Moses to Blyth, CR Collection, SHSW. See also SNCC "Urgent Action Memorandum," n.d., CR Collection, SHSW.
51. Hampton and Fayer, *Voices of Freedom*, 180. See also James C. Cobb, *The Most Southern Place on Earth: The Mississippi Delta and the Roots of Regional Identity* (New York: Oxford University Press, 1992), 232–33.
52. Quoted in Barbara Carter, "The Fifteenth Amendment Comes to Mississippi," *The Reporter* 28 (January 17, 1963): 24.
53. Clayborne Carson, *In Struggle: SNCC and the Black Awakening of the 1960s* (Cambridge, Mass.: Harvard University Press, 1981), 88.

Notes to Chapter Five

1. *Moses et al. v. Kennedy and Hoover* 219 F Supp. 762 (1963). On December 4, 1962, Moses wrote to Bill Higgs, a white lawyer long active in integration activities in Mississippi, and asked him for representation "in court action designed to secure protection for applicants to register to vote and for workers who are helping others to register to vote." He concluded, "I find it hard to believe that the most powerful nation in the world is not able to provide security for its citizens who attempt to vote and work to get others registered and voting." Southern Regional Council Papers, series VI, Voter Education Project, reel 177, Civil Rights Microfilm Collection, Woodruff Library, Atlanta University, Atlanta, Ga. (hereafter cited as SRC Papers, Atlanta University). William M. Kunstler and William L. Higgs filed as attorneys for the plaintiffs.

   The suit was publicized locally as well. See, for example, *The Atlanta Constitution*, January 3, 1963; *Atlanta Inquirer*, January 12, 1963; *Jackson Daily News*, January 3, 1963.

2. *Civil Rights Hearings Before Subcommittee No. 5 of the Committee on the Judiciary, House of Representatives*, serial no. 4, pt. 2 (Washington, D.C.: U.S. Government Printing Office, 1963), May 28, 1963, 1,276ff.; cf. May 8, 1963, 1,089ff. (hereafter cited as *CR Hearings*, House Judiciary).

3. Wiley Branton interview, quoted in Kenneth O'Reilly, *"Racial Matters": The FBI's Secret File on Black America, 1960–1972* (New York: Free Press, 1989), 75.

4. "Outline for COFO Program—1964," undated but before December 15, 1963. This four-page proposal written on legal-size sheets is perhaps the most comprehensive statement Moses had made to this time about the Freedom Vote and plans to challenge the regular Mississippi delegation at both Republican and Democratic national conventions. Civil Rights Collection, Social Action Vertical File, MS 577, State Historical Society of Wisconsin (hereafter cited as CR Collection, SHSW).

   On August 28, 1965 The *Saturday Evening Post* noted that the basic wage for SNCC workers was still at subsidence levels of $20 per week. At the same time, the annual budget for SNCC had risen to $1 million, most of it raised by "Friends of S.N.C.C." organizations on college campuses and in cities in the North. Richard Armstrong, "Will Snick Overcome?" *Saturday Evening Post* 238 (August 28, 1965): 80, 82.

5. Blyth to Moses, February 15 and 26, 1963; Moses to Blyth, February 22 and 24, 1963, CR Collection, SHSW. Blyth's efforts in conjunction with Moses resulted in a grant, which helped to get the project started. Letter from Blyth to the author, March 19, 1993.

6. In addition, Moses was investigating the possibility of a grant for the Mississippi voting project from the Rockefeller Foundation via the legal counsel for the civil rights commission. The chief counsel for the commission was Clarence Clyde Ferguson, Jr. Moses to Blyth, February 22, 1963. See also Moses to Arthur I. Waskow, Institute for Policy Studies, Washington, D.C., September 20, 1963, CR Collection, SHSW.

7. Moses to Philip M. Stern, July 15 and 30, 1963, CR Collection, SHSW. John Fischer of *Harper's Magazine* had put Moses in touch with Stern. Fischer to Moses, July 3, 1963, SNCC Papers, series XV, State Project Files 1960–68, box 104, Martin Luther King, Jr. Center for Non-Violent Social Change, Atlanta, Ga. (hereafter cited as MLK Center).

8. Mendy Samstein, interview by Anne Romaine, September 4, 1966, Knoxville, Tenn. in "The Mississippi Freedom Democratic Party Through August, 1964" (Master's thesis, University of Virginia, 1970), 136–37 (hereafter referred to as Interview by Romaine). Samstein notes that the program, developed first at Tougaloo and then expanded to Miles College in Birmingham, was funded by the Field Foundation.

9. Moses to executive committee, "Outline for COFO Program— 1964," n.d., CR Collection, SHSW.

   Stephen Currier, who headed the Taconic Foundation, began a series of meetings with civil rights groups that included the NAACP, CORE, SCLC, and the Urban League. The press referred to them as the "Big Four," unintentionally establishing a hierarchy within gatherings that also included SNCC and the National Council of Negro Women. James Farmer remarks, "Age bias and sexism were even more rampant then than now," in *Lay Bare the Heart: An Autobiography of the Civil Rights Movement* (New York: Arbor House, 1985), 215.

10. Moses to Julian [Bond], February 24, 1963, addressed to SNCC headquarters in Atlanta. CR Collection, SHSW.

11. Independent sources emphasize the intention of the freedom schools to pursue social science research. See, for example, a report filed by Robert H. Benthins, a Presbyterian minister from Portland, Oregon, who had volunteered in the Hattiesburg

Minister's Project for two weeks during the summer of 1964. "Research will disclose the actual accomplishments," he reported. He commented that "almost the idol of the movement is Bob Moses." Robert H. Benthins Report, July 19, 1964, SNCC Papers, series XV, State Project Files, box 104, file 16, MLK Center.

12. The report is dated January 9–11, 1963. Series IV, Voter Education Project, reel 177, SRC Papers, Atlanta University. Yet the bulk of the food and clothing came from contributions of sympathizers throughout the country. Minnis later would work directly for SNCC.

13. Quoted in Taylor Branch, *Parting the Waters: America in the King Years, 1954–63* (New York: Simon and Schuster, 1988), 714.

14. VEP, a program of the Southern Regional Council, awarded COFO a fourteen-thousand-dollar grant from the period of August 1, 1962, through March 31, 1963. Branton to Aaron Henry, September 5, 1962; Branton to Moses, November 20 and 29, 1963; Minnis to Moses, October 3, 1962. Voter Education Project, series VI, reel 177, SRC Papers, Atlanta University.

15. *Jet* 23 (March 7, 1963): 8. A feature story on Block by the columnist James A. Wechsler appeared in the *New York Post*, March 19, 1964, 34.

16. The *Mississippi Free Press* noted that 125 people had filed voter registration forms in Greenwood in a two-day period. 2, no. 12 (March 2, 1963): 1.

17. "To the Chicago Friends of S.N.C.C.," series VI, Voter Education Project, reel 177, SRC Papers, Atlanta University. A "Diary of Greenwood" appeared in the *Mississippi Free Press*, outlining the near-daily acts of physical violence and economic intimidation starting there in August 1962 when SNCC began its voter registration drive. 3, no. 17 (April 11, 1964): 1, 3.

18. *Mississippi Free Press*, 2, no. 13 (March 9, 1963): 1.

19. Travis testified on June 16, 1964, that he first was taken to the campus of Mississippi Vocational College, where a doctor from Greenwood was called in; he directed them to the hospital in Greenwood. Travis was transferred to Jackson's University Hospital the following day. *Congressional Record*, House, 88th Cong., 2d sess., 110, no. 121. The *Mississippi Free Press* gave a detailed report of the incident. 2, no. 13 (March 9, 1963): 1, 4. See also SNCC news release dated March 1, 1963, CR Collection, SHSW. Randolph Blackwell's account is given via a memo writ-

ten by Jack Minnis and based on a telephone call Blackwell made to Wiley Branton at 4:00 a.m. on March 1, 1963. Series VI, Voter Education Project, reel 177, SRC Papers, Atlanta University. Moses later told a congressional committee: "They left a tattoo of 13 bullet holes along the car." *CR Hearings,* House Judiciary, 1,268.
20. The Reverend Edwin King, unpublished memoir in possession of the author.
21. *Mississippi Free Press* 2, no. 13 (March 9, 1963): 4.
22. Timothy Jenkins, interview in Howell Raines, ed., *My Soul Is Rested* (New York: G. P. Putnam, 1977), 230–31.
23. SNCC news release dated November 29, 1964, CR Collection, SHSW.
24. The *Mississippi Free Press* boasted a banner headline entitled, "Vow All-Out Vote Drive in LeFlore," and printed a facsimile of the telegram. 2, no. 13 (March 9, 1963).
25. *New York Times,* March 2, 1963, 4.
26. A few months later, in May 1963, Moses would comment on some of the items in the proposed legislation, particularly the presumption that all registrants possess a sixth-grade education when the state made no attempt to ensure that for every black. *CR Hearings,* House Judiciary, May 28, 1963, 1,256.
27. *New York Times,* April 6, 1963, 20.
28. Robinson to Horton, March 25, 1963, Carl and Anne Braden Papers, MSS 6, box 55, folder 14, SHSW.
29. SNCC Newsletter 1, no. 16 (April 1, 1963), headed "Greenwood, Mississippi." Series VI, Voter Education Project, reel 173, SRC Papers, Atlanta University. All of these events happened in a period of four days, March 24–27, 1963. See also Jack Minnis, ed., "A Chronology of Violence and Intimidation in Mississippi Since 1961," SNCC publication, 12–13, CR Collection, SHSW.
30. The weekly edition of the *Mississippi Free Press* gave a day-by-day summary of events in Greenwood for the week of Tuesday, March 28, to Tuesday, April 2. 2, no. 17 (April 6, 1963): 1, 3. See also the *New York Times,* March 28, 1963, 4; March 29, 1963, 1; *Newsweek* 61 (April 8, 1963): 25–26; *CR Hearings,* House Judiciary, May 28, 1963, 1,300ff.
31. *Newsweek* 61 (April 8, 1963), 26.
32. *Mississippi Free Press,* April 6, 1963, 1,3. Later in the same week Judge Claude Clayton denied the Justice Department suit that asked for an injunction to stop interfering with blacks attempting to register.

33. James Forman, *The Making of Black Revolutionaries* (New York: Macmillan, 1972), 299–303.

34. Lawrence Guyot, November 23, 1966, Jackson, Miss., interview by Romaine, 82. See also the *Mississippi Free Press*, "Diary of Greenwood," 3, no. 17 (April 11, 1964): 1, 3; *New York Times*, April 5, 1963, 16.

35. Clayborne Carson, *In Struggle: SNCC and the Black Awakening of the 1960s* (Cambridge, Mass.: Harvard University Press, 1981), 86–87.

36. Robert H. Brisbane, *Black Activism: Racial Revolution in the United States, 1954–1970* (Valley Forge, Pa: Judson Press, 1974), 81. The *New York Times* was filing optimistic reports about the future of voter registration; dozens of reporters were covering incidents for major news magazines and papers. See *New York Times*, July 16, 1963, 7; *Atlanta Daily World*, February 6, 1963, 2.

37. *New York Times*, April 6, 1963, 20.

38. *New York Times*, April 6, 1963. At the end of that week, Gregory was turned back with a group attempting to reach the court house to register. Again, a police dog was there but taken away once news photographers began taking pictures. *Mississippi Free Press* 2, no. 17 (April 6, 1963): 3. Later King called Gregory to Birmingham. This request was followed by a telephone conversation with President Kennedy, who called to plead, *"Please* don't go down to Birmingham. We've got it all solved. Dr. King is wrong, what he's doing." And Gregory immediately went to Birmingham. Gregory, interview in Raines, *My Soul Is Rested*, 291–93.

39. The government's position is best illustrated in Burke Marshall, *Federalism and Civil Rights* (New York: Columbia University Press, 1964). See also, Neil R. McMillen, "Black Enfranchisement in Mississippi: Federal Enforcement and Black Protest in the 1960s," *Journal of Southern History* 53, no. 3 (August 1977): 358–59.

40. For a summary, largely positive, of the Kennedy administration's civil rights record, see Carl M. Brauer, *John F. Kennedy and the Second Reconstruction* (New York: Columbia University Press, 1977), 318–20.

41. *Jet* 23 (April 18, 1963): 23; Burke Marshall to Robert F. Kennedy, March 11, 1963, Box 16; March 29, 1963, box 3; Marshall to John F. Kennedy, April 8, 1963, box 23, Lee White Papers, John F. Kennedy Presidential Library, Dorcester, Mass.; *New York Times*, April 4, 1963, 16. The effort to help blacks in the

county learn the intricacies of voter registration was considerable; eight people taught separate classes, four in Greenwood, two in Itta Bena, and two in Ruleville, summing to 150 at a time. All classes were held in churches. *Mississippi Free Press*, 2, no. 17 (April 6, 1963): 3.
42. September 3, 1966, Knoxville, Tenn., Interview by Romaine, 23. This is an unedited version; copy in Mississippi Department of Archives and History.
43. During the spring, over 3,000 demonstrators were arrested in Birmingham, and during the whole of 1963 some 930 demonstrations in 115 cities in eleven Southern states resulted in over 20,000 arrests. Carson, *In Struggle*, 90.

Notes to Chapter Six

1. James Forman, *The Making of Black Revolutionaries* (New York: Macmillan, 1972), 305–7.
2. As Harvard Sitkoff notes, the median income for a black family in Mississippi was less than fifteen hundred dollars, and one out of twenty blacks registered to vote. Sitkoff, *The Struggle for Black Equality, 1954–1980* (New York: Hill and Wang, 1981), 168. See also August Meier, "Negro Protest Movements and Organization," *The Black Man in America Since Reconstruction*, ed. David M. Reimers (New York: Thomas Y. Crowell, 1970), 244–45.
3. *Civil Rights Hearings before Subcommittee No. 5 of the Committee on the Judiciary, House of Representatives*, serial no. 4, pt. 2 (Washington, D.C.: U.S. Government Printing Office, 1963), May 28, 1963, "SNCC Fieldwork in Mississippi," 1278–79. Hereafter cited as *CR Hearings*, House Judiciary. Moses, "Report to Voter Education Project of the Southern Regional Council," December 1962, Series VI, Voter Education Project, reel 177, Southern Regional Council Papers, Civil Rights Microfilm Collection, Woodruff Library, Atlanta University, Atlanta, Ga. (hereafter cited as SRC Papers, Atlanta University).
4. SNCC news release dated June 1, 1963, and headed "Arson Charges Recessed by Cox," Civil Rights Collection, Social Action Vertical File, MSS 577, State Historical Society of Wisconsin (hereafter cited as CR Collection, SHSW).
5. Hartman Turnbow, interview, Howell Raines, *My Soul Is Rested* (New York: G. P. Putnam, 1977), 265. Turnbow is an example of the poor rural farmer who came to be more and more the

infantry of the young SNCC civil rights workers. But in joining with SNCC workers who practiced nonviolence, these rural blacks did not themselves remain nonviolent in the face of attack. Meier, "Negro Protest Movements and Organizations," 244–45.

6. Greenwood, *Commonwealth,* May 10, 1963, 2. The *Mississippi Free Press* on May 25, 1963, reported that the deputy had told the Department of Justice that Moses was arrested because his camera looked "suspicious." 2, no. 24, 1.

7. Fay Bennett to Hon. Robert F. Kennedy, May 9, 1963, Series VI, Voter Education Project, reel 179, SRC Papers, Atlanta University. See also the *New York Times,* May 10, 1963, which included a number of other stories concerning civil rights arrests and racial incidents in Birmingham, Nashville, and Raleigh picked up from the wire services.

8. SNCC Newsletter, undated, CR Collection, SHSW.

9. *CR Hearings,* House Judiciary, May 28, 1963, 1,254, 1,256; *Mississippi Free Press* 2, no. 38 (August 31, 1963): 3. The Voting Rights Act of 1965, passed by Congress two years later, would forbid literacy tests as qualification for voting. John Doar and Dorothy Landsberg, "The Performance of the FBI in Investigating Violations of Federal Laws Protecting the Right to Vote— 1960–1967" (Unpublished essay, 1971), 18. Copy in the John F. Kennedy Presidential Library, Dorcester, Mass. (hereafter cited as JFK Library).

Because adult education for blacks simply did not exist in Mississippi, SNCC's voter registration classes became a substitute, educating blacks about current events, health, and economic issues. For the majority, the classes began lessons in basic literacy. The most important achievement was that the blacks were taught to know their own self-worth and power.

10. *Public Papers of the Presidents of the United States,* John F. Kennedy, 1963: 469. (Washington, D.C.: Federal Register Division, National Archives and Records Service, General Services Administration.)

11. *Mississippi Free Press* 2, no. 24 (May 25, 1963): 1.

12. Seth Cagin and Philip Dray, *We Are Not Afraid: The Story of Goodman, Schwerner, and Chaney and the Civil Rights Campaign in Mississippi* (New York: Macmillan, 1988), 306.

13. SNCC news release, July 8, 1963, CR Collection, SHSW; Edwin King Memoirs, pt. 5, in the possession of the author.

14. Greenwood *Commonwealth,* July 12, 1963.

15. *Mississippi Free Press* 2, no. 31 (July 13, 1963): 1.
16. *Mississippi Free Press,* July 13, 1963. See the text of Moses' message issued as a press release from SNCC headquarters in Atlanta; it is directed to Berl Bernhard, staff director of the U.S. Commission on Civil Rights. CR Collection, SHSW.

Byron de la Beckwith was a fertilizer salesman in Greenwood; he was tried twice for the killing of Medgar Evers and not convicted. A group of fourteen business and professional men directed a fund established by the Citizens' Council to help pay Beckwith's legal expenses.
17. Burke Marshall to Robert F. Kennedy, March 29, 1963, Marshall Papers, box 3, JFK Library.
18. Moses, interview by Anne Romaine, September 3, 1966, Knoxville, Tenn., in "The Mississippi Freedom Democratic Party Through August, 1964" (Master's thesis, University of Virginia, 1970), 64–65 (hereafter cited as Interview by Romaine).
19. Interview by Romaine, 64–65.
20. Richard Cummings, *The Pied Piper: Allard K. Lowenstein and the Liberal Dream* (New York: Grove Press, 1985), 41, 43–44, 52, 58, 73, 108, and passim.
21. Cummings, *The Pied Piper,* 129, 145, 229–33. Cummings suggests that Lowenstein went into Mississippi as a CIA operative to investigate civil rights activities. He points out that Lowenstein had no case trial experience and as an out-of-state counsel would be at a real disadvantage (232).
22. Clayborne Carson, *In Struggle: SNCC and the Black Awakening of the 1960s* (Cambridge, Mass.: Harvard University Press, 1981), 97; Cummings, *The Pied Piper,* 234–35; Doug McAdam, *Freedom Summer* (New York: Oxford University Press, 1988), 36–37.
23. Interview by Romaine, 66. The protesters were asserting their rights under a Mississippi law providing that a voter accidentally omitted from its election rolls could vote by submitting an affidavit showing qualification. One scholar has attributed the finding of this elusive law to Timothy Jenkins, a black law school student from Yale and a SNCC worker. William Chafe, "Allard Lowenstein and the Civil Rights Movement in Mississippi," talk presented at the Annual Meeting of the Organization of American Historians, Chicago, April 5, 1992.

Allard Lowenstein noted, "A Harvard law student was down there [Jackson] that summer doing research in Mississippi law and found a law which said that if you were illegally excluded

from registering, you could vote anyway. March 4, 1967, Charlottesville, Va., Interview by Romaine, 118.

24. The *Mississippi Free Press* asserted that the August "Vote for
Freedom" had elicited 27,000 unregistered blacks who cast protest ballots. 2, no. 41 (September 21, 1963): 1. Moses' reference
to "hundreds" makes the figure of 1,000 cited by Carson (*In
Struggle*, 97) more plausible.

25. SNCC news release dated August 1963 and entitled, "Delta Ne-
groes to Make Vote Attempts in August 6 Democratic Primary,"
CR Collection, SHSW; SNCC letter dated August 2, 1963, "Dear
Friend." The letter invites the recipient to serve as an official
SNCC observer and to participate in making a joint statement
to the press and any other individual statement. CR Collection,
SHSW.

26. *Mississippi Free Press* 2, no. 41 (September 21, 1963): 1.

27. For a detailed analysis of the genesis of this idea and its implementation, see Joseph A. Sinsheimer, "The Freedom Vote of
1963: New Strategies of Racial Protest in Mississippi," *Journal
of Southern History* 55, no. 2 (May 1989): 217–44. See also Cagin
and Dray, *We Are Not Afraid*, 104, 210–13. Lowenstein was also
a lecturer in political science. *Lowenstein: Acts of Courage and
Belief*, Gregory Stone and Douglas Lowenstein (New York: Harcourt Brace Jovanovich, 1983), 15.

28. See, for example, Forman, *The Making of Black Revolutionaries*,
331–36; Carson, *In Struggle*, 92–93; Taylor Branch, *Parting the
Waters: America in the King Years, 1954–63* (New York: Simon
and Schuster, 1988), 873–76; James Farmer, *Lay Bare the Heart:
An Autobiography of the Civil Rights Movement* (New York:
Arbor House, 1985), 243.

29. Thomas Gentile, *March on Washington: August 28, 1963* (Washington, D.C.: Dew Day Publishing, 1983), 160.

30. For a detailed description of SNCC's activities and its participation in the March on Washington, see Carson, *In Struggle*, 83–95.

31. SNCC Papers, Series XV, State Project Files 1960–68, box 104,
Martin Luther King, Jr. Center for Non-Violent Social Change,
Atlanta, Ga.

32. Moses has put the number of students from Stanford and Yale
at about eighty. The students brought to SNCC "the college
base of the white broad middle class country.... Again, that
was Lowenstein's specific dimension of contribution." Interview by Romaine, 69. An initial group of seventeen volunteers
from Yale went to Jackson in mid-October, and they were fol-

lowed by fifty more. Stanford sent fifteen volunteers. "Commitment in Mississippi," fund-raising statement, undated but notes that all students arrived on October 18, 1963. CR Collection, SHSW.

33. In an interview, SNCC member Lawrence Guyot denied emphatically that Lowenstein had originated the Freedom Vote project. He could not remember whose idea it had been. November 23, 1966, Jackson, Miss., interview by Romaine, 15. This unedited version is in the Mississippi Department of Archives and History (hereafter cited as MDAH). See also Carson, *In Struggle*, 97; Cummings, *The Pied Piper*, 234–36, 284.

34. Chafe, "Allard Lowenstein and the Civil Rights Movement in Mississippi," OAH Annual Meeting, April 5, 1992.

35. *Mississippi Free Press* 2, no. 39 (October 5, 1963): 1.

36. Bill Higgs met with Moses and Medgar Evers in Jackson and suggested the idea of running a black for a statewide office. He adds that the mock election followed "quite logically" from running Reverend Smith in 1962. William Higgs, January 12, 1967, Washington, D.C., Interview by Romaine, 282.

37. The *Mississippi Free Press* 2, no. 41 (September 21, 1963): 1.

38. "Two Run in Mississippi Freedom Vote," SNCC press release, October 1963, SNCC Papers, MDAH.

39. In June 1960 King had been assigned to a chain gang after inviting a black friend to the whites-only Jefferson Davis Hotel in downtown Montgomery. Cagin and Dray, *We Are Not Afraid*, 214. That same year the John Birch Society and the Citizens Council had his family run out of Vicksburg. In April 1963 Tougaloo College made him chaplain. Edwin King Memoirs, pt. 4, typescript copy in the possession of the author.

40. Edwin King Memoirs, pt. 4.

41. Donaldson, field report, Howard Zinn Papers, MSS 588, Box 1, Folder 22, Social Action Collection, SHSW.

42. About 75,000 to 80,000 participated; the *Mississippi Free Press* put the number at 90,000. 2, no. 47 (November 9, 1963): 1. See Carson, *In Struggle*, 98; Cummings, *The Pied Piper*, 240.

43. McMillen, "Commentary," in *The Civil Rights Movement in America*, ed. Charles W. Eagles (Jackson: University Press of Mississippi, 1986), 95.

44. Forman, *The Making of Black Revolutionaries*, 356.

45. Mendy Samstein believed that the organizational development achieved made the Summer Project realizable. "Notes on Mississippi," n.d. but c. 1964. Civil Rights Workers, Miscellaneous

Small Collections, SC 3093, SHSW (hereafter cited as SC, SHSW).

46. Edwin King Memoirs, pt. 16, 1.

47. "Federal Intervention Must Be Forced," *The Student Voice* 4 (December 9, 1963): 2. This was a weekly paper published out of Atlanta by SNCC.

48. Edwin King Memoirs, pt. 16.

49. *Mississippi Free Press* 2, no. 51 (November 30, 1963): 1.

50. Mary King, *Freedom Song* (New York: William Morrow, 1987), 243. The conference was held November 29 through December 1. Over 500 attended; James Baldwin delivered the keynote speech. *The Student Voice*, December 9, 1963, 2. Moses' talk at the SNCC conference is quoted in the *Mississippi Free Press*; here he asserts that change in the lives of black Americans and their assurance of civil rights will come only through "a change in the power structure." And this will result only from pressure on the part of the federal government. 2, no. 52 (December 7, 1963): 8.

51. Allard Lowenstein noted two lessons learned from the Freedom Vote: "If you wanted to change Mississippi you had to do it with outside help ... [and] the vote was the most effective, vulnerable point in the established power." Interview by Romaine, 120.

52. Samstein, "Notes on Mississippi," SHSW.

53. "Schedule for COFO Workshop," November 11–17, 1963, Greenville, Miss. Papers of Highlander Research and Education Center, Box 41, folder 6, SHSW.

54. Samstein, "Notes on Mississippi," SHSW.

55. Nearly three years later he would recall that at a workshop in Greenville sponsored by the Highlander Center the debate on the Freedom Vote campaign and the use of out-of-state white volunteers first emerged and was debated. Interview by Romaine, 71.

56. Memorandum entitled "Outline for COFO Program—1964," to executive committee from Moses regarding the Mississippi project, n.d., CR Collection, SHSW.

57. "Outline for COFO Program—1964," CR Collection, SHSW.

58. "SNCC Field Work in Mississippi, Spring 1963," Howard Zinn Papers, box 1, folder 21, SHSW. Moses was the oldest of the group; most were aged nineteen and twenty.

59. Cummings, *The Pied Piper*, 237. Cummings cites a telephone interview with Moses as his source here. He notes that the

Raleigh Times on April 21, 1964, reported Lowenstein as dinner guest of Senator and Mrs. William Fulbright at a gathering in Washington, D.C., along with the president and his wife, Defense Secretary Robert McNamara, and Adlai Stevenson (257). See also Federal Bureau of Investigation: file 105–103168, vol. 2, U.S. Department of Justice, Washington, D.C.

60. Wiley Branton to Aaron Henry and Robert Moses, November 12, 1963, series VI, Voter Education Project, reel 174, SRC Papers, Atlanta University. See also Pat Watters and Reese Cleghorn, *Climbing Jacob's Ladder: The Arrival of Negroes in Southern Politics* (New York: Harcourt, Brace & World, 1967), 213.

61. Branton to Henry, September 5, 1962, series VI, Voter Education Project, reel 177, SRC Papers, Atlanta University.

62. Moses to Branton, October 12, 1963, series VI, Voter Education Project, reel 179, SRC Papers, Atlanta University.

63. Telephone memo to file by Branton dated October 15, 1963, series VI, Voter Education Project, reel 179, SRC Papers, Atlanta University.

64. Interview by Neil McMillen, April 14, 1972, Ruleville, Miss. Mississippi Oral History Program of the University of Southern Mississippi 31 (1977), 2 (hereafter cited as Oral History Program, USM).

65. *Mississippi Free Press* 3, no. 15 (March 28, 1964): 1.

66. Howard Zinn, *SNCC: The New Abolitionists* (Boston: Beacon Press, 1964), 183. Carson remarks that SNCC veterans already had fears that the organization was moving in a more radical and more separatist direction. Carson, *In Struggle*, 100. Perhaps Zinn, himself involved in SNCC, believed that his book should not raise issues of disharmony.

67. Quoted in Robert Penn Warren, *Who Speaks for the Negro?* (New York: Random House, 1965), 95–96.

68. Quoted in Warren, *Who Speaks for the Negro?*, 97.

69. Lowenstein, Interview by Romaine, 131.

70. Lawrence Guyot, interview in Raines, *My Soul Is Rested*, 286–87.

71. Sally Belfrage, *Freedom Summer* (New York: Viking Press, 1965), 62. Itta Bena, a small town populated by fewer than 3,000 people, is a few miles west of Greenwood.

72. Samstein, "Notes on Mississippi," SC 3093, SHSW.

73. Samstein, "Notes on Mississippi."

74. Quoted in editor's note in Raines, *My Soul Is Rested*, 286–87.

75. Edwin King Memoirs, 83.

76. Interview by Michael Garvey, March 29, 1977, Cleveland, Miss., 184 (1981), 67. Oral History Program, USM.
77. Edwin King Memoirs, pt. 12-B, 7.
78. On July 14, 1964, Sandra (Casey) Hayden circulated to the Jackson FD staff notes on a conversation with Al Lowenstein; the copy has the notation "Bob" at the top. Seven major points are outlined, ranging from the representation on the MFDP delegation to the makeup of the advisory committee to the platform. CR Collection, SHSW.
79. Cagin and Dray, *We Are Not Afraid*, 225.
80. See the discussion in Forman, *The Making of Black Revolutionaries*, 356–58. According to Forman, Lowenstein represented the "liberal-labor syndrome" who sought to protect SNCC from becoming too radical. He noted that Lowenstein, UAW counsel Joe Rauh, Michael Harrington, and Bayard Rustin, Martin Luther King, Jr.'s adviser, met several times during 1962 and 1963 to determine action to keep communist influences within SNCC at a minimum.
81. Hollis Watkins, interview in Henry Hampton and Steve Fayer, eds., *Voices of Freedom: An Oral History of the Civil Rights Movement from the 1950s Through the 1980s* (New York: Bantam Books, 1990), 182–83.
82. Mary Aickin Rothschild, *A Case of Black and White: Northern Volunteers and the Southern Freedom Summers, 1964–1965* (Westport, Conn.: Greenwood Press, 1982), 26–27.
83. "Notes on Mississippi Staff Meeting, Greenville, November 14–16," CR Collection, SHSW.
84. "Notes on Mississippi Staff Meeting."
85. Lawrence Guyot, interview in Raines, *My Soul Is Rested*, 286–87.
86. According to Lowenstein, the SNCC Mississippi or Atlanta staff also decided at one point to allow only a ratio of fifty blacks to six whites in the Summer Project. Interview by Romaine, 128–29. The ratio, in fact, was nearly reversed: almost nine whites to one black.
87. Carson, *In Struggle*, 99.
88. Carson, *In Struggle*, 100.
89. Transcript of an interview (partially edited) with Moses on May 19, 1986, for the television series, "Eyes on the Prize," transcript SR 1, CR 405, show 5, 15, produced by Blackside, Inc., Boston, Mass.
90. McAdam, *Freedom Summer*, 38–39.

91. The *Mississippi Free Press* reported in grueling detail the killing of Allen, shot in the head three times by a shotgun and found in the driveway of his home in Liberty by his son. 3, no. 10 (February 15, 1964): 1.
92. Moses interview, May 19, 1986, "Eyes on the Prize," 15–16.

Notes to Chapter 7

1. SNCC paper entitled "The 'Freedom Ballot' in Mississippi," undated but reference is made to "roughly where we stand in the summer of 1964." Civil Rights Collection, Social Action Vertical File, MSS 577, State Historical Society of Wisconsin (hereafter cited as CR Collection, SHSW).
2. Bob Moses, interview by Anne Romaine, September 3, 1966, Knoxville, Tenn., in "The Mississippi Freedom Democratic Party Through August, 1964" (Master's thesis, University of Virginia, 1970), 72 (hereafter cited as Interview by Romaine).
3. Branton to Aaron Henry and Bob Moses, November 12, 1963. Copied on this letter were the names of Roy Wilkins, James Forman, Martin Luther King, Jr., Whitney Young, and James Farmer Southern Regional Council Papers, series VI, Voter Education Project, reel 179, Civil Rights Microfilm Collection, Woodruff Library, Atlanta University, Atlanta, Ga. (hereafter cited as SRC Papers, Atlanta University). See also Calvin Trillin, "Letter from Jackson," *The New Yorker* 40 (August 29, 1964): 95.
4. Clayborne Carson, *In Struggle: SNCC and the Black Awakening of the 1960s* (Cambridge, Mass.: Harvard University Press, 1981), 96.
5. *Mississippi Free Press* 3, no. 6 (January 18, 1964): 2.
6. "Minutes, COFO Convention," February 9, 1964, Lois Chaffee, Recorder, Social Action Collection, MSS 191, box 1, folder 3, SHSW.
7. SNCC News Release (#24), March 20, 1964, CR Collection, SHSW.
8. *The Student Voice* 5 (March 3, 1964): 3.
9. Undated memorandum, but the letter requests a response before April 18, 1964, SNCC Papers, series XV, State Project Files, 1960–68, box 104, Martin Luther King, Jr. Center for Non-Violent Social Change, Atlanta, Ga. (hereafter cited as MLK Center).
    On April 28, Moses, Aaron Henry, and Dave Dennis wrote

again to this group announcing a hearing in Washington on June 9 concerning intimidation of blacks participating in civil rights activities and a demonstration scheduled for the next day. The idea was to effect an audience with the president. COFO memorandum, April 28, 1964, CR Collection, SHSW.

10. The letter suggests that the meeting take place on June 18 or 19; it was forwarded to Lee White. White House Central Files, box 600, Lyndon Baines Johnson Presidential Library (hereafter cited as WHCF, LBJ Library).

11. Betty Garman, Northern Campus Coordinator for SNCC to Frank Millspaugh, National Student Association (Philadelphia), June 3, 1964. Mississippi Freedom Democratic Party Records, 1962–71, MSS 586, micro 788, reel 1, Social Action Collection, SHSW (hereafter referred to as MFDP Records, SHSW).

12. Moses to Albert Shanker, vice president, United Federal of Teachers, March 10, 1964, CR Collection, SHSW. Identical letters were sent to other UFT officials, including President Charles Cogen, Dick Parrish, Sid Harris, and Ted Bleeker. See also Moses, Aaron Henry, and Dave Dennis to "Dear Faculty Member," dated April 8, 1964 with a cover memorandum to "Dear Department Chairman" from Moses. MFDP Papers, box 5, file 7, MLK Center.

13. Edwin King Memoirs, pt. 12–B.

14. The release listed the following schools where Freedom Centers had been established: University of California, Michigan, Southern California, Oregon, North Carolina, Pennsylvania, Illinois, Southern Illinois, Harvard, Yale, Howard, Stanford, Atlanta, Oberlin, Morehouse, Spelman, Emory, Radcliffe, Queens, Clark, Morris Brown, and Pomona. SNCC news release (#53), CR Collection, SHSW.

15. Moses to Lowenstein, n.d., Alfred E. Lowenstein Papers, no. 4340, subseries 2.14, Box 32, folder 353. Southern Historical Collection, Library of the University of North Carolina, Chapel Hill.

16. *San Francisco Chronicle*, December 7, 1963, 4.

17. Carson, *In Struggle*, 107–8.

18. See, for example, Sandra C. Hayden (SNCC Mississippi Staff) to Jon L. Regier, executive secretary, Division of Home Missions of the National Council of Churches, February 14, 1964. SNCC Papers, box 12, file 16, MLK Center.

19. Edwin King Memoirs, pt. 6–B.

20. Edwin King Memoirs, pt. 6–B, 2. For a detailed chronicle of a

Jackson church's efforts to preserve the exclusionary practice, see W. J. Cunningham, *Agony at Galloway* (Jackson: University Press of Mississippi, 1980).

21. Several college-based "Friends of SNCC" organizations also distributed reprints and added information about the Mississippi project, urging support. For example, an article by Richard Woodley, "It Will Be a Hot Summer in Mississippi" that appeared in *The Reporter* was distributed by the Philadelphia area college-based "Friends of SNCC," 30 (May 21, 1964): 21–24.

22. SNCC Papers, CR Collection, SHSW.

23. Edwin King Memoirs, "COFO Office," 90, 92.

24. David Wise, "The Campaign to Destroy Martin Luther King," *New York Review of Books,* November 11, 1976, 38–42.

25. Carson, *In Struggle,* 106–7.

26. *Jackson Daily News,* August 31, 1962; *Courier-Journal* (Louisville, Ky.), September 1, 1962; *Advertiser* (Montgomery, Ala.), September 2, 1962. See also the response printed in the *Mississippi Free Press,* no. 39 (September 8, 1962): 1.

    Lowenstein and Joseph Rauh, who would become counsel for the Mississippi Freedom Democratic Party, came to suspect SNCC of communist infiltration because of its association with such groups as the National Lawyers Guild and SCEF.

27. Carl Braden to Jim Dombrowski and John M. Coe, SCEF, September 2, 1962. Carl and Anne Braden Papers, MSS 6, box 55, folder 13, SHSW.

28. Braden to Moses and Higgs, September 7, 1962, Braden Papers, box 55, folder 13, SHSW.

29. Anne Braden to Moses, September 25, 1962; Anne Braden to Wiley Branton, September 25, 1962; Anne Braden to Moses, October 24, 1962; Moses to Anne Braden (bottom of Braden letter), Braden Papers, box 55, folder 13, SHSW.

30. Moses to Fay Bennett, February 24, 1963, CR Collection, SHSW.

31. Moses to Wiley Branton, Roy Wilkins, Andrew Young, James Forman, undated but stamped by receiving office August 2, 1963; Moses refers to a copy of a voter registration report for Hattiesburg for the week ending July 28. In the memorandum, he notes, "the Department of Justice won an order from a three judge court of the fifth circuit, setting forth rules for fair registration of Negroes in that county. It is the first such order handed down in Mississippi." He urges a concerted drive to register blacks before the 1964 elections and adds that because of the Justice Department's statewide suit, the government will

be watching events closely. Series VI, Voter Education Project, reel 179, SRC Papers, Atlanta University.

32. SNCC news release, February 21, 1964, headed "Over 100 Ministers Aid Mississippi Vote Drive," CR Collection, SHSW; Lawrence Guyot, November 23, 1966, Jackson, Miss., Interview by Romaine, 104–5.

    John Doar relates a similar long-term victory over registration records in Bolivar County. John Doar and Dorothy Landsberg, "The Performance of the FBI in Investigating Violations of Federal Laws Protecting the Right to Vote—1960–1967" (unpublished essay, 1971), nn. 21–22. Copy in the John F. Kennedy Presidential Library, Dorcester, Mass.

33. Moses put the number of ministers at "about sixty." Moses, 74. See also Mendy Samstein, September 4, 1966, Knoxville, Tenn. Interview by Romaine, 143. The Hattiesburg event brought its measure of repression. Moses was arrested and another black, Oscar Chase, was charged with "leaving the scene of an accident" and was badly beaten in jail that same day. Howard Zinn, "Incident in Hattiesburg," *The Nation* 198 (May 18, 1964): 501–4.

34. SNCC news release dated February 21, 1964, CR Collection, SHSW. The *Atlanta Inquirer*, March 7, 1964, carried an article headed "KKK on Rise in Miss.," and outlined the many beatings, shootings, and cross-burnings throughout Mississippi and the South. In the article Moses is quoted as saying that the rights organizations were "issuing a call for 1,000 students, ministers and educators to participate in a 'Mississippi Freedom Summer' program." See also *New York Times*, March 16, 1964, 26.

35. See, for example, *The Student Voice* 5, no. 8 (March 3, 1964): 2; the Freedom Days resulted in bringing hundreds of Negroes to local courthouses to attempt to register.

36. See, for instance, an internal SNCC paper by Charles Sherrod, summarizing the reasons for establishing a separate political party: "The Freedom Democratic Party was formed through precinct, county, district, and state conventions. An attempt to register with the state was frustrated.... We had tried to work within the structure of the State Party.... In eight precincts in six different counties, we went to polling stations before the time legally designated for the precinct meeting, ... but were unable to find any evidence of a meeting.... In six different counties where we found the white precinct meetings, we were

excluded from the meetings." SNCC Papers, box 107, folder 9, MLK Center.

37. 3, no. 15 (March 28, 1964): 1. See also "Meeting," *The New Yorker* 40 (April 11, 1964): 36.

38. Interview by Romaine, 145–46.

39. "The Freedom Democratic Party was established in April of this year [1964]. At a meeting on April 26, approximately 200 delegates established a temporary State Executive Committee of the Freedom Democratic Party." SNCC paper entitled "The 'Freedom Ballot' in Mississippi," CR Collection, SHSW. This paper also gives the date for the new party's district caucuses, July 24, and for the state convention, July 26.

40. *Jackson Daily News*, March 16, 1964; *Mississippi Free Press*, March 28, 1964, 1. A detailed SNCC paper entitled "Freedom Candidates—Mississippi" describes the plan for freedom registration and voting in the June primary and November elections in Mississippi and includes brief biographical sketches of the four candidates. See also SNCC news release (#51) dated May 27, 1964, headed "Mississippi Voters Could Choose Negro Candidates," CR Collection, SHSW. One of the legislators challenged was Sen. John Stennis, opposed by a black woman from Hattiesburg, Victoria Gray. Mrs. Hamer, contemplating defeat, announced she would challenge the incumbent's right to sit in the House. *Mississippi Free Press* 3, no. 17 (April 11, 1964): 1. In November, when they decided to run as independents, the State Board of Elections would reject their petitions.

41. Lawrence Guyot and Mike Thelwell, "The Politics of Necessity and Survival in Mississippi," *Freedomways* 6, no. 1 (1966): 131–32.

42. Higgs, January 12, 1967, Washington, D.C., Interview by Romaine, 286.

43. Henry Hampton and Steve Fayer, eds., *Voices of Freedom: An Oral History of the Civil Rights Movement from the 1950s Through the 1980s* (New York: Bantam Books, 1990), 196. Rauh confirms Moses' question: [Moses] "asked whether there would be support for the Freedom Party at Atlantic City.... I answered the question myself and answered it affirmatively." Later, at the UAW Convention in Atlantic City, Rauh met with Moses, Ella Baker, and a Michigan Democratic National Committee member, Mildred Jeffrey. A third meeting with Moses and others took place in mid-May after the Americans for Democratic Action convention, which unanimously approved the MFDP chal-

lenge. Rauh, June 16, 1967, Washington, D.C., Interview by Romaine, 301–3.

44. Rauh, Interview by Romaine, 301.

45. Walter Tillow, September 4, 1966, Knoxville, Tenn., Interview by Romaine, 187. Tillow also notes that the NAACP did not contribute funds to the MFDP.

46. CR Collection, SHSW. The Hederman papers were the conservative morning daily, the Jackson *Clarion-Ledger*, and the evening paper, the *Daily News*, fervent supporters of the Citizens' Council.

47. Lowenstein, March 4, 1967, Charlottesville, Va., Interview by Romaine, 126, 129–31. Edwin King in his interview with Romaine discusses in some detail the relationship of the NAACP with SNCC in the summer project and MFDP, particularly after Medgar Evers's murder. September 5, 1966, Knoxville, Tenn., 255–62. According to King, the summer project suffered both financially and in personnel from the eagerness of the Mississippi NAACP under Charles Evers to capitalize in the media and its funneling of contributions for its own purposes in the guise of being one of the civil rights organizations in COFO supporting the Project. Edwin King Memoirs, pt. 4.

48. Mary King, *Freedom Song* (New York: William Morrow, 1987), 310.

49. King, *Freedom Song*, 319–20.

50. I am indebted to Edwin King's detailed analysis of Lowenstein and his role—both actual and expected—in Freedom Summer. Memoirs, pt. 12-B, 7–28.

51. Jerry Tecklin Papers, Social Action Collection, MSS 538, box 1, folder 5, SHSW.

52. Letter to "Dear Faculty Member," April 8, 1964, MFDP Papers, box 5, file 7, MLK Center. A typical letter, dated April 6, 1964, begins: "This letter is being sent to hundreds of faculty members across the country in an effort to involve the intellectual community in America's most serious social problem—racial discrimination." The letter is signed jointly by Moses, Aaron Henry, and Dave Dennis. Howard Zinn Papers, Social Action Collection, MSS 588, box 1, folder 22, SHSW.

53. Richard Cummings, *The Pied Piper: Allard K. Lowenstein and the Liberal Dream* (New York: Grove Press, 1985), 259. See also Doug McAdam, *Freedom Summer* (New York: Oxford University Press, 1988), 50–51, 292–93n. A group of teachers from New

York City, after working in Mississippi, returned and continued to help the project through the United Federation of Teachers. Eric Morton, materials coordinator for the summer project, stated the one condition required on each volunteer: "train a Mississippian to do whatever work he was doing and eventually work himself out and the Mississippian in." Morton, "Tremor in the Iceberg," *Freedomways* 5, no. 2 (1965): 319–20.

54. See, for example, Donald M. Winkelman to Moses, August 5, 1964. It begins "Prof. Roland, Duerksen, Rabbi Joseph Radensky, and I were planning to travel to Mississippi to join COFO for ten days to two weeks." CR Collection, SHSW.

55. King, *Freedom Song*, 322.

56. King, *Freedom Song*, 318. A month earlier, on May 6, Moses testified before the State Advisory Committee to the U.S. Civil Rights Commission. In recent months, he said, five blacks had been killed in southeast Mississippi, yet no arrests had been made. SNCC news release (#50), May 16, 1964, CR Collection, SHSW.

Early in 1964 Howard Zinn questioned the limits of nonviolence and called for a permanent federal presence in the Delta. Zinn, "The Limits of Nonviolence," *Freedomways* 4, no. 1 (1964): 145.

57. *New York Times*, May 17, 1964, 66ff.

58. Richard Woodley, "It Will Be a Hot Summer in Mississippi," *The Reporter* 30, no. 11 (May 21, 1964): 21, 23–24.

59. Burt Schoor, "Mississippi Summer: State Appears Ready to Tolerate Peaceful Civil Rights 'Invasion,'" *Wall Street Journal*, May 25, 1964. The state's attorney general, however, advised that the bill go no farther, because it could adversely affect the state's defense in pending federal civil rights cases.

60. "Allen's Army," *Newsweek* 63 (February 24, 1964): 30.

61. Moses to the president, undated but reference is made in the letter to "next weekend, June 22." A notation dated July 15, 1964, on the letter indicates it was forwarded to the Justice Department for a direct reply; "6/17" is noted also by hand at the top of the letter. Robert Moses name file, box 600, WHCF, LBJ Library.

62. James Atwater, "If We Can Crack Mississippi . . . ," *Saturday Evening Post* 237 (July 30, 1964): 16. Atwater put the number of college volunteers at 450. That the first group, sent to work on voter registration, totaled 175; the second group, assigned to

community centers and freedom schools, was larger—275. (See 15–17) Only about one hundred of the nine hundred who would come at different times throughout that summer were black.

63. Interview by Emily Stoper in *The Student Nonviolent Coordinating Committee: The Growth of Radicalism in a Civil Rights Organization*, rev. ed. (Brooklyn, N.Y.: Carlson Publishing, 1989), 213.

64. Dave Dennis, interview in Howell Raines, ed., *My Soul Is Rested* (New York: G. P. Putnam, 1977), 274.

65. SNCC News Release (#53), CR Collection, SHSW. This press release, issued on May 27, 1964, announced the official beginning of the Mississippi Summer Project as July 1. See also *New York Times*, July 1, 1964, 23.

66. Zellner, New England Regional Office, Boston Friends of SNCC, to Jackson COFO office, April 9, 1964, MFDP Records, reel 2, SHSW.

67. Zellner, reel 2, MFDP Records, SHSW.

68. The application, a three-page questionnaire, asked about the applicant's arrest history, civil rights activities, and contacts who would be useful "in securing you[r] release from jail if you were arrested or who could help with publicity about your activities." MFDP Papers, box 5, file 2, MLK Center.

69. Cleveland Sellers, *The River of No Return* (New York: William Morrow, 1973), 82.

70. Seth Cagin and Philip Dray, *We Are Not Afraid: The Story of Goodman, Schwerner, and Chaney and the Civil Rights Campaign in Mississippi* (New York: Macmillan, 1988), 225–26; see also Sally Belfrage, *Freedom Summer* (New York: Viking Press, 1965), 9–11, 81.

71. Sellers, *The River of No Return*, 82.

72. Atwater, "If We Can Crack Mississippi," 18. According to Staughton Lynd, director of the Freedom School project in Mississippi, 2,500 black children attended the schools staffed by 250 Northern volunteer coordinators. "The Freedom Schools: Concept and Organization," *Freedomways* 5, no. 2 (1965): 302.

73. Samstein, interview by Romaine, 156. See also Morton, "Tremor in the Iceberg," 320.

74. See Stoper, *The Student Nonviolent Coordinating Committee*, 88–89, 102–3, 105–13 and passim. She argues that well before Stokely Carmichael's enunciation of "black power," SNCC's major intention was to raise black consciousness. Her extensive use of interviews collected in the late 1960s makes her evidence

compelling. It is possible, however, that the memories of her sources were filtered through their familiarity with the rhetorical violence into which SNCC members had descended by the time she interviewed them. Moses' use of the concept of black consciousness was quite different from Carmichael's concept of black power.

75. *New York Times*, June 21, 1964, 64.
76. Cagin and Dray, *We Are Not Afraid*, 29–30. See also Belfrage, *Freedom Summer*, 9–11; King, *Freedom Song*, 372–77.
77. Anne Braden, draft article, dateline Meridian, Miss., 1964, Braden Papers, box 56, folder 1, SHSW.
78. Belfrage, *Freedom Summer*, 10–11; Carson, *In Struggle*, 114; Atwater, "If We Can Crack Mississippi," 17. The phrase "the closed society" was coined by Prof. James Silver, a University of Mississippi professor, when he gave a presidential address to the Southern Historical Association at Asheville, North Carolina, on November 7, 1963, and the following year published *Mississippi: The Closed Society* (New York: Harcourt, Brace & World, 1964).
79. Edwin King Memoirs. The time is fall of 1963.
80. Belfrage, *Freedom Summer*, 11.
81. See the interview with Dave Dennis in Raines, *My Soul Is Rested*, 275–76. The story of the three rights workers is ably told by Cagin and Dray, *We Are Not Afraid*.
82. Belfrage, *Freedom Summer*, 22. Moses also pointed out that Harvard University was the largest stockholder of Mid-South Utilities, holding company for Mississippi Power and Light, a major utility on whose board sat several Citizens Council leaders. Several student volunteers were from Harvard. Moses was illustrating that the whole nation was deeply involved in the crimes of Mississippi. Anne Braden, draft article, dateline Meridian, Miss., 1964, Braden Papers, box 56, folder 1, SHSW.
83. Belfrage, *Freedom Summer*, 22.
84. Edwin King Memoirs, pt. 4.
85. Belfrage, *Freedom Summer*, 25.
86. "Questions Raised by Moses," Transcript of a talk given by Moses at the fifth anniversary of SNCC and published in *The Movement* 1, no. 4 (April 1965). See also Lerone Bennett, Jr., "SNCC: Rebels With a Cause," *Ebony* 20 (July 1965): 193.
87. Steven Bingham, "Mississippi Letter," typescript, 1964, 7. Social Action Collection, Civil Rights Workers, Miscellaneous Small Collections, 1963–1967, SHSW. Ed King recalled, "All

of us in Freedom Summer leadership were targets and [we] expected murder attempts." Edwin King Memoirs.

88. Letter from Casey Hayden to the author, May 6, 1993.

89. Although John Doar in the Justice Department, immediately alerted, indicated that he would tell the FBI to investigate, the local agents responded that they had been given no such authority. It took at least twenty-four hours for the bureau to begin investigating the disappearance. This lag in action by the FBI was typical. "Memo to Mississippi Summer Project Contacts from Robert Moses," June 27, 1964, CR Collection, SHSW.

90. Belfrage, *Freedom Summer*, 15.

91. COFO Memorandum dated June 27, 1964, from Moses as COFO program director, SNCC Mississippi project director, and Summer Project director; COFO Memorandum to "Parents of all Mississippi Summer Volunteers" signed by Moses as director. CR Collection, SHSW.

92. MFDP Papers, appendix A, box 5, file 12, MLK Center.

93. SNCC Press Release, June 27, 1964. MFDP Papers, appendix A, box 5, file 12, MLK Center.

94. See the description of the search in Cagin and Dray, *We Are Not Afraid*, 393–402.

95. November 23, 1966, Jackson, Miss., Interview by Romaine, 288.

96. Moses hoped that federal intervention, if it came, would secure the rights of all Southern blacks, not just the middle class. See the comments concerning the reaction of the Mississippi black middle class to the activities of SNCC in King, *Freedom Song*, 163.

97. *Newsweek* 64 (July 13, 1964): 20.

98. Atwater, "If We Can Crack Mississippi," *Saturday Evening Post*, 18.

99. Moses, his wife Dona Richards, whom he had married in December 1963, and the Reverend Ralph Abernathy also spoke. *Free Press* 3, no. 32 (July 25, 1964): 2.

100. Quoted in Belfrage, *Freedom Summer*, 182–83.

101. Belfrage, *Freedom Summer*, 183; Stoper, *The Student Nonviolent Coordinating Committee*, 84.

102. "Moses of Mississippi Raises Some Universal Questions," *Pacific Scene* 5 (February 1965): 2.

103. COFO internal document entitled "Mississippi Summer Project: Running Summary of Incidents," CR Collection, SHSW.

104. Cagin and Dray, *We Are Not Afraid*, 384–85. The complainants included Rita Schwerner, Fannie Lou Hamer, and Edwin King.

105. Quoted in Kenneth O'Reilly, *"Racial Matters": The FBI's Secret File on Black America, 1960–1972* (New York: Free Press, 1989), 158.

106. Neil R. McMillen, "Black Enfranchisement in Mississippi: Federal Enforcement and Black Protest in the 1960s," *Journal of Southern History* 43 (August 1977): 367.

107. Edwin King Memoirs, pts. 4 and 2, 12.

108. Samstein, "Prospectus for an Educational Workshop Program," [1964], Mendy Samstein Papers, 1963–1966, SC 3093, Civil Rights Workers, Miscellaneous Small Collection, SHSW.

109. Interview by Neil McMillen and George Burson, May 1, 1972, Clarksdale, Miss. Mississippi Oral History Program of the University of Southern Mississippi 33 (1980), 22, 76.

110. Quoted from an interview with Claude Sitton in Raines, *My Soul Is Rested*, 380; Lawrence Guyot, interview in Raines, *My Soul is Rested*, 288. Hoover described the Klan as "white scum."

111. Guyot, interview in Raines, *My Soul Is Rested*, 289.

112. Doar and Landsberg, "The Performance of the FBI," 47–48; see also *New York Times*, December 6, 1964, 14.

113. Edwin King Memoirs, pts. 4 and 6, 85–86.

114. Harvard Sitkoff, *The Struggle for Black Equality, 1954–1980* (New York: Straus and Giroux, 1981), 177.

115. Stephen B. Oates, *Let the Trumpet Sound: The Life of Martin Luther King, Jr.* (New York: Harper & Row, 1982), 301. The number of arrests and appeals pending in criminal proceedings prompted Moses in early September to establish a legal advisory committee, and COFO hired for a few months a staff counsel. The initial meeting was held in New York City on October 3, 1964, with Moses, Ella Baker, Dave Dennis, Arthur Kinoy, Ben Smith, and Bill Kunstler. Benjamin E. Smith Papers, Social Action Collection, MSS 513, box 1, folder 14, SHSW.

Notes to Chapter Eight

1. COFO news release, June 19, 1964, Civil Rights Collection, Social Action Vertical File, MSS 577, State Historical Society of Wisconsin, (hereafter cited as CR Collection, SHSW).

2. *Mississippi Free Press* 3, no. 33 (August 1, 1964): 2.

3. Joseph Rauh, interview by Anne Romaine, June 16, 1967, Washington, D.C., in "The Mississippi Freedom Democratic Party Through August, 1964" (Master's thesis, University of Virginia, 1970), 305 (hereafter cited as Interview by Romaine). A workshop including Rauh, Bill Higgs, and Walter Johnson from the University of Chicago had been planned for the Highlander Center as well. See Carole Merritt to Moses, July 11, 1964. Merritt was at the Institute for Policy Studies in Washington. CR Collection, SHSW.

4. "Over 800 Meet at MFDP Convention," *The Student Voice* 5 (August 12, 1964): 1. See the description of the convention with three hundred delegates attending, in Mary King, *Freedom Song* (New York: William Morrow, 1987), 341–42, 344.

5. For a brief analysis of the MFDP and its relation to the national Democratic party, see Christopher Jencks, "Mississippi: From Conversion to Coercion," *The New Republic* 151 (August 22, 1964): 17–21.

6. Len Holt, *The Summer That Didn't End* (London: Heinemann, 1966), 165; Reese Cleghorn, "Who Speaks for Mississippi?" *The Reporter* 31 (August 13, 1964): 32; Leslie Burl McLemore, "The Mississippi Freedom Democratic Party: A Case Study of Grass-Roots Politics," (Ph.D. diss., University of Massachusetts, 1971), 128ff.

   Ella Baker had agreed to set up an office in Washington, D.C., to organize national support for the MFDP, working mostly through the Democratic party leadership. Ella Baker, March 25, 1967, New York, Interview by Romaine, 375–77.

7. Rauh, Interview by Romaine, 305.

8. David J. Garrow, *The FBI and Martin Luther King, Jr.: From "Solo" to Memphis* (New York: W. W. Norton, 1981), 118–19.

9. Harold F. Bass, Jr., "Presidential Party Leadership and Party Reform: Lyndon B. Johnson and the MFDP Controversy," *Presidential Studies Quarterly* 21, no. 1 (Winter 1991): 90–92.

10. David Harris, *Dreams Die Hard* (New York: St. Martin's Press, 1982), 69.

11. Edwin King, September 5, 1966, Knoxville, Tenn., Interview by Romaine, 264–66. A close ally of Lowenstein, Rustin was repeating a tactic Lowenstein had employed that spring in proposing himself for Ella Baker's role, arguing that he had the contacts and prestige and was free of any "pink" connections, such as the SCEF, with which she was associated. Similarly,

Lowenstein had pushed for William Sloane Coffin of Yale to head the Mississippi Summer Project in place of Moses. As Ed King comments, "What a summer project that might have been—led by a liberal troika of Al Lowenstein, Bill Coffin, and Bayard Rustin! SNCC—and the new movement radicalizing so many American students—would have been destroyed." Edwin King Memoirs, in the possession of the author.

12. See a short summary of Rauh's brief, illustrating earlier precedents for the seating of two delegations from the same state, in Richard Cummings, *The Pied Piper: Allard K. Lowenstein and the Liberal Dream* (New York: Grove Press, 1985), 540n.

13. Adam Fairclough, *To Redeem the Soul of America: The Southern Christian Leadership Conference and Martin Luther King, Jr.* (Athens, Ga.: University of Georgia Press, 1987), 202.

14. Walter Tillow, September 4, 1966, Knoxville, Tenn., Interview by Romaine, 196.

15. Rauh, Interview by Romaine, 307–9, 311, 318.

16. The MFDP through Ella Baker's office rented the entire motel because the group needed one hundred beds. Walter Tillow, Interview by Romaine, 186–87. This made bugging the facility by the FBI relatively easy.

17. Mississippi Freedom Democratic Party Records, 1962–71, MSS 586, micro 788, reel 1, Social Action Collection, State Historical Society of Wisconsin, (hereafter cited as MFDP Records, SHSW).

18. Harris, *Dreams Die Hard*, 69–70.

19. Interview by Romaine, 324.

20. "Notes on the Democratic National Convention, August 1964," MS, 38. Arthur Waskow Papers, Social Action Collection, MSS 5, box 22, SHSW.

21. *New York Times*, August 24, 1964, 19.

22. Fannie Lou Hamer, interview in Howell Raines, ed. *My Soul Is Rested* (New York: G. P. Putnam, 1977), 253–54.

23. In an interview given a few years later, John Stewart, an attorney on Humphrey's staff at the 1964 convention, claims that the televised testimony of the MFDP delegation "did clearly have an impact on the Convention and on the country as a whole.... It helped dramatize the whole issue in a way that no amount of printed material, documents, second-hand descriptions, quotations, what have you, could do." But the hearings had "more impact on the average delegate and the country at large" than on President Johnson or Senator Hubert Humphrey. April 1967,

Boston, Mass. (interview by taped correspondence), Interview by Romaine, 362.

24. Walter Tillow comments that the president "called the news media [to] shift it to the White House." Interview by Romaine, 193.

25. Bass, "Presidential Party Leadership and Party Reform," *Presidential Studies Quarterly*, 94.

26. King, *Freedom Song*, 348. Rauh would later estimate that even before the testimony given at the Saturday Credentials Committee meeting, the MFDP had as many as seventeen committed committee members and twelve states ready to give support in a roll call vote. Interview by Romaine, 323.

27. *New York Times*, August 24, 1964, 19.

28. *New York Times*, August 24, 1964, 19. Gov. John J. McKeithen of Louisiana urged that state's delegation to walk out if Alabama and the regular Mississippi delegates were not seated. *New York Times*, August 25, 1964, 23. Johnson also may have had personal reasons for not antagonizing the regular Mississippi delegation. He was close to some of its members, including Doug Wynn, whose wife was a goddaughter of the Johnsons and the daughter of Ed Clark, an old Texas friend of the president's. Walter Tillow, Interview with Romaine, 194. Edwin King also comments on this relationship, noting that Doug Wynn did not walk out with the rest of the regular Mississippi delegation. Wynn was from Greenville and got "a good federal appointment with the state since then." September 6, 1966, Knoxville, Tenn., Interview with Romaine, 276.

29. *New York Times*, August 24, 1964, 1, 16.

30. *New York Times*, August 24, 1964, 1, 16.

31. September 4, 1966, Knoxville, Tenn., Interview with Romaine, 166.

32. Rauh, Interview by Romaine, 327–28.

33. *New York Times*, August 24, 1964, 19.

34. Arthur Waskow, a fellow at the Institute for Policy Studies in Washington, D.C., remarks that the meeting as somewhat disjoined, with people coming and leaving: Kastenmeier came, waited, and then left, giving a proxy vote to Edith Green; members of the credentials committee "straggled in"; Roy Wilkins and James Farmer, Fannie Lou Hamer and Ella Baker and other FDP people came later. "Notes," 13–14, Waskow Papers, folder 22, SHSW.

35. Samstein, Interview by Romaine, 173–74.

36. Rauh, Interview by Romaine, 330–31. See also Cummings, *The Pied Piper*, 266–67. Waskow indicates that the idea of two votes for the FDP, an idea proposed by Al Ullman of Oregon, was discussed, and this was "not totally unacceptable." "Notes," 14, Waskow Papers, folder 22, SHSW.
37. March 25,1967, New York, Interview by Romaine, 381–82.
38. Romaine, "The Mississippi Freedom Democratic Party," 42.
39. November 22, 1966, Canton, Miss., Interview by Romaine, 244.
40. "Notes," 17–18, Waskow Papers, folder 22, SHSW.
41. *New York Times*, August 25, 1964, 22.
42. *New York Times*, August 25, 1964, 23.
43. Hubert H. Humphrey, *The Education of a Public Man: My Life and Politics*, ed. Norman Sherman (Garden City, N.Y.: Doubleday, 1976), 299.
44. "Moses of Mississippi Raises Some Universal Questions," *Pacific Scene* 5 (February 1965): 3; Tillow, Interview by Romaine, 202–03.
45. *New York Times*, August 25, 1964, 23.
46. Rauh, Interview by Romaine, 306.
47. Interview by Romaine, 360.
48. Speech at *National Guardian* Dinner, November 24, 1964, MFDP Papers, box 23, file 3, Martin Luther King, Jr. Center for Non-Violent Social Change, Atlanta, Ga., (hereafter cited as MLK Center).
49. Rauh, Interview by Romaine, 340. Humphrey knew whatever the MFDP and COFO people were thinking; Rauh's discussion repeatedly mentions daily talks with Humphrey during the convention.
50. Johnson had been instrumental in helping to settle on terms favorable to labor an auto strike at Chrysler. Edwin King, Interview by Romaine, 272–73. King notes that Reuther "had been breaking delegations all day."
51. Rauh, Interview by Romaine, 341–42. According to Adam Fairclough, Humphrey explained that LBJ had wanted to name the two delegates to exclude Fannie Lou Hamer, who had angered and embarrassed him. Reuther, he says, flew in from Detroit on August 24 to sell the compromise and indicated that Rauh would be out of a job and SCLC would receive no more contributions from his union unless the MFDP accepted the compromise. *To Redeem the Soul of America*, 203.
52. Interview by Romaine, 344. In Rauh's characterization "This

little punk, Sherman Markum, who works at the White House," refused to delay the meeting.

53. Samstein, Interview by Romaine, 175, 178–79. In addition, Walter Tillow recalls that Rauh had announced that he was prepared to be the only one to sign the minority report if it came down to that. Interview by Romaine, 201.

54. Rauh, Interview by Romaine, 344–47. See also the interview with Rauh in *Voices of Freedom: An Oral History of the Civil Rights Movement from the 1950s Through the 1980s,* ed. Henry Hampton and Steve Fayer (New York: Bantam Books, 1990), 201–02. In yet another interview, Rauh noted that the count was five against the compromise. Cummings, *The Pied Piper,* 271. Others say seven stood with Rauh. All agree, however, that the vote total was not enough to bring the issue to the convention floor.

55. *Voices of Freedom,* 202. In an interview three years after the event, Rauh remarks of the announcement, "But that is just the trick they played, . . . The White House probably put that out. Anyway, he, Moses, did get infuriated, that is absolutely true." Interview by Romaine, 347. Mendy Samstein declares that when he talked to Rauh about the incident in March or April 1966, Rauh asserted that Mondale had simply lied when he announced to the press, "Here is the majority report, and the FDP accepts it." Interview by Romaine, 177–79.

56. Interview by Romaine, 269.

57. Edwin King, Interview by Romaine, 267–71.

58. Edwin King, present at the meeting with Moses, Reuther, Aaron Henry, and others in Humphrey's rooms during the credentials committee meeting, recounts Humphrey's own surprise and consternation when Senator Mondale announced a unanimous agreement to the compromise over national television. Moses' reaction, he remembers, was to slam the door in Humphrey's face. And Moses himself remembers, "I guess I was furious.... [It was] the final sort of sledge hammer." "Freedom Democrats," National Public Radio Station WATC, aired August 19, 1989, ed. Lynn Neary and Dan Collison.

59. Edwin King Memoirs, pt. 8-B.

60. Cummings, *The Pied Piper,* 272; see also Rauh, Interview by Romaine, 348–50.

61. Various meetings took place throughout the angry days both before and during the Democratic Convention, and accounts vary considerably. John Frederick Martin, *Civil Rights and the*

Crisis of Liberalism: The Democratic Party, 1945–1976 (Boulder, Colo.: Westview Press, 1977), 211. Martin's version is based primarily on an unpublished memoir written by Joe Rauh as well as interviews (209–12). See also the account given by Walter Tillow. Interview by Romaine, 204–7.

62. Interview with Courtland Cox in *Voices of Freedom*, 199; James Forman, *The Making of Black Revolutionaries* (New York: Macmillan, 1972), 388. David Lee Lawrence's full-time job was that of chairman of the President's Committee on Equal Opportunity in Housing. The *New York Times* reported, "The convention assignment might be described as equal opportunity in seating." August 24, 1964, 16.

63. Fairclough, *To Redeem the Soul of America*, 202.

64. Interview by Romaine, 318.

65. Martin, *Civil Rights and the Crisis of Liberalism*, 210.

66. Mrs. Annie Devine, Interview by Romaine, 244. According to Al Lowenstein, Aaron Henry insisted that the executive committee of the MFDP, not SNCC, make any decisions; he had asked Al to serve as advisor. Cummings, *The Pied Piper*, 265.

67. Interview by Romaine, 249.

68. Rauh, Interview by Romaine, 351.

69. Robert H. Brisbane, *Black Activism: The Racial Revolution in the United States, 1954–1970* (Valley Forge, Pa.: Judson Press, 1974), 91. Rauh quotes Lowenstein as saying, "Moses' turning on you later on was so absurd, he was willing to take two [at-large delegates] on Sunday night." Interview by Romaine, 330–31. But Moses on August 26 at the MFDP meeting spoke for Edith Green's compromise, not for the selection of the two delegates by the administration. Given Moses' absolute distaste for centralized leadership, it is highly unlikely that he would have made any commitment for the group.

70. Cummings, *The Pied Piper*, 266.

71. Edwin King, Interview by Romaine, 269.

72. Brisbane, *Black Activism*, 91. See the account in Stephen B. Oates, *Let the Trumpet Sound: The Life of Martin Luther King, Jr.* (New York: Harper and Row, 1982), 302.

73. Fairclough, *To Redeem the Soul of America*, 204.

74. Fannie Lou Hamer, November 22, 1966, Ruleville, Miss., Interview by Romaine, 214.

75. Quoted in Hamer, Interview by Romaine, 279.

76. Higgs, January 12, 1967, Washington, D.C., Interview by Romaine, 289–90.

77. Interview by Romaine, 279.
78. Rauh, when he returned to the committee's counsel the credentials Ed King and Aaron Henry had refused, discovered that there were eleven signatures on the minority report. Several people had signed it after it didn't matter, simply to put themselves on record as having done the right thing. Cummings, *The Pied Piper*, 273.
79. Quoted in *Voices of Freedom*, 112.
80. *Voices of Freedom*, 202. In his detailed firsthand reminiscence about the MFDP and the Democratic National Convention, Arthur Waskow insists that "Moses' full pitch was to continue with the Democratic party, within the regular politics, not to abandon it . . . to carry the intentions, the hopes, the morality, the demands of the civil rights movement into politics." "Notes," 33, Waskow Papers, box 22, SHSW.
81. "Unfinished Business: Issues of the '60s," *Proceedings of the 1990 Convention of the American Society of Newspaper Editors*, April 3–6, 1990 (Washington, D.C.: American Society of Newspaper Editors, 1990), 46.
82. "Freedom Democrats," ed. Neary and Collison, National Public Radio Station WATC, aired August 19, 1989.
83. Harvard Sitkoff, *The Struggle for Black Equality, 1954–1980* (New York: Hill and Wang, 1981), 181.
84. The compromise might have worked had the administration allowed the group to select its delegates. As Moses has observed, "If the MFDP had been seated, the attitude toward politics would have been different. The disillusionment with traditional politics began there." Cummings, *The Pied Piper*, 273–74.
85. Milton Viorst, *Fire in the Streets* (New York: Simon and Schuster, 1979), 267–68.
86. Richard Armstrong, "Will Snick Overcome?" *Saturday Evening Post* 238 (August 28, 1965): 82.
87. Interview by Neil McMillen and George Burson, May 1, 1972, Clarksdale, Miss. Mississippi Oral History Program of the University of Southern Mississippi 33 (1980), 28.
88. Brisbane, *Black Activism*, 92. Goldwater won eighty-seven percent of the vote in Mississippi in 1964.
89. Lawrence Guyot, November 23, 1966, Jackson, Miss., Interview by Romaine, 95–97.
90. Quoted in Armstrong, "Will Snick Overcome?" *Saturday Evening Post*, 83.

91. Lerone Bennett, Jr., "SNCC: Rebels With a Cause," *Ebony* 20 (July 1965): 148.
92. "Freedom Democrats," National Public Radio Station WATC, aired August 19, 1989.
93. Transcript (partially edited), SR 1, CR 405, show 5, May 19, 1986, 4. Produced by Blackside, Inc., Boston, Mass.
94. MFDP Records, Reel 2, SHSW.
95. Moses noted, "Now what happened at the Atlantic City convention is about to be replayed in the Congress of the U.S." Speech at *National Guardian* Dinner, November 24, 1964. MFDP Papers, box 12, file 3, MLK Center.
96. King referred to the challenge when speaking at a program in his honor held in New York City on December 17, 1964, after receiving the Nobel Peace Prize. Memorandum, White to LBJ, December 18, 1964, White House Central Files, "Mississippi, F-K," box 477, Lyndon Baines Johnson Presidential Library.
97. *Mississippi Freedom Press* 3, no. 15 (March 28, 1964), 1.
98. *Mississippi Free Press*, March 28, 1964, 1.
99. "Moses of Mississippi," *Pacific Scene*, 4.
100. Moses interview, "Eyes on the Prize," May 19, 1986, 39.
101. Bennett, "SNCC: Rebels with a Cause," 151.
102. Quoted from a talk given by Moses at the fifth anniversary of SNCC, published in *The Movement* 1, no. 4 (April 1965).
103. Robert Penn Warren, *Who Speaks for the Negro?* (New York: Random House, 1965), 95–96. This interview took place in early February 1964.
104. Thomas Powers, "A Chance Encounter," reprinted from *Commonweal* 107 (April 11, 1980): 197–99, in *Lowenstein: Acts of Courage and Conflict*, ed. Gregory Stone and Douglas Lowenstein (New York: Harcourt Brace Jovanovich, 1983), 279.
105. This source also noted that newspaper red-baiting attack would probably be launched soon—and certainly Evans and Novak of the *Washington Post* printed a series of articles that fulfilled that prediction. Memorandum entitled "Red-baiting of SNCC and MFDP," Allard K. Lowenstein Papers, subseries 2.14, box 32, folder 371. Southern Historical Collection, University of North Carolina, Chapel Hill, NC.
106. Cummings, *The Pied Piper*, 307.
107. Powers, "A Chance Encounter," 279.
108. Cummings, *The Pied Piper*, 249, 261.
109. Edwin King Memoirs, pt. 12–B, 34; pt. 3, 4, 27.

110. Quoted in James Silver, *Mississippi: The Closed Society* (New York: Harcourt, Brace & World, 1964), 344.
111. Carson, *In Struggle*, 128.
112. See McLemore, "The Mississippi Freedom Democratic Party," 153–55.
113. Minnis, "The MFDP: A New Declaration of Independence," *Freedomways* 5, no. 2 (Spring 1965): 269.

Notes to Chapter Nine

1. James Forman, *The Making of Black Revolutionaries* (New York: Macmillan, 1972), 420.
2. Forman, *Making of Black Revolutionaries*, 416; Clayborne Carson, *In Struggle: SNCC and the Black Awakening of the 1960s* (Cambridge, Mass.: Harvard University Press, 1981), 138. At an October meeting SNCC staffers rejected the plan. It was typical of Moses that he had not spoken up for it but let the group reach its own consensus. This, perhaps, was the beginning of strained relations between Forman, who urged better structure and organization, and Moses, who continued to provide leadership by indirection.
3. n.d., Civil Rights Collection, Social Action Vertical File, MSS 577, State Historical Society of Wisconsin (hereafter cited as CR Collection, SHSW). See also *New York Times*, August 20, 1964, 1.
4. CORE Vertical Files, CR Collection, SHSW.
5. Harry Belafonte sponsored the delegation through associations he had with the government of Guinea. Included in the group were Moses' first wife, Dona, and Julian Bond. Carson, *In Struggle*, 134.
6. SNCC internal document entitled "Brief Report on Guinea," dated September 23, 1964, Conakry, Guinea. CR Collection, SHSW.
7. SNCC Papers, n.d., "Name Withheld by Request," CR Collection, SHSW.
8. Carson, *In Struggle*, 140–43. The retreat in Waveland, Mississippi, generated about thirty-seven papers; one, unsigned, but perhaps written by Moses, urged a flexible approach to making decisions (141). See also Cleveland Sellers, *The River of No Return* (New York: William Morrow, 1973), 113–15.

9. Carl and Anne Braden Papers, MSS 6, box 50, folder 3, SHSW.
10. Dick Kelley, November 28, 1964, Stewart Ewen Papers, MSS 531, box 1, folder 1, Social Action Collection, SHSW.
11. Report from Nick Hampton, Stuart Ewen Papers, box 1, folder 1, SHSW.
12. Lewis to "All SNCC Staff," undated but notes he had been back from Africa for more than two weeks, which puts the date around mid-November, 1964. CR Collection, SHSW.
13. Thomas Powers, a Yale recruit to Mississippi in November 1963, has recounted his summary of the events after the election of 1964: "In 1965 Robert Moses dropped out of sight, saying he didn't think the Movement ought to have leaders." Reprint from *Commonweal* 107 (April 11, 1980) as "A Chance Encounter," in *Lowenstein: Acts of Courage and Conflict,* ed. Gregory Stone and Douglas Lowenstein (New York: Harcourt Brace Jovanovich, 1983), 345.
14. Doug McAdam, *Freedom Summer* (New York: Oxford University Press, 1988), 125.
15. Interview by Emily Stoper in *The Student Nonviolent Coordinating Committee: The Growth of Radicalism in a Civil Rights Organization,* rev. ed. (Brooklyn, N.Y.: Carlson Publishing, Inc. 1989), 128, 140.
16. Jack Newfield, "Moses in Mississippi: The Invisible Man Learns his Name," *Village Voice* December 3, 1964, 3, 21. Moses and Staughton Lynd, who served as the SNCC freedom schools' director, spoke at the dinner.
17. Newfield, "Moses in Mississippi," 21. Moses urged local black autonomy as opposed to a broad radical movement. See also Richard Cummings, *The Pied Piper: Allard K. Lowenstein and the Liberal Dream* (New York: Grove Press, 1985), 279.
18. Mary King, *Freedom Song* (New York: William Morrow and Co., 1987), 430. Cleveland Sellers describes this incident in some detail. *The River of No Return,* 137–39.
19. Lerone Bennett, Jr., "SNCC: Rebels With A Cause," *Ebony* 20 (July 1965): 148.
20. Interview by Michael Garvey, March 29, 1977, Cleveland, Miss. Mississippi Oral History Program of the University of Southern Mississippi 184 (1981), 67 (hereafter cited as Oral History Program, USM).
21. "Moses of Mississippi Raises Some Universal Questions," *Pacific Scene* 5 (February 1965), 5.

22. SNCC internal document entitled "Executive Committee Meeting," Holly Springs, Mississippi, April 12–14, 1965. CR Collection, SHSW.

23. Amzie Moore, interview by Michael Garvey, Oral History Program, USM.

24. Allard Lowenstein, Interview by Anne Romaine, March 4, 1967, Charlottesville, Va., in "The Mississippi Freedom Democratic Party Through August, 1964" (Master's thesis, University of Virginia, 1970), 128 (hereafter cited as Interview by Romaine).

25. Moses to Trumpauer, December 6, 1962, CR Collection, SHSW.

26. If accepted at Tougaloo, the students who elected to take time off from their college studies during the academic year and serve as field secretaries of SNCC would be able to attend Tougaloo for a year with tuition paid by the Field Foundation. SNCC internal statement on work study program with a memorandum from Dona Richards Moses to Mississippi field staff, n.d. (but probably spring 1964), SNCC Papers, box 104, file 17, Martin Luther King, Jr. Center for Non-Violent Social Change, Atlanta, Ga. (hereafter cited as MLK Center).

See also Moses to Philip Stern (Stern Foundation), May 1, 1964, regarding the SNCC work study project and the Freedom Schools. CR Collection, SHSW.

As campaign manager for the "Committee to Elect Henry" for governor of Mississippi on the Freedom Ballot, Moses in the summer and fall of 1963 was responsible for extensive letter writing, brochure preparation, a fact sheet on the candidate, and much detail work in organizing the balloting. See, for example, a typical letter from Moses explaining Henry's coming announcement, on October 14, 1963, of his candidacy in SNCC Papers, n.d., box 107, folder 10, MLK Center.

27. Letter to "Summer Project Applicant," May 5, 1964, MFDP Papers, box 23, file 2, MLK Center.

28. The initial work for the implementation of the freedom schools was handled by Charlie Cobb, a SNCC field representative and a Northerner. Minutes, February 13, 1964, Summer Steering Committee; SNCC internal document entitled "Curriculum Planning for Summer Project; Prospectus for Summer Freedom School Program in Mississippi," MFDP Papers, box 5, file 6, MLK Center. See also a SNCC internal paper written by Liz Fusco, coordinator, COFO Freedom Schools, entitled "Freedom Schools in Mississippi, 1964," SNCC Papers, box 106, folder 6, MLK Center. Finally, an annotated list of "People

Invited to the Curriculum Conference" indicates the extent to which Moses was involved in personnel and planning for this component of the Summer Project. MFDP Papers, box 5, file 6, MLK Center.

29. Mary Aickin Rothschild, "The Volunteers and the Freedom Schools: Education for Social Change in Mississippi," *History of Education Quarterly*, 22 (Winter 1982): 406–7. Rothschild's article is a detailed analysis of the change of direction in the freedom schools from political to academic (401–20). See also Howard Zinn, "Schools in Context: The Mississippi Idea," *The Nation* 198 (March 23, 1964): 3–10.

30. Memorandum dated August 11, 1964, Jackson, Miss., SNCC Papers, box 107, folder 9, MLK Center.

31. SNCC Papers, box 104, folder 10, MLK Center.

32. Jack Newfield, "The Question of SNCC," *The Nation* 201 (July 19, 1965): 38–40.

33. Sellers, *The River of No Return*, 137. Sellers recalls this confrontation as taking place at an annual fall meeting in 1965 (134–37). Carson puts the incident in the spring of 1965. *In Struggle*, 157.

34. Rowland Evans and Robert Novak, "Freedom Party Postscript," *Washington Post*, September 3, 1964. Additional articles on this topic appeared in their columns on March 18, April 9, and July 17 of 1965. The new impetus shifted from Mississippi directly to the nation as a whole and began with the Free Speech Movement at the University of California's Berkeley campus, led by a volunteer in Mississippi during Freedom Summer named Mario Savio. The incident that started the movement there began with an attempt by the university to restrict a fund-raising drive for SNCC and the FDP congressional challenge. Mario Savio, "An End to History," *Humanity* (Berkeley, Calif., 1964), 1.

35. Carson, *In Struggle*, 137. But Rauh had decided opinions. For example, when Moses asked him to work as MFDP counsel with the white Mississippi activist lawyer, Bill Higgs (who with William Kunstler had filed Moses' suit in January 1963 against the Justice Department and the FBI), he had responded that Higgs was "not a particularly good lawyer . . . [and] a totally irresponsible person." Rauh, Interview by Romaine, 303. For a sketch of some of Higgs's activities with civil rights work in Mississippi, see Seth Cagin and Philip Dray, *We Are Not Afraid: The Story of Goodman, Schwerner, and Chaney and the Civil*

Rights Campaign for Mississippi (New York: Macmillan, 1988), 174, 189–90, 208–9.

36. Cummings, *The Pied Piper*, 267.

37. For a detailed discussion about the "communist threat" in SNCC, see Cummings, *The Pied Piper*, 246–54.

38. Christopher Jencks, "Mississippi: From Conversion to Coercion," *The New Republic* 151 (August 22, 1964): 19; Quoted in Richard Armstrong, "Will Snick Overcome?" *Saturday Evening Post* 238 (August 28, 1965): 83.

39. Sellers, *The River of No Return*, 130–37. As early as December 1963 disagreements had arisen about the direction of SNCC; Courtland Cox, among others, had urged that the projects be economic in their thrust rather than address enfranchisement of poor blacks. Carson, *In Struggle*, 104.

40. "Moses of Mississippi," *Pacific Scene*, 5.

41. SNCC internal document entitled "Executive Committee Meeting," Holly Springs, Mississippi, April 12–14, 1965. CR Collection, SHSW.

    In an interview with a reporter for the *Village Voice* in late November 1964, Moses announced his plan to travel around Mississippi with his wife in the coming year to teach blacks their history and to work toward awakening blacks to their own self worth. Newfield, "Moses in Mississippi," 21. But in March 1965 Moses and his wife left for Birmingham, Alabama, to work on programs there with urban blacks.

42. SNCC Papers, April 28, 1965, CR Collection, SHSW.

43. King, *Freedom Song*, 447. At a SNCC session in Atlanta in the spring of 1965, Forman defeated Moses in a policy vote on the direction of SNCC. Cummings, *The Pied Piper*, 280. See also Carson, *In Struggle*, 140.

44. Gene Roberts, "From Freedom High to Black Power," *New York Times Magazine*, September 25, 1966, 21.

45. See Stoper, *The Student Nonviolent Coordinating Committee*, 83–85.

46. Newfield, "The Question of SNCC," 40.

47. "A Talk with Bob Parris . . . One Freedom Worker's Views," *Southern Patriot* 23 (October 1965), 3.

48. Newfield, "The Question of SNCC," 38–40. Newfield remarks, "After the convention there began a venomous flow of red-baiting, beatnik-baiting attacks from syndicated columnists Rowland Evans and Robert Novak" (40). See also "A Talk with Bob Parris," 3.

The syndicated columnists Rowland Evans and Robert Novak continued to pound away at SNCC and Moses, hinting of communist alliances and subversive activities. For a sample of a smear tactic against Moses, see Rowland Evans and Robert Novak in their column "Inside Report" an article entitled "The Moses Rally," *Washington Post*, July 27, 1965, 13.

49. Cummings, *The Pied Piper*, 282; David Harris, *Dreams Die Hard* (New York: St. Martin's Press, 1982), 120.
50. "A Talk with Bob Parris," 3–5; Cagin and Dray, *We Are Not Afraid*, 438.
51. The *Saturday Evening Post*, commenting on the SNCC philosophy against leaders and organization, remarked, "So deeply runs this mistrust of leadership that Robert Moses, who directed S.N.C.C.'s summer project in Mississippi last year amid a glare of national publicity, decided he owed it to the movement to change his name (to Robert Parris) and drop temporarily out of sight." Armstrong, "Will Snick Overcome?" 80. Mary King also says that Moses took a leave of absence from SNCC because of criticism from members who believed the opposition to the Vietnam war was diverting the organization from its main thrust—bettering the lives of blacks in the United States. *Freedom Song*, 495.
52. Harvard Sitkoff, *The Struggle for Black Equality, 1954–1980* (New York: Hill and Wang, 1981), 197.
53. Cummings, *The Pied Piper*, 295. Lowenstein had been in Mississippi early in 1965 and saw Moses about this. Lowenstein commented that Moses was now convinced of the need for a temporary black party but was friendly and "seems less bitter."
54. Interview with Wise by Clayborne Carson, April 19, 1972, and quoted in Carson, *In Struggle*, 330 n. 11. See also King, *Freedom Song*, 503; John Lewis interview in Stoper, *The Student Nonviolent Coordinating Committee*, 242–43.
55. Lawrence Guyot, interview in Howell Raines, *My Soul Is Rested* (New York: G. P. Putnam, 1977), 289.
56. Interview by Michael Garvey, 65, Oral History Program, USM. Aaron Henry confirms the impression: "Bob has lost confidence in the system. He doesn't talk to whites, he doesn't talk to blacks who talk to whites." Interview by Neil McMillen and George Burson, May 1, 1971, Clarksdale, Miss., 33 (1980), 29. Oral History Program, USM.
57. Julian Bond, Notes, CR Collection, SHSW.

58. Bond, Notes, CR Collection, SHSW.
59. Carson, *In Struggle*, 163–66; 200–3. Cagin and Dray, *We Are Not Afraid*, 440–41. One former SNCC activist notes that in practice whites were out of SNCC by February 1965. Letter from Mariam Cohen Glickman to the author, March 1993.
60. Carson, *In Struggle*, 180.
61. See, for example, Vincent Harding, *Hope and History* (Maryknoll, N.Y.: Orbis Books, 1990), 115.
62. Moses to Mr. Schoenfeld (presumably in New York, because Moses gives a changed address in c/o his father), June 25, 1961, series IV, Executive Secretary Files, SNCC Papers, box 17, folder 7, MLK Center.
63. "Resumé of the Inquiry Re: Robert Parris Moses, Conscientious Objector," March 21, 1962, U.S. Department of Justice, Southern District of New York, 10 and passim. Copy in the Mississippi Department of Archives and History, Jackson, Miss.
64. Kenneth O'Reilly, *"Racial Matters": The FBI's Secret File on Black America, 1960–1972* (New York: Free Press, 1989), 399n35.
65. Cagin and Dray, *We Are Not Afraid*, 453.
66. Ivanhoe Donaldson, interview in Raines, *My Soul Is Rested*, 259.
67. Connie Curry, interview in Raines, *My Soul Is Rested*, 107–8.
68. A detailed explanation of the civil rights groups' hesitancy to become involved in the Vietnam war protest movement is given in an article by Robert S. Browne, "The Freedom Movement and the War," *Freedomways* 5, no. 4 (1965): 467–80.
69. Carson, *In Struggle*, 187.
70. Reprinted in *Freedomways* 6, no. 1 (1966): 7.
71. Cagin and Dray, *We Are Not Afraid*, 452–53; Gregory Moses, Jr., interview with the author, June 2, 1993, Detroit, Mich..
72. King, *Freedom Song*, 535; Robert P. Moses, Mieko Kamii, Susan McAllister Swap, and Jeffrey Howard, "The Algebra Project: Organizing in the Spirit of Ella," *Harvard Educational Review* 59, no. 4 (November 1989): 426.
73. Robert P. Moses et al., "The Algebra Project," *Harvard Educational Review*, 425, 441.
74. "Unfinished Business: Issues of the '60s," *Proceedings of the 1990 Convention of the American Society of Newspaper Editors*, April 3–6, 1990 (Washington, D.C.: American Society of Newspaper Editors, 1990), 25.
75. Quoted in Alexis Jetter, "Mississippi Learning," *New York Times Magazine*, February 21, 1992, 29.
76. Harding, *Hope and History*, 24.

77. Moses, "Commentary," *We Shall Overcome: Martin Luther King, Jr., and the Black Freedom Struggle,* ed. Peter J. Albert and Ronald Hoffman (New York: Pantheon Books, 1990), 73, 76.

78. Harding, *Hope and History,* 38.

79. "Unfinished Business," 41.

INDEX

Peacock, Willie, 1
Pike County, Miss., 66
Plague, The, 5
Poll tax, 40
Price, Cecil, 157

Rauh, Joseph, 170, 172, 173; address
 to MFDP delegates, 180–81; and
 administration compromise, 179,
 187; as attorney for MFDP, 179;
 and credentials committee, 176,
 182; and Ella Baker, 181; and Lyndon Johnson's maneuvers at Democratic National Convention of
 1964, 184; and MFDP, 145, 184–
 85; and Mississippi delegates,
 173; and Moses, 145–46; and National Lawyers Guild, 210; as representative of white liberalism,
 197; and Walter Reuther, 181
Rebel, The, 5–6, 213
Reporter, 151
Reuther, Walter, 176, 181; at Democratic National Convention of
 1964, 182
Richards, Donna, 211, 214; and Moses, 219
Roberts, Gene: and SNCC, 213
Robinson, Bernice, 72, 99
Robinson, Harold, 66
Robinson, Reggie, 43
Roosevelt, Eleanor, 67, 111
Ruleville, Miss.: incidents cited in
 Kennedy's Press conference, 84;
 voter registration in, 79; white re-
 taliation in, 74
Rustin, Bayard, 19, 171–72; on ad-
 ministration compromise, 186;
 meeting with Hubert Humphrey,
 182; and SNCC, 26
Ryan, William Fitts, 161

Samstein, Mendy, 92, 121, 144, 165–
 66, 176, 177, 182, 185
Sanders, Carl, 172
Saturday Evening Post, 189

Schwerner, Michael, 157, 164, 166
SCLC (Southern Christian Leader-
 ship Conference), 18–19, 20–22;
 and COFO, 24; and communism,
 139; and Freedom Rides, 33; and
 March on Washington, 114; and
 Moses, 38, 39; and SNCC, 39, 106;
 support for MFDP, 171. *See also*
 King, Martin Luther, Jr.
Screws v. United States of America
 (1944), 64
SDS (Students for a Democratic Society), 213
Seeger, Pete, 109
Sellers, Cleveland, 2, 209, 210–11
Shanker, Albert, 136
Shenden, Walter, 161
Sherrod, Charles, 38, 198
Sitton, Claude, 37
Smith, Andrew, 107
Smith, Rev. Robert L. T., 67–68, 73,
 116, 164
SNCC (Student Nonviolent Coordinating Committee), 20, 23, 30,
 206; and Allard Lowenstein, 126–
 28, 149, 195, 196, 210; and Cleveland Sellers, 210–11; and COFO,
 134–35, 147, 201; communist allegations about, 78–79, 109, 139–
 40, 195, 210; conferences, 23, 61;
 and Courtland Cox, 210; direct action in, 162; and FBI, 59; and federal government, 88, 134, 191;
 Easter 1963 Conference, 104; exclusion of whites from, 217; factionalism in, 90, 202; financing,
 90; and Fannie Lou Hamer, 174;
 floaters in, 203, 211; formation of,
 21; Freedom Rides, 33; Freedom
 Summer, 130–31, 135, 136, 138,
 152; Freedom Vote, 119, 126; and
 Gene Roberts, 213; Greenwood Office, 1, 109; hardliners in, 204; hostility to liberalism, 194; jailings of
 workers, 66; Justice Department
 and, 47, 101, 102; and Martin